Research in Social Work series

Series Editors: **Anna Gupta**, Royal Holloway, University of London, UK and **John Gal**, Hebrew University of Jerusalem, Israel

---

Published together with The European Social Work Research Association (ESWRA), this series examines current, progressive and innovative research applications of familiar ideas and models in international social work research.

Also available in the series:

Interprofessional Collaboration and Service User Participation: Analysing Meetings in Social Welfare

Edited by **Kirsi Juhila**, **Tanja Dall**, **Christopher Hall** and **Juliet Koprowska**

The Settlement House Movement Revisited: A Transnational History

Edited by **John Gal**, **Stefan Köngeter**, and **Sarah Vicary**

Social Work and the Making of Social Policy

Edited by **Ute Klammer**, **Simone Leiber**, and **Sigrid Leitner**

Research and the Social Work Picture

By **Ian Shaw**

Find out more at:

policy.bristoluniversitypress.co.uk/
research-in-social-work

Research in Social Work series

Series Editors: **Anna Gupta**, Royal Holloway, University of London, UK and **John Gal**, Hebrew University of Jerusalem, Israel

---

Forthcoming in the series:

*Involving Service Users in Social Work Education,
Research and Policy:
A Comparative European Analysis*

Edited by **Kristel Driessens** and **Vicky Lyssens-Danneboom**

Social Work Research Using Arts-Based Methods

Edited by **Ephrat Huss** and **Eltje Bos**

Critical Gerontology for Social Workers

Edited by **Sandra Torres** and **Sarah Donnelly**

*Power and Control in Social Work:
An Ethnographic Account of Mental Health Practice*

By **Hannah Jobling**

Find out more at:

policy.bristoluniversitypress.co.uk/
research-in-social-work

Research in Social Work series

Series Editors: **Anna Gupta**, Royal Holloway, University of London, UK and **John Gal**, Hebrew University of Jerusalem, Israel

---

Forthcoming in the series:

Migration and Social Work:
Approaches, Visions and Challenges

Edited by **Emilio J. Gómez-Ciriano**, **Elena Cabiati** and **Sofia Dedotsi**

The Origins of Social Work:
Western Roots, International Futures

By **Mark Henrickson**

Find out more at:

policy.bristoluniversitypress.co.uk/
research-in-social-work

Research in Social Work series

Series Editors: **Anna Gupta**, Royal Holloway, University of London, UK and **John Gal**, Hebrew University of Jerusalem, Israel

---

International Editorial Board:

Find out more at:

policy.bristoluniversitypress.co.uk/
research-in-social-work

ADOPTION FROM CARE

International Perspectives on Children's Rights, Family Preservation and State Intervention

Edited by
Tarja Pösö, Marit Skivenes and June Thoburn

First published in Great Britain in 2021 by

Policy Press, an imprint of
Bristol University Press
University of Bristol
1–9 Old Park Hill
Bristol
BS2 8BB
UK
t: +44 (0)117 954 5940
e: bup-info@bristol.ac.uk

Details of international sales and distribution partners are available at
policy.bristoluniversitypress.co.uk

British Library Cataloguing in Publication Data
A catalogue record for this book is available from the British Library

ISBN 978-1-4473-5103-0 paperback
ISBN 978-1-4473-5104-7 ePub
ISBN 978-1-4473-5105-4 OA PDF

Cover design: Bristol University Press
Image credit: iStock
Bristol University Press uses environmentally responsible
print partners.
Printed in Great Britain by CMP, Poole

Contents

List of figures and tables

Figures

Tables

Notes on contributors

Ana Cristina Gomez Aparicio is Deputy Director General of Child Protection at the Community of Madrid, Spain.

Jill Duerr Berrick is Professor II at the Department of Administration and Organization Theory and the Centre for Research on Discretion and Paternalism, University of Bergen, Norway, and a professor at the School of Social Welfare, UC Berkeley, USA.

Ina Bovenschen is a research associate at the German Youth Institute, Germany.

Kenneth Burns is Senior Lecturer and a research associate with the Institute for Social Science in the 21st Century (ISS21) at the School of Applied Social Studies, University College Cork, Ireland.

Pia Eriksson is a lecturer at the Swedish School of Social Science, University of Helsinki, Finland.

Esther Abad Guerra is Chief Executive Officer of the Area of Adoption and Fostering at the Autonomous Community of Madrid, Spain.

Hege Stein Helland is a PhD candidate at the Centre for Research on Discretion and Paternalism, University of Bergen, Norway.

Katrin Križ is Professor at Emmanuel College, USA.

Jenny Krutzinna is a senior researcher at the Centre for Research on Discretion and Paternalism, University of Bergen, Norway.

Katre Luhamaa is a senior researcher at the Centre for Research on Discretion and Paternalism, University of Bergen, Norway, and lecturer of European law and international law at the School of Law, University of Tartu, Estonia.

Simone McCaughren is a lecturer and research associate at the ISS21, School of Applied Social Studies, University College Cork, Ireland.

Thomas Meysen is Managing Director of the SOCLES International Centre for Socio-Legal Studies, Germany.

Sveinung Hellesen Nygård is a researcher at the Centre for Research on Discretion and Paternalism, University of Bergen, Norway.

Conor O'Mahony is Professor at the Centre for Children's Rights and Family Law, School of Law, University College Cork.

Tarja Pösö is Professor II at the Department of Administration and Organization Theory and the Centre for Research on Discretion and Paternalism, University of Bergen, Norway, and Professor in Social Work, Faculty of Social Sciences, Tampere University, Finland.

Sagrario Segado is Associate Professor at the Department of Social Work, Faculty of Law, National University of Distance Education (UNED), Spain.

Marit Skivenes is Professor at the Department of Administration and Organization Theory and Director of the Centre for Research on Discretion and Paternalism, University of Bergen, Norway.

Judit Strömpl is Associate Professor at the University of Tartu, Estonia.

June Thoburn is Emeritus Professor of Social Work at the University of East Anglia, UK.

Acknowledgements

This book has benefited from the work of the insightful authors and many good colleagues. The book project is a result of ongoing research projects at the Centre for Research on Discretion and Paternalism, University of Bergen, Norway, and the fact that there are huge knowledge gaps in the field of adoption from care. Most chapters were presented at a seminar at the University of Bergen in the autumn of 2019, at a 'pre-COVID-19' time when physical meetings were still possible, and we are obliged and grateful for all comments and input that were received at this seminar. We have received assistance from research assistant Florian Wingens with editing and organising throughout the process, as well as from research assistant Vanessa T. Seeligmann in the final editing rounds. Research coordinator Daniel Nygård has ensured that this will be an Open Access publication.

The project has received funding from the European Research Council (ERC) under the European Union's Horizon 2020 research and innovation programme (grant agreement no. 724460) and from the Research Council of Norway under the Independent Projects – Humanities and Social Science programme (grant no. 262773). The publication has received additional funding from the Open Access publication fund at the University of Bergen.

1

Introducing the field of adoption from care

Tarja Pösö, Marit Skivenes and June Thoburn

Introduction

All countries are signatories to the principles and rights laid out in the Convention on the Rights of the Child (CRC),[1] and comparative studies show that, at the national level, there are some similar basic principles underpinning the family welfare and child protection systems in many high-income countries (Gilbert et al, 2011; Skivenes et al, 2015; Burns et al, 2017; Berrick et al, forthcoming). These basic principles include: the central importance of the best interest and well-being of the child when key decisions are taken; an emphasis on family preservation and valuing the child's relationships with birth parents and siblings; principles of least intrusion from the state; and the child protection system only having secondary responsibility for children compared with the family. However, the degree to which governments focus on each of these principles differs, and this is especially so if one considers the potentially contradictory principles that are most relevant when considering placement policies when children need to be removed and come into public care. In the majority of cases, therefore, there is scope for interpretation about what course of action will be 'in the child's best interest', leaving space for courts, child protection front-line staff and, indeed, whole countries to determine the balance between these commonly accepted principles. It is not an exaggeration to point out that parental rights and family preservation have a strong standing in most states and systems, with the result that the rights of the child often come second to parental rights and are challenging for nation states and courts to respect and promote. Perhaps an example of this is when the European Court of Human Rights stated that only in exceptional circumstances and with an overriding child's best interest consideration could parental rights be terminated (Breen et al, 2020). Child protection is about the 'government's responsibility to establish a system that has the authority to intervene into the family to support, restrict and even terminate parental rights if parents or caregivers are unable or unwilling to protect the child' (Berrick et al, forthcoming). Adoptions as a child projection measure – or, as we refer to it in this book, adoptions from care – are to be understood as those adoptions where a child who is currently in public care or is under guardianship of the state, after full or partial removal of custody from the parents, is placed with prospective adopters and/or legally adopted by their foster carers with or without the consent of the parents.

Morally and legally, adoption from care should only happen when a child's reunification with birth parents is deemed impossible. Article 21 of the CRC states that the best interests of the child are the paramount consideration in all types of adoption, and this consideration prevails over the interests of birth parents and prospective adoptive parents. In Europe, all states provide a legal opportunity to terminate parental rights and place a child for adoption without parents' consent (Fenton-Glynn, 2015), but there are substantial variations in practice. Adoption is a measure that, like all child protection interventions, should only be undertaken with the highest regard to the specific child's best interests, and in accordance with due process and decision-making procedures that fulfil rational criteria of reasoning and critical reflection (Burns et al, 2019).

One should also have in mind that adoptions are normatively and ideologically contested, as the chapter by Krutzinna (this volume) displays. One reason for this is that, historically, governments have used adoptions to punish and correct individuals that are considered immoral, as with single mothers in the UK prior to the 1960s, or with the kidnappings of newborns under oppressive regimes, such as in Chile in the 1970s/1980s and in Spain under the Franco regime. In transnational adoptions, marked by the geographies of unequal power, when children are moved from poorer countries to wealthier ones, adoptions may be seen simultaneously as acts of love and as acts of (structural) violence (Briggs and Marre, 2009).

The chapters in this book will highlight a topic that has, to date, had little exposure in the international child protection literature, though there is more extensive coverage of adoption more generally. It introduces general topics on human rights and attachment, as well as a country-specific in-depth analysis of the legal and policy imperatives guiding adoptions from care, with a particular interest on the rights of children and their care-taking adults, including their birth parents. We argue that the seemingly 'minor' issue of adoptions from care provides a unique and topical point to explore how children's rights are practised and weighed against parents' rights in present-day societies, and how governments and legal and welfare professionals balance those rights and discharge their duties of care to all who need their services, especially children following a decision that they cannot grow up in their parents' care.

Adoption from care among other types of adoption

Our primary focus in this book is on those situations in which the child has been taken into public care by child protection systems or due to abandonment, and while in public care, an adoption process is initiated. They are 'domestic adoptions', in the sense that the adoptees and adopters have the same country of residence, for example, in the same way as domestic step-parent adoptions. Domestic adoptions are different from inter-country adoptions, in which a child is adopted from another country. Children of inter-country adoptions might be in public care when inter-country adoption proceedings are initiated but we focus here only on domestic adoptions from care.

The global trends are, however, that domestic and inter-country adoptions are decreasing. These trends are reflected in Figure 1.1, representing the number of children adopted in the European Union (EU) and the relative shares of domestic and inter-country adoptions in the period 2004–14 (European Parliamentary Research Service, 2016). The overall pattern is that domestic adoptions of any type outnumber inter-country adoptions and that both types of adoption are declining. The share of adoptions from care is not presented as a separate category of domestic adoptions in Figure 1.1 as it is often not a distinctive adoption category in a variety of countries, as the chapters of this book will demonstrate. We will return to the trends of adoptions from care in the country chapters and finally in the conclusion chapter.

Figure 1.1: Domestic and inter-country adoptions in the EU, 2004–14

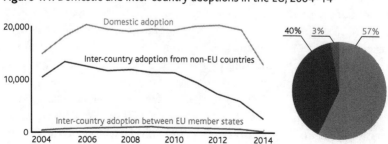

Source: European Parliamentary Research Service (2016)

The reasons for the declining trends are many: fewer unwanted pregnancies (through increased availability of contraception and abortions); social measures supporting parents; and changes in policies on the desirability of sending children out of the country (Selman, 2009; Palacios et al, 2019). The availability of adopters is also changing due to reproduction technology; it is estimated that, in 2013, the number of children born by surrogacy was higher than the number of inter-country adoptions (Palacios et al, 2019).

The changes also inform us about governments' understanding and interpretation of the principle of the child's best interest in the sphere of adoptions from care. Article 20 of the CRC concerns children in public custody that do not and cannot live with their parents:

1. A child temporarily or permanently deprived of his or her family environment, or in whose own best interests cannot be allowed to remain in that environment, shall be entitled to special protection and assistance provided by the State.
2. States Parties shall in accordance with their national laws ensure alternative care for such a child.
3. Such care could include, inter alia, foster placement, kafalah of Islamic law, adoption or if necessary placement in suitable institutions for the care of children. When considering solutions, due regard shall be paid to the desirability of continuity in a child's upbringing and to the child's ethnic, religious, cultural and linguistic background.

Regarding alternative care, the importance of creating a family environment for children in care is reflected in the resolution adopted by the General Assembly of the United Nations prioritising family-based care over residential care as an overall principle but especially for children under the age of three (UN General Assembly, 2010; 2019: #22). There is a variety of forms of family-based care, as will be described in the next section. Adoptions are about 'creating families' and thus relevant for the ambition to support children separated from their birth parents to grow up in a family environment.

There seem to be policy changes in terms of the increasing use of adoption from care in Japan, Denmark, Norway and Sweden, to mention just four countries (Helland and Skivenes, 2019; Tefre, 2020). A range of researchers in the child protection field are recommending policymakers to use adoptions from care (Vinnjerlung and Hjern, 2011;

Christoffersen, 2012; Palacios et al, 2019). Based on the evidence of their study, Swedish researcher Hjern and his colleagues (2019: 72) conclude that 'when foster parents want to adopt, there is no valid support from research for social workers to act against that wish, if the reasons for a negative attitude are related to concerns about the child's long term development'. They also recommend a shift in Swedish child protection policy from long-term foster care towards adoption. At the same time, there is a rise in critique of the 'overuse' of adoptions from care in England (Thoburn and Featherstone, 2019), a country that has used adoption as a permanency measure for 20 years or more. Even though adoption as a child protection measure should only be considered for children that are otherwise likely to grow up in public care because they cannot be reunified with birth parents or wider family, this book shows that there are wide differences in how states view the border between public and private responsibility for children, and when it is legitimate to provide supportive welfare services or to compulsorily intervene into the family (Gilbert, 2011; Berrick et al, forthcoming).

Adoption from care among child protection removal decisions

When children need to be separated from their parents' care for protective reasons, the removal processes across the different child welfare systems fall into four categories: emergency removals, voluntary admissions, involuntary admissions and adoptions (Burns et al, 2017: 223–6). Emergency removals, often short-term (hours, days or weeks), aim to provide immediate security and care for a child in a concerning or even dangerous situation. Voluntary admissions rest on consent given by parents and children of certain ages, and they aim to support or rehabilitate the family and are often short-term. While the child is in voluntary care, the parents keep their rights as parents, with only few restrictions; following that, social workers, parents and carers share day-to-day decision-making. Far more intrusive interventions – often referred to as 'care orders' in European and US literature – restrict parents' rights as it is the state that has full or partial custody of the child and the child is looked after by the public authorities for a longer period of time. Decisions on care orders are made by courts or court-like decision-making bodies. Care orders are formally temporary and should aim for family reunification (Burns et al, 2017; Farmer, 2018). However, there are children that cannot be reunified with their birth parents, and it is for this group of children that the government may consider adoption from care. Adoption as a child protection measure terminates the rights of birth parents and aims to be a lifelong arrangement.

As a result of the removal decision, the child is placed in family-based care (foster care, kinship care, guardianship or adoption) or residential care. There are considerable differences in the use of these types of alternative care among the countries as, in practice, 'foster care' or 'residential care' may mean quite different things in terms of the recruitment of carers, supervision and home or unit sizes, among other issues. The tendency during recent decades has been towards foster care, resulting in 90 per cent of children in foster care in some countries and only less than 10 per cent in residential care (for example, in Australia and Ireland), yet only 44–9 per cent in foster care in others (for example, in Italy and Germany) (del Valle and Bravo, 2013). Alongside adoption, some countries include guardianship with kin and long-term foster care to provide an option for long-term care, while some other countries focus only on long-term care, with permanent placement options not included in legislation. Some jurisdictions have legislation or statutory guidance providing a 'hierarchy' of preferred permanence options. In the US and some states in Canada and Australia, leaving care by return to a parent is the first option. Failing that, only leaving care by adoption or guardianship are recognised permanence options, the only other recorded exit route in the US is 'emancipation'. In England, the preferred options are leaving care by return to a parent or a legally secured kinship placement. Following that, long-term foster care (with kin or unrelated foster carers), adoption and (for older young people) group care are recognised permanence options, depending on the needs of the child.

Once an adoption order has been made, children are in 'private care' in contrast to 'public care', and all the responsibilities of bringing up the child are transferred to the adoptive parents. The child protection authorities have no rights to intervene unless new child protection concerns arise. In some jurisdictions, the child welfare authorities or adoption agencies have a duty to assist if asked to do so, and there may be duties associated with court orders or agreements about continuing birth family links, though these are typically not enforceable. There are several complex issues included in the use of adoption as a form of child protection alternative, such as decision-making practices, non-consensual adoptions, support services, sharing information and contact after adoption (Skivenes, 2010; Palacios et al, 2019). Governments differ in their approaches to birth parents and future adoptive parents, how they assess their motives and skills, and how they provide support, and thereby indirectly influence children's rights after adoption. When children are already placed in the care of long-term foster parents, the transformation from 'substitute carers' to adoptive parents includes a variety of legal, financial, emotional, existential, social and cultural changes in the lives and social positions of the children to be adopted, future adoptive parents and birth parents. How these changes are incorporated into child protection policy and practices is of high importance to both the child and the adults and other children whose lives are touched in the short and longer term by the adoption.

If parents' rights are already restricted at that point and the long-term separation of the child from their parents has taken place for their best interest, how is the step towards adoption taken and, in particular, how are the decisions regarding the human and basic rights of children and their adult birth relatives and siblings made? In a recent study examining national legislation, organisational guidelines (for courts and child protection or supervisory agencies), statistics and expert knowledge in eight European countries, all included in this book, serious concerns were raised about the limited accountability regarding adoptions from care (Burns et al, 2019). The study reported on a lack of information about the proceedings, as well as a lack of transparency, both for those involved and the wider public, and concluded that there is a missing connection between wider democratic society and this part of the legal systems in the countries studied. In addition, research is either limited or non-existent. The legitimacy of decision-making procedures, the involvement of parents and children, and the nature of the expertise guiding the decisions and services provided before, during and after the adoption decision are, however, of major importance for all involved.

Long-term care and adoption from care as alternatives

As can be seen from the chapters that follow, different countries, while committed to the basic principles of the CRC, have arrived at different positions with respect to the place of adoption within child placement legislation and practice. Shared understanding of child and adult psychological development has led to broad consensus across national boundaries that children who have been exposed to maltreatment, trauma and loss must be provided with stability and belonging within a family when birth parents cannot care for them. Preferably, then, children should grow up with relatives, but if not, then within a stable and committed substitute family. The important question for governments to handle is how to care for the children that are in public care. What is the best interest option for these children of different ages, with different needs and with differing prior relationships and experiences of loss and trauma? This question is urgent as child protection systems tend to expand and the number of children in public care is not decreasing, but rather increasing, in many countries (Gilbert et al, 2011; Berrick et al, forthcoming). However, a general message from research seems to be that, overall, the welfare states are not sufficiently protecting these children's rights,[2] and this knowledge has resulted in questions about the quality of the child protection system and the services and support to children and families.

Regarding the different alternatives for children needing long-term care, there is general agreement that adoption will be the best way of securing 'permanence' and enduring family membership for some children since it combines legal permanence (a lifetime, legal relationship between an adult and child), residential permanence (continuity of caregiving in a designated home) and relational permanence (in which an adult and child see each other as family) (see Palacios et al, 2019). The combination of these three elements of permanence makes adoptions different from long-term foster care. Triseliotis (2002), for example, based on an extensive research review, concludes that the main difference between adoption and long-term fostering is in the higher levels of emotional security, sense of belonging and general well-being expressed by those who have been adopted compared to those in foster care. This conclusion has been well documented and further substantiated in a range of solid studies that find evidence to support adoption as a better alternative for children needing long-term care in terms of better developmental consequences, placement stability, emotional security and transitions into adulthood, among other issues (for a meta-study, see Christoffersen et al 2007, 2008; for comprehensive register data studies, see Vinnjerlung and Hjern, 2011; Hjern et al, 2019; for overviews of this literature, see also Tregeagle et al, 2019).

In the chapters that follow, readers will discover how the countries represented in this book arrived at the present use of adoption from care. The evidence provided by research and used by the particular countries will be presented in each chapter; however, it is clear that in most jurisdictions, there is little use of evidence to support the present balance between the different options. The knowledge base is more advanced in some countries than others. This book cannot conclude about whether the approach of a particular country to adoptions from care is preferable to that of another country with different historical, social and cultural factors related to adoption and child welfare.

The aim of the book

In this book, we explore adoptions from care in countries with different policies and practices. We know that children who have been taken into public care are adopted in each of the countries included in this volume, yet the legislation, practices and responsible bodies for pre-adoption, adoption and post-adoption decisions vary, and countries consider the option of non-consensual adoptions differently. Adoptions from care are, for example, included in child protection legislation and organisations in England and Norway, whereas adoptions and child protection removals are separated in legislation, organisations and decision-makers in Finland. When studying adoptions from care, we will also look at other options for children who need permanent or long-term care, and consider how countries arrived at their current placement policies and legal arrangements.

The book provides an opportunity to look beyond the parents' rights–children's rights dichotomy as it explores the notions of responsibilities and outcomes. Fundamental questions are: is adoption a service for the child's best interests, for parents unable to provide adequate care for a child, for children or for adults who wish to create – or expand – their family in this way? Or, is adoption a service for states who wish to make use of a cheaper way of discharging their responsibilities towards maltreated children 'throughout their childhood'? The lens of 'responsibilities' leads to a more nuanced analysis of differences in different countries. Central are birth parents', foster carers', residential childcare workers' and adopters' responsibilities towards a child. However, weight is also given to clarification of the state's responsibilities towards the child it has removed from a dangerous or life-limiting situation, and we also explore the state's responsibilities towards the vulnerable adults unable to meet the 24/7 0–19+ needs of their children. Where is the 'middle way' (and for which children/family circumstances) between creating a totally new family by changing the child's legal identity and creating a 'shared parental responsibility' that may vary over time and with different ways of sharing parental duties?

The countries chosen for this book have a range of usage of adoptions from care – with England and US at one end of continuum, Spain and Estonia more inclined to use adoptions than the other European countries, and Finland least likely. However, we also have a range of judicial processes (the extent to which care processes and adoption processes are fully integrated, as with England, or very separate legal systems). Other differences include adoption by specially recruited adopters and early placement, contrasted with adoption only by foster carers with whom the child is already well settled. The book departs from the premise that there is a connection between the welfare state and child protection system, which is why the jurisdictions included in the book cover different child protection systems (see Gilbert et al, 2011). Four countries – England, Estonia, Ireland and the US – have a risk-oriented child protection system,[3] in which the emphasis is primarily to protect children from maltreatment. These systems have a relatively high threshold for family service provision and compulsory intervention, such as a care order. The five remaining countries – Austria, Finland, Germany, Norway and Spain – all have systems that are categorised as family service systems oriented towards the protection of children's needs. In these systems, there are generous service provisions and a focus on families and children's well-being. Thus, the thresholds for interventions are lower. Although the basic philosophy of family service-oriented systems is similar, there are two branches within it: a family-based branch, represented by Austria, Germany and Spain; and a child-based branch, represented by Finland and Norway. As noted by Gilbert et al (2011), typologies of this kind inform about orientations and patterns rather than about fixed systems of protecting children. Nevertheless, this cross-cutting of service provision and intervention approaches helps to understand the differential use of adoption from care among the jurisdictions included in this volume, an issue to which we return in the concluding chapter.

As the chapters will demonstrate, the authors are highly experienced in the field of child welfare in their respective countries and have contributed to several inter-country explorations of child protection. The book is organised into three parts. Part I includes analyses of country practices of adoptions from care in risk-oriented child protection systems. Part II includes analyses of country practices of adoptions from care in service-oriented child protection systems. Within each of these two parts, we have asked each country contributor to cover the following topics:

- adoptions from care in legislation, national guidelines and the knowledge base;
- other types of adoption;
- the social, historical and cultural context in which adoptions from care take place;
- decision-making regarding adoptions;
- adoptions from care and children in long-term care (number and profiles);
- critical points in present policy and practice regarding adoptions from care; and
- anticipation about the future of adoptions from care.

Part III covers specific key issues related to adoptions from care that further demonstrate their complexity, including international human rights, the recognition of attachment in decisions regarding adoptions, adoptive kinship networks and the creation of family. The issues typically attached to adoption – whether nature matters more than nurture, or vice versa – expand to the topics of narratives (how we make sense of identity and social bonds, as suggested by Howe [2009]), as well as to those of safeguarding children's rights in the context of broader human rights. In the concluding chapter, we bring the findings together and discuss the role of adoptions from care in different societal contexts.

Acknowledgements

This project has received funding from the Research Council of Norway under the Independent Projects – Humanities and Social Science program (grant no. 262773) and European Research Council under the European Union's Horizon 2020 research and innovation programme (grant agreement No 724460). Disclaimer: This chapter reflects only the authors' views and the funding agencies are not responsible for any use that may be made of the information contained therein.

Notes

[1] The US has not formally ratified the CRC.
[2] In terms of outcomes for children in out-of-home care, two recent systematic reviews (Gypen et al, 2017; Kääriälä and Hiilamo, 2017) on existing knowledge and research on children growing up in public care reveal that they are discouraging and bleak.
[3] England is positioned between these two approaches, with family service-oriented legal provisions but operating in practice within a risk-oriented framework.

References

Berrick, J., Gilbert, N. and Skivenes, M. (eds) (forthcoming) *International Handbook of Child Protection Services*, New York: Oxford University Press.

Breen, C., Krutzinna, J., Luhamaa, K. and Skivenes, M. (2020) 'Family life for children in state care. An analysis of the European Court of Human Rights' reasoning on adoption without consent', *International Journal of Human Rights*, 28: 715–47. Available at: https://brill.com/view/journals/chil/aop/article-10.1163-15718182-28040001/article-10.1163-15718182-28040001.xml?body=pdf-35540 (accessed 9 December 2020).

Briggs, L. and Marre, D. (2009) 'Introduction. The circulation of children', in D. Marre and L. Briggs (eds) *International Adoption. Global Inequalities and the Circulation of Children*, New York: New York University Press, pp 1–28.

Burns, K., Pösö, T. and Skivenes, M. (eds) (2017) *Child Welfare Removals by the State. A Cross-Country Analysis of Decision-Making Systems*, New York: Oxford University Press.

Burns, K., Kriz, K., Krutzinna, J., Luhamaa, K., Meysen, T., Pösö, T., Sagrario, S., Skivenes, M. and Thoburn, J. (2019) 'The hidden proceedings – an analysis of accountability of child protection adoption proceedings in eight European jurisdictions', *European Journal of Comparative Law and Governance*, 6(4): 339–71.

Christoffersen, M.N. (2012) 'A study of adopted children, their environment, and development: a systematic review', *Adoption Quarterly*, 15(3): 220–37.

Christoffersen, M.N., Soothill, K. and Francis, B. (2007) 'Violent life events and social disadvantage: a systematic study on the social background of various kinds of lethal violence, other violence crime, suicide, and suicide attempts', *Journal of Scandinavian Studies in Criminology and Crime Prevention*, 8(2): 157–84.

Christoffersen, M.N., Hammen, I., Raft Andersen, K. and Jeldtoft, N. (2008) 'Adoption som indsats: en systematisk gennemgang af udenlandske erfaringer' ['Adoption as an effort: A systematic review of foreign experiences'], SFI - Det Nationale Forskningscenter for Velfærd. SFI-Rapport Nr. 07:32.

Del Valle, J. and Bravo, A. (2013) 'Current trends, figures and challenges in out of home care: an international comparative analysis', *Psychosocial Intervention*, 22: 251–7.

European Parliamentary Research Service (2016) 'Briefing. Adoption of children in the European Union'. Available at: www.europarl.europa.eu/RegData/etudes/BRIE/2016/583860/EPRS_BRI(2016)583860_EN.pdf (accessed 24 June 2020).

Farmer, E. (2018) 'Reunification from out-of-home care. A research overview of good practice in returning children home from care', University of Bristol. Available at: https://research-information.bris.ac.uk/ws/portalfiles/portal/189519934/Reunification_from_Out_of_Home_Care_A_Research_Overview_of_Good_Practice.pdf (accessed 6 March 2020).

Fenton-Glynn, C. (2015) 'Adoption without consent. Directorate General for Internal Policies', Policy Department, Citizens' Rights and Constitutional Affairs, European Parliament. Available at: www.europarl.europa.eu/RegData/etudes/STUD/2015/519236/IPOL_STU(2015)519236_EN.pdf (accessed 20 June 2020).

Gilbert, N. (2011) 'A comparative study of child welfare systems: abstract orientations and concrete results', *Children and Youth Services Review*, 34(3): 532–6.

Gilbert, N., Parton, N. and Skivenes, M. (eds) (2011) *Child Protection Systems: International Trends and Orientations*, New York: Oxford University Press.

Gypen, L., Vanderfaeille, J., de Maeyer, S., Belenger, L. and van Holen, F. (2017) 'Outcomes of children who grew up in foster care: systematic review', *Children and Youth Services Review*, 76(C): 74–83.

Helland, H. and Skivenes, M. (2019) 'Adopsjon til barnets beste' ['Adoption in the best interest of the child'], *Tidsskriftet Fosterhjemskontakt*, 2: 2–7.

Hjern, A., Vinnerljung, B. and Brännström, L. (2019) 'Outcomes in adulthood of adoption after long-term foster care: a sibling study', *Developmental Child Welfare*, 1(1): 61–75.

Howe, D. (2009) 'Nature, nurture and narratives', in M. Wrobel and E. Neil (eds) *International Advances in Adoption Research for Practice*, Chichester: Wiley-Blackwell, pp 1–16.

Kääriälä, A. and Hiilamo, H. (2017) 'Children in out-of-home care as young adults: a systematic review of outcomes in the Nordic countries', *Children and Youth Services Review*, 79: 107–14.

Palacios, J., Brodzinsky, D., Grotevant, H., Johnson, D., Juffer, F., Marninez-Mora, L. Muhamedrahimov, R., Selwyn, J., Simmons, J. and Tarren-Sweeney, M. (2019) 'Adoption in the service of child protection. An international interdisciplinary perspective', *Psychology, Public Policy, and Law*, 25(2): 57–72.

Selman, P. (2009) 'From Bucharest to Beijing: changes in countries sending children for international adoption 1990 to 2006', in G. Wrobel and E. Neil (eds) *International Advances in Adoption Research for Practice*, Chichester: Wiley-Blackwell, pp 41–70.

Skivenes, M. (2010) 'Judging the child's best interests: rational reasoning or subjective presumptions?', *Acta Sociologica*, 53(4): 339–53.

Skivenes, M., Barn, R., Kriz, K. and Pösö, T. (eds) (2015) *Child Welfare Systems and Migrant Children – A Cross-Country Study of Policies and Practice*, New York: Oxford University Press.

Tefre, Ø. (2020) 'The child's best interest and the politics of adoptions from care in Norway', *The International Journal of Children's Rights*, 28(2): 288–321.

Thoburn, J. and Featherstone, B. (2019) 'Adoption, child rescue, maltreatment and poverty', in S. Webb (ed) *The Routledge Handbook of Critical Social Work*, London: Routledge, pp 401–11.

Tregeagle, S., Moggach, L., Trivedi, H. and Ward, H. (2019) 'Previous life experiences and the vulnerability of children adopted from out-of-home care: the impact of adverse childhood experiences and child welfare decision-making', *Children and Youth Services Review*, 96(1): 55–63.

Triseliotis, J. (2002) 'Long-term foster care or adoption? The evidence examined', *Child and Family Social Work*, 7: 23–33.

UN General Assembly (2010) 'Guidelines for the alternative care of children', resolution adopted by the General Assembly 64/142. Available at: https://digitallibrary.un.org/record/673583 (accessed 9 December 2020).

UN General Assembly (2019) 'Promotion and protection of the rights of children: follow-up on the outcome of the special session on children', report of the 3rd Committee: General Assembly, 74th Session. Available at: www.un.org/en/ga/62/plenary/children/bkg.shtml (accessed 23 June 2019).

Vinnerljung, B. and Hjern, A. (2011) 'Cognitive, educational and self-support outcomes of long-term foster care versus adoption. A Swedish national cohort study', *Children and Youth Services Review*, 33(10): 1902–10.

PART I

Adoption from care in risk-oriented child protection systems

2

Adoption from care in England: learning from experience

June Thoburn

Introduction

Prior to the 1980s, most adoptions in England[1] were of infants whose birth parent(s) requested adoption or were adoptions by a step-parent. In the early years after the Adoption Act 1927, numbers rose gradually and reached a peak in the 1960s. Although these were technically placements at the request of parent(s) (usually only the mother), in reality, those 'giving up' a child for adoption (most often shortly after birth) to (mainly) childless couples did so because of the stigma of illegitimacy and the lack of housing and income that would have made it possible for them to parent the child. From the 1950s onwards, improved welfare provision, a reduction in stigma and the availability of contraception led to a fall in numbers. For children who may need out-of-home care, the emphasis especially since the Children and Young Persons Act 1963 (strengthened by Section 17 of the Children Act 1989) was to assist parents to avoid the need for care and work for speedy reunification. Limitation of parents' rights was only possible via a court order or the assumption of parental rights by the local authority (LA) if return home seemed unlikely. Small numbers were adopted from care but placement for adoption from care was not generally pursued for children who were past infancy, had disabilities or were of minority ethnic heritage. In summary, until the mid-1970s the position in England was very similar to that which currently applies in most European jurisdictions.

Professional concern began to be expressed about the lack of legal rights of parents when an administrative decision could lead to adoption without parental consent. Also, in the early 1970s, media reports began to appear about children being 'dragged away' from 'loving foster parents' where they were well settled. This coincided with political and public outrage at the death of Maria Colwell, a child returned from her kinship foster carers to her mother and the stepfather, who murdered her (DHSS, 1974; Butler and Drakeford, 2011). One result was the Children Act 1975, which determined that parental rights could only be removed by a court order. This Act also increased the power of LAs to oppose reunification if it was not in a child's interest and strengthened the rights of foster carers to adopt children who had been settled with them for two years.

Another key contributor to the 1975 legislation was an influential research-based book by Jane Rowe and Lydia Lambert (1974), entitled *Children Who Wait*. This demonstrated that although policy was for children to return to parents after short stays in care, a substantial number remained in care and were often exposed to unplanned placement changes. Around the same time, messages from the US about success in placing 'hard-to-place' children in care for adoption aroused interest among policymakers and child welfare professionals. Professional debates around this time started to encourage placement of children in care with adopters not previously known to them. Specialist voluntary sector agencies, based on US models, recruited, trained and supported families who adopted 'hard-to-place' children from care. This included younger children previously considered 'unadoptable', especially black children and those with disabilities, as well as older children in children's homes (Fratter et al, 1991). These agencies emphasised the rights of children to 'stability' and 'permanence'. Although placing mainly with adopters, they also made placements with specially recruited 'permanent' foster carers, especially if there were strong birth family links. Post-adoption birth family contact was also encouraged where appropriate. Some LAs set up their own specialist adoption services and introduced 'time limits' such that if the child was in care for six months, a permanence plan (preferably via adoption) should be made.

This shift of balance in legislation between 'parents' rights' and 'children's rights', as well as the strengthening of foster carer/adopter rights, did not go unchallenged. The government committee set up following the death of Maria Colwell and in response to these other concerns (Short, 1984), although broadly following the direction of travel with respect to the importance of stability, introduced a note of caution about the move towards adoption without parental consent. The report's conclusion that 'permanence should not have been considered synonymous with adoption' (Short, 1984, pp 75–8) set in train a process of reviewing the balance between parents', children's and carers' rights and led to the Children Act 1989. This strengthened not only children's protection rights, but also birth parents' rights to receive a service to help them care for their children.

From the late 1990s, changes in policy emphasis and practice guidance led to increasing numbers leaving care through adoption, facilitated by increased funding to LAs and adoption agencies to recruit potential adoptive parents. These policy and funding changes (Cabinet Office, 2000) led to adoptions from care peaking at 5,050 in 2014 (a rate of around 40 per 100,000 children aged 0–17). A note of caution then came from the judiciary in the form of a series of appeal court judgements (summarised by Sir James Munby, the President of the Family Division, in Court of Appeal, Re B-S [2013] EWCA Civ 1146), restating the legislation that adoptions from care without parental consent could only be agreed 'if nothing else will do'. Around the same time, there was an increase in the placement of children from care with family members (using the Special Guardianship Order [SGO] introduced in 2002). Numbers leaving care via adoption fell from 5,050 in 2013/14 to 3,820 in 2017/18 (see Tables 2.1 and 2.2). This rate of 32 per 100,000 children aged 0–17 is still much higher than in other European countries, though the drop in numbers contrasts with a rise in those adopted from care in the US (Burns et al, 2019; see also Berrick, this volume).

Although considerable effort was made to increase the adoption of older children, the data indicate that from the mid-1990s onwards, the trend has been for most children placed for adoption from care to be singleton white British children aged under 24 months when placed. Efforts have also been made to improve stability for children in long-term foster care. Despite some amendments and statutory guidance updates, the emphasis continues to be on balancing the rights of families to support within the community and providing more intrusive protective services only when necessary, with adoption from care being a small but important part of the child protection service.

Legislation and guidance

The principles covering placement of children entering care by voluntary agreement ('accommodated') or by a court order ('in care') were laid down by the England and Wales Children Act 1989 and the accompanying guidance (the legal term for all children in care is 'looked after'). Although not formally designated as a family court until the Crime and Courts Act 2013, after the Children Act became operational in 1991, magistrates and county courts worked more closely together and judges hearing family matters became more specialist.

Central to this legislation are the Section 1 principles and checklist that must be considered when a court is making any order with respect to the care of a child:

- the child's welfare shall be the paramount consideration;
- unnecessary delay is to be avoided;
- courts and LAs must ascertain and give due consideration to the ascertainable wishes and feelings of the child;
- consideration should be given to physical, emotional and educational needs; the likely effect of any change in circumstances; age, sex, background and any characteristics which the court considers relevant; any actual or likely harm;
- parents' views and capability of each parent to meet the child's needs must be considered.

Courts must consider the range of available orders, whether or not they have been specifically applied for by a party to the proceeding.

When considering making an adoption placement order, there are slight changes to the checklist, substituting the detailed list of child characteristics with the more general 'the child's particular needs' in order to give greater flexibility in finding suitable adopters.

Four checklist considerations are added:

- the likely effect on the child (throughout his life) of having ceased to be a member of the original family and become an adopted person;
- the relationship which the child has with relatives, and with any other person in relation to whom the court or agency considers the relationship to be relevant;
- the ability and willingness of any of the child's relatives, or of any such person, to provide the child with a secure environment in which the child can develop, and otherwise to meet the child's needs;
- the wishes and feelings of any of the child's relatives, or of any such person, regarding the child. (Section 1,4,f of the Adoption and Children Act 2002)

Decision-making on adoption

There is a very small number of cases (estimated as fewer than 100 each year) when each (known) parent requests adoption and signs (no earlier than six weeks after the birth) informed and witnessed consent. In such cases, a parent may withdraw consent and the child must be returned within seven days unless an application for a placement order has been made. In all other cases, the LA applies for a care order, which the court may make if it is satisfied that the child has suffered or is likely to suffer significant harm and that the harm is attributable to a parent. The court must also be satisfied that making an order 'would be better for the child than making no order at all' (s 1 Children Act 1989).

The LA may apply for a placement order if each parent gives informed and witnessed consent, or the court dispenses with their consent. The checklist provisions apply but the court must also be satisfied (s 52) that parent(s) cannot be found or lack capacity, or that the *welfare of the child requires* the consent to be dispensed with.

Once the 'significant harm' threshold is judged to have been crossed, dispensing with consent to adoption is not linked to specific parental behaviours, but rather to the welfare needs of the particular child, as determined with reference to the checklists. Case law has determined that the term 'requires' is to be interpreted as all realistic alternatives having been considered and balanced against each other, and 'nothing else will do'.

When a care order has been made, the LA shares parental responsibility (PR) with the parent(s) but may limit the extent to which parents can make decisions about the child. There is the assumption of 'reasonable contact' (for parents, other adult family members who are important to the child and siblings living separately), and efforts have to be made to place siblings together. There is a provision (rarely used except to limit contact) for the court to make a (s 34) contact order. Once a placement order has been made, the exercise of PR passes to the LA, and once placed with prospective adopters, PR is shared with them. The right of the parent to contest the placement order is removed unless granted leave by the court because of substantial changes in circumstances. The court may make an order for continuing contact with parents, relatives or siblings before the adoption is finalised (s 26). However, this provision, even with respect to siblings wishing to remain in contact, is rarely used (Monk and McVarish, 2018). If applications for care and placement orders are concurrent, judgments will combine the reasons for each order being made.

If the child has not been placed with prospective adopters or prospective adopters have not applied to adopt within a reasonable period of time, the LA, the child or a parent may apply to court for the placement order to be rescinded. In most such cases, the child will remain in care, though the court may determine that the child should return to the parent(s) or be placed with relatives under an SGO.

Once a child has lived with prospective adopters for at least ten weeks, and subject to satisfactory social work reports, the prospective adoptive parent(s) may apply to the family court for an adoption order, which has the result that 'an adopted person is to be treated in law as if born as the child of the adopters or adopter' (s 46). Parents must be notified of the adoption hearing unless they ask not to be. They have a right to attend and be heard but may only contest the adoption if they have leave of the court, which will only be given if circumstances have substantially changed. The child does not usually attend the adoption hearing itself, but may attend a separate informal hearing to 'meet the judge'.

All previous orders lapse but the court, at the time or at a later date, may make an order (s 51) requiring the adopters to arrange for the child to have contact with 'former' parent(s), relatives or siblings. Applicants for such an order can be the adopters or the child, or (if leave is first given by the court) a parent or other person with a connection with the child. Such applications are unusual, though some form of post-adoption contact (usually indirect) is often agreed at the time the order is made. There is provision and, indeed, encouragement for foster carers to apply to adopt children who have been living with them for 12 months if there is no plan for reunification with a parent.

The previously outlined process only applies to children placed for adoption by an approved LA or voluntary adoption agency (VAA). Privately arranged adoptions are not permitted, but people with whom a child has lived continuously for three years may apply to adopt. The application has to be assessed and a report provided to the court by a VAA or LA social worker.

The adoption service and the practice of adoption from care

Section 3 of the Adoption and Children Act 2002 places the duty on LAs to ensure the availability of a service to children, prospective adopters and birth relatives of a child who may be or has been adopted. To further its aims of improving the adoption service and increasing numbers adopted from care, in 2014, the government set up the Adoption Leadership Board 'to provide leadership to the adoption system and drive improvements in performance'(Coram-BAAF, https:// coram-i.org.uk/asglb/ (accessed 9 December 2020). From 2018, this became the Adoption and Special Guardianship Leadership Board.

Almost all children adopted in England do so via a registered VAA or LA. There is broad agreement, including from the national inspectorate, that the quality of adoption work is generally high. LA adoption sections and VAAs are mostly staffed by registered and experienced social workers who receive specialist post-qualifying training. For over 70 years, practitioners have had access to training materials and research publications via the British Agencies for Adoption and Fostering (now Coram-BAAF) and its specialist journal *Adoption and Fostering*. Fostering Network, a member-led national body, also provides advice, publications and research for foster carers and adopters. Since 2016, VAAs and LA adoption services have been required to combine as a network of Regional Adoption Agencies intended to improve effectiveness and reduce costs.

The service for children and adopted persons

The child's LA social worker leads on the preparation of a *permanence plan* for all children entering care on a voluntary or court-ordered basis. Family group meetings (sometimes referred to as family group conferences – a specialist service bringing together family members to seek an agreed way of meeting the child's protection and care needs) are increasingly part of this work, which may start even before a child is born and/or when entry to care is a possibility (Dickens et al, 2019). The national guidance on permanence planning (DfE, 2015), in line with the United Nations Convention on the Rights of the Child, Human Rights Convention and 'no [court] order unless necessary principle', states that the first option should be return to one or both birth parents. If this is not possible, preference is for placement with family members or close friends, preferably leaving care via an SGO. Other permanence options are long-term foster care, adoption or, usually for teenagers, a group care placement. Unlike in most other countries, long-term foster care is recognised in statutory guidance as a permanence option and is further encouraged by 'staying put' provisions for the young person to remain a part of the foster family after the age of 18.

At any time during or after court proceedings, a decision can be taken by an LA senior manager that adoption should be the plan for a child. At this stage, the child may be placed with prospective adopters who are also approved as foster carers but will usually be placed in short-term foster care and moved to a specially recruited adoptive family if the court makes a placement order. The adoption specialist worker works jointly with the child's social worker to prepare the child for adoption.

Once matched with prospective adopters, the child's worker or the adoption worker will prepare the child for the move and arrange introductory visits. After placement, the child is visited by (usually) the adoption social worker, who may continue to work with the child regarding identity issues and will assist with contact arrangements and family meetings. Further services may be provided after adoption at the request of the new parents. Mental health or LA social work teams may become involved if the child experiences serious difficulties, and this may include the child going into care (usually on a voluntary basis).

An important service is to assist with access to case records (both when the child was in care and at any time after adoption). There may also be assistance for adoptees of any age in re-establishing birth family contact if this has been lost (Howe and Feast, 2000).

Service for prospective adopters and adoptive families

The LA adoption team will match the child with adopters it has recruited and trained, or will contact VAAs to see if there are any suitable waiting adopters. A government-funded system allows prospective adopters to access anonymised information about children for whom there is an adoption plan. For children in care who have had an adoption plan for some time (mostly children past infancy, with disabilities, of minority heritage or needing to be placed with siblings), adoption agencies may arrange 'adoption parties' so that potential adopters may meet 'waiting' children in an informal way. These are the subject of controversy among professionals, as well as parent and children interest groups and in the media. There will sometimes be a meeting between the adopters and the birth parents either just before or just after placement. Space precludes further details of adoption practice. Reference is made in the following sections to research findings, and details about practice can be found on the Coram-BAAF website.[2]

The 2002 Act requires the LA to provide a post-adoption support service. Adoption allowances are available with respect to placement of some children who may be 'hard to place', and since 2015, adopters and adopted young people can apply for grants to pay for therapeutic care from the government-funded Adoption Support Fund (DfE, 2018).

Services to birth relatives

Section 3 of the 2002 Act lists services and support to parents of children to be placed for adoption. Around the time of the care application and placement, when there will usually be arrangements for supervised contact, birth parents are the focus of much social work activity. This often includes encouraging the parent to 'accept' the need for adoption and possibly to meet the adopters, and arranging the sensitive last meeting with the child if, as is usually the case, there will be no direct contact after placement. Parents may also be helped to write 'letters for later life' to help the child understand why they were adopted. However, the service is weakest in respect of parents once the child has been adopted. Most often, longer-term support is restricted to providing a 'letter-box service' (Neil et al, 2010, 2014), unless the agency assists with direct family meetings after placement. However, the 2002 Act made provision for specialist adoption support agencies, and these, and some of the VAAs, provide specialist support to birth parents and relatives. More recently, self-help groups have emerged to provide support to birth parents, and these work closely with the post-adoption services. The 2002 Act authorised birth parents to seek identifying information about an adopted child who has reached the age of 21, and the birth parents and siblings of adopted children, as well as the adoptees themselves, increasingly seek to make links using social media.

Numbers and profiles of adoptions in England

The Law Commission and government teams drawing up the 1989 Act were also responsible for drawing up legislation governing arrangements after separation and divorce and the Adoption and Children Act 2002, and ensured close alignment of philosophy and detailed provisions. Legislation for step-parent and other in-family adoption was included within the 2002 Act, as was provision for the adoption in England of children from other jurisdictions. Inter-country adoption has never been popular in England (see Table 2.1). Although a non-governmental organisation (NGO) was set up to provide advice to those wishing to adopt from overseas, there has never been an agency in England set up specifically to arrange overseas adoptions. Those who wish to adopt from overseas follow the same assessment processes as those adopting from care, as well as the agreed processes under the Hague Convention, and there is a separate section in the *Statutory Guidance on Adoption* (DfE, 2013). Table 2.1 shows that adoptions by step-parents used to be high but the 2002 Act and guidance discouraged in-family adoptions and provided other ways in which step-parents could become legal guardians with shared parental responsibility.

As noted earlier, numbers leaving care via adoption have been decreasing (see Tables 2.1 and 2.2). Nationally provided administrative data (DfE and National Statistics, 2019) on children with an adoption plan and adopted from care in 2017/18 document that:

- A total of 11,300 children at year end (roughly equal numbers male and female) had an adoption plan but only 2,230 were already living with prospective adopters; 3,282 had left care via adoption during the year (13 per cent of all care leavers), of whom 78 per cent were aged less than four and 60 per cent came into care when under 12 months; and 84 per cent were of white British heritage (compared with 75 per cent of the children in care).

- Most children adopted from care are placed with specially recruited adopters, though 220 (10 per cent) of those living with prospective adopters were to be adopted by their current foster carers.
- Parental consent was dispensed with in 48 per cent of cases (but more would have been opposed at the placement order stage – not opposing in court does not necessarily equate with consenting).
- A total of 58 per cent of those with an adoption plan had been waiting for a placement for 12 months or more. During the year, the placement decision was reversed for 670 children, in 28 per cent of cases because the court declined to make a placement order and in 17 per cent of cases because no adopters could be matched with the child.
- In 2018/19, 89 per cent of orders were made to a couple (12 per cent of whom were same-sex couples) and 11 per cent were made to a single adopter.

The provision in the 2002 Act for SGOs also provided a route for other family members (including kinship foster carers of children in care, who

Table 2.1: Adoption numbers and rates: England, 1980–2018

	In-family (including step-parent) adoptions	Inter-country adoptions	Numbers adopted from care (rate per 100,000)	All adoptions
1980	3,668	–	1,634	10,609
1989	3,000 (approx.)	–	2,411	7,044
2000	–	326 (all UK 2001)	–	4,943
2006	–	363 (all UK)	3,300 (30)	5,556
2010/11	516	(In column 4)	3,200 (28)	4,709
2015	435	(In column 4)	5,360 (45)	6,197
2018	410	(In column 4)	3,820 (32)	4,932

Note: Office for National Statistics figures combine England and Wales. All adoptions figures from 2006 include step-parent and inter-country adoptions.

Source: Office of National Statistics (2011) and Department for Education and National Statistics (2015, 2019)

Table 2.2: Children entering care, in care and adopted from care: England, 2005–18

	2005	2010	2015	2018
Entrants to care (rate per 100,000 children)	25,000 (223)	28,090 (243)	31,350 (280)	32,050 (290)
Children in care at year end (rate per 100,000)	60,300 (550)	64,400 (580)	69,470 (600)	75,420 (640)
% in care by voluntary agreement (at year end)	29%	32%	28%	20%
In care on court order (at year end) (% of all in care)	42,813 (71%)	43,440 (68%)	49,840 (72%)	61,710 (80%)
Total in care living with adopters at year end[a] (% of all in care)	3,000 (5%)	2,300 (4%)	3,580 (5%)	2,230 (3%)
Total leaving care via adoption order during year (rate per 100,000 child population)	3,700 (32)	3,200 (28)	5,360 (45)	3,820 (32)
Total leaving care to return to a parent during year	11,000	9,800	10,700	8,810
Total leaving care (guardianship to relative or former foster carer)	70	760	3,570	3,430
Average stay (years) (all leaving care in that year)	2.13	2.37	2.15	2.1

Note: [a] These are children in local authority care but placed either as foster children or under the provisions of an adoption placement order with the person(s) who will be applying to adopt them. The percentage given is of all children in care at year end. Separate data are provided for those who left care during the year following an adoption order.

Source: Department for Education and National Statistics (2015, 2019)

might have sought an adoption order in the past) to provide long-term legally secure care for young relatives. The provision is also available to foster carers. This is a partial explanation for the smaller number of adoptions by foster carers, especially when compared with the US (see Berrick, this volume), which otherwise has a similar adoption policy.

Research on adoption and alternatives to adoption

A large volume of research going back to the mid-1970s reports on adoptions from care and alternative long-term placements. Adoption practice has been much influenced by US research but the aim here is to provide an overview of conclusions from UK studies, especially with respect to outcomes (for an overview of research, see Thomas, 2013).

Starting with birth parents, studies and personal accounts concur that losing a child to adoption has long-term negative impacts on many birth mothers and fathers (Howe and Feast, 2000). With respect to adoptive families, much long-term outcome research concerns children adopted as infants; however, only studies of children placed from care are referred to here. Those reporting on the views and well-being of children and young adults include Thoburn et al (1986, 2000), Hill et al (1988), Thomas et al (1999), Neil et al (2014) and Selwyn et al (2014). Since English legislation requires those planning and making judgements about placements from care to look to the future and decide whether 'the child's welfare' 'throughout his life' 'requires it', longitudinal outcome research is of particular relevance. Key longitudinal adoption studies are those of Selwyn et al (2014) and Neil et al (2014). These report a very low rate of adoption breakdown. Selwyn and colleagues estimate a post-adoption disruption rate of around 3 per cent over a 12-year period, though those disrupting before the order was made are not included. Neil and colleagues, reporting on children placed under three, found no actual disruptions when followed up as teenagers. However, both these studies report considerable distress for around half of the families, especially during teenage years. Neil et al (2014) assessed fewer than half as doing averagely well at the age of 15–17. More than half of the 3,000 adopters (a self-selected sample) responding to a recent BBC *File on Four* survey reported living with a child who was violent, including being punched, kicked or threatened with knives; almost half said their adoption was 'challenging but stable' but only around a quarter described it as 'fulfilling and stable' (Harte and Drinkwater, 2017).

Another source of information comes from support and self-help groups of adopters, birth parents and adopted teenagers and adults.

Featherstone and Gupta (2018) report on focus groups, with adopters, birth parents, adoptees, social workers and lawyers brought together to debate the ethics of adoption, in particular, human rights and children's rights issues. Although not making claims for the generalisability of their conclusions, they find some consensus from these different groups that the total legal severance and undifferentiated contact arrangements model of adoption may not be an appropriate option for many children in long-term care needing to put down roots with new families.

Each of these studies, especially that by Neil et al (2014), provides information on differing post-adoption contact arrangements, and there is growing interest in sibling contact (Monk and McVarish, 2018). With respect to alternative permanence options for children who cannot return to a parent, most studies report that children placed with long-term foster or adoptive families when young do better than those placed when past infancy. Reporting on alternative permanence options, Biehal et al (2010) reported that, on most outcome measures (other than on measures of participation and progress on educational outcomes, for which there were no significant differences), the adopted children were doing better than those in long-term foster care. However, they concluded that since most of the adoptees had joined their new families as infants but very few in the sample had joined their long-term foster families when under five, valid outcome comparisons could not be made. Schofield and Beek (2009), Biehal et al (2010) and Sebba et al (2015) report encouraging messages about outcomes for most children placed in well-managed and stable foster care. With respect to kinship care, there is a growing body of research indicating that, despite the kinship guardians, on average, being older and living in poorer economic circumstances, the actual placement breakdown rate is low (Wade et al, 2014).

Conclusion

The fall in numbers adopted from care results, in part, from positive messages about the increased use of kinship care. This, and policy changes to enable children to put down roots in their foster families, has meant that the balancing required between alternative permanence options has become more nuanced. Increased concern about the separation of siblings to facilitate adoption and the evidence of sibling groups waiting longer in temporary placements has led to questions about whether an earlier long-term foster placement to keep them together or at least maintain comfortable contact would be preferable to adoption in some cases.

Perhaps most important to policymakers and practitioners is the knowledge from foster and adoptive families, therapist, teachers, and social workers that most children who need long-term out-of-home care are children with special needs. At the very least, they have to come to terms with why they went into care, and most will have experienced one or more separations and the traumas of neglectful or abusive parenting. Whether placed with relatives, with foster carers or with adopters, they and their carers will need special services, at least episodically at times of stress. The recent fall in the numbers of applicants to adopt from care may result, in part, from adoption workers being clearer in what they tell prospective adopters about the special challenges, as well as rewards, in parenting a child adopted from care.

Adoption from care in England is at something of a crossroads (Thoburn and Featherstone, 2019). With the election of a new government in 2019, it seems likely that the present policy aims to increase the numbers adopted from care will continue. In January 2020, there was a government commitment to increase funding for post-adoption services in order to encourage more prospective adopters to come forward. However, a space may be opening up between the courts' determination that non-consensual adoption should be a 'last resort' and government policy to increase the numbers leaving care through adoption. The chapter concludes with the following quote from Sir Andrew McFarlane, President of the Family Division, who, in a widely publicised lecture, reflects on the place of adoption, which 'radically shifts the tectonic plates of an individual's legal identity (and those of others) for life', and asks: 'But is adoption the best option?' ... How is it possible to say that by making adoption orders, particularly in the middle to low range of abuse cases, we are indeed getting the balance right' McFarlane (2017, p 24).

Notes

[1] Although the four UK nations place children from care for adoption, the legislation and processes for child protection and adoption services differ, as do the numbers and rates placed, though there are many similarities. This chapter focuses on England.

[2] For further information see the Coram-BAAF website https://corambaaf.org.uk/

References

Biehal, N., Ellison, S., Baker, C. and Sinclair, I. (2010) *Belonging and Permanence. Outcomes in Long-Term Foster Care and Adoption*, London: BAAF.

Burns, K., Kritz, K., Krutzinna, J., Luhamaa, K., Meysen, T., Pösö, T., Segado, S., Skivenes, M. and Thoburn, J. (2019) 'The hidden proceedings – an analysis of accountability of child protection adoption proceedings in eight European jurisdictions', *European Journal of Comparative Law and Governance*, 6: 1–35.

Butler, I. and Drakeford, M. (2011) *Social Work on Trial: The Colwell Inquiry*, Bristol: Policy Press.

Cabinet Office (2000) *The Prime Minister's Review of Adoption*, London: Performance and Innovations Unit.

DfE (Department for Education) (2013) *Statutory Guidance on Adoption*, London: DfE.

DfE (2015) *Permanence, Long-Term Foster Placements, and Ceasing to Look after a Child: Statutory Guidance for Local Authorities*, London: DFE.

DfE (2018) *The Adoption Support Fund Guidance*, London: DfE.

DfE and National Statistics (2015) *Children Looked after in England and Adoptions 2013–2014*, London: National Statistics.

DfE and National Statistics (2019) *Children Looked after in England and Adoptions 2017–2018*, London: National Statistics.

DHSS (Department of Health and Social Security) (1974) *Report of the Committee of Inquiry into the Care and Supervision Provided by Local Authorities and Other Agencies in Relation to Maria Colwell and the Co-ordination between Them*, London: HMSO.

Dickens, J., Masson, J., Garside, L., Young, J. and Bader, K. (2019) 'Courts, care proceedings and outcomes uncertainty: the challenges of achieving and assessing "good outcomes" for children after child protection proceedings', *Child and Family Social Work*, 24(4): 574–81.

Featherstone, B. and Gupta, A. (2018) *The Role of the Social Worker in Adoption- Ethics and Human Rights*, Birmingham: BASW.

Fratter, J., Rowe, J., Sapsford, D. and Thoburn, J. (1991) *Permanent Family Placement: A Decade of Experience*, London: BAAF.

Harte, A. and Drinkwater, J. (2017) 'Over a quarter of adoptive families in crisis, survey shows', BBC, *File on Four*, 28 September.

Hill, M., Lambert, L. and Triseliotis, J. (1988) *Achieving Adoption with Love and Money*, London: NCB.

Howe, D. and Feast, J. (2000) *Adoption, Search and Reunion: The Long Term Experience of Adopted People*, London: BAAF.

McFarlane, Lord Justice A. (2017) *Holding the risk: The balance between child protection and the right to family life*, London: Family Justice Council.

Monk, D. and McVarish, J. (2018) *Siblings, Contact and the Law: An Overlooked Relationship*, London: Nuffield Foundation.

Neil, E., Cossar, J., Lorgelly, P. and Young, J. (2010) *Helping Birth Families: Services, Costs and Outcomes*, London: BAAF.

Neil, E., Beek, M. and Ward, E. (2014) *Contact after Adoption: A Longitudinal Study of Adopted Young People and Their Adoptive Parents and Birth Relatives*, London: BAAF.

Office for National Statistics (2011) *Adoptions in England and Wales*, London: ONS.

Rowe, J. and Lambert, L. (1974) *Children Who Wait*, London: BAAF.

Schofield, G. and Beek, M. (2009) 'Growing up in foster care: providing a secure base through adolescence', *Child and Family Social Work*, 14: 255–66.

Sebba, J., Berridge, D., Luke, N., Fletcher, J., Bell, K., Strand, S., Thomas, S., Sinclair, I. and O'Higgins, A. (2015) *The Educational Progress of Looked after Children in England*, Oxford: Rees Centre.

Selwyn, J., Wijedasa, D.N. and Meakings, S.J. (2014) *Beyond the Adoption Order: Challenges, Interventions and Disruptions*, London: DfE.

Short, R. (1984) *Report of the Social Services Select Committee on Children in Care*, London: HMSO.

Thoburn, J. and Featherstone, B. (2019) 'Adoption, child rescue, maltreatment and poverty', in S.A. Webb (ed) *The Routledge Handbook of Critical Social Work*, London: Routledge, pp 401–11.

Thoburn, J., Murdoch, A. and O'Brien, A. (1986) *Permanence in Child Care*, Oxford: Blackwell.

Thoburn, J., Norford, L. and Rashid, S.P. (2000) *Permanent Family Placement for Children of Minority Ethnic Origin*, London: Jessica Kingsley.

Thomas, C. (2013) *Adoption for Looked after Children: Messages from Research – An Overview of the Adoption Research Initiative*, London: BAAF.

Thomas, C., Beckford, V., Lowe, M. and Murch, N. (1999) *Adopted Children Speaking*, London: BAAF.

Wade, J., Sinclair, I., Stuttard, L. and Simmonds, J. (2014) *Investigating Special Guardianship: Experiences, Challenges and Outcomes*, London: DFE.

3

Overcoming the Soviet legacy? Adoption from care in Estonia

Katre Luhamaa and Judit Strömpl

Introduction

Adoption is a topic that has received undeservedly little attention in Estonian policy development, as well as academic discussions. Nevertheless, Estonian children are adopted both in country and inter-country. Most of these adoptions are step-parent adoptions but adoption is also part of the child protection system. In Estonia, the term 'adoption from care' is not used in policy discourse. It is defined as 'adoption to a new family' and statistics also include cases when the child is adopted from a maternity hospital or direct from the birth family.

While adoption regulation of the newly independent Estonia continued to follow the regulation of the Soviet era, adoption practice has gone through rapid change over the last few years. Adoption in family[1] and from care show a decrease, even though the policy papers recognise the need to move towards alternative care in a family (as opposed to institutional care) in the form of guardianship, foster placement and adoption (Ministry of Social Affairs, 2011). In recent years, the number of placements in public care has remained relatively stable (1,000 children per 100,000 child population), while the number of adoptions has decreased from 41 children per 100,000 in 2010 to nine per 100,000 in 2018 (see Table 3.1).

Estonian legislation and practice focus on the total secrecy of adoptions, including the identity of the biological parents. The background to this approach is the idea that any child should and could have only one mother and father. This principle derives from the Soviet legislation that was not changed in the 1990s, and it is still a prevalent concept in adoptions from care. The institutional system that supports all adoptions was fully reformed and centralised in 2017.

This chapter discusses these changes in law, policy and practice, and analyses the current state of affairs of both international and national adoptions in and from Estonia. It draws on national policy documents, legislation, court practice and expert interviews that give an insight into the institutional framework and practice, as well as the way prospective adoptive parents and families are found and prepared for adoption.[2] For a better understanding of the current situation, the chapter starts with a historical overview of its development and the impacts on adoption from care in Estonia, followed by an overview of different stages of the adoption process, starting from the preparations for and ending with the consequences of adoption.

Adoption in Estonia: a historical overview

The roots of a parent-centred adoption system are in the Russian Empire, where adoptions were the privilege of childless noblemen who wanted to have heirs, or the rights of those who adopted their extramarital children (Commission of Laws, 1817). During Estonia's first period of independence (1918–45), this tradition continued and the legislation prescribed that: adoption should not harm the adoptee; adoptees older than 14 had to consent to the adoption; and adoption decisions were made by the court (Junkur, 1940; Roosaare, 1944).

During the Soviet occupation (1945–91),[3] prospective adoptive parents (s 112 Marriage and Family Code [MFC]) initiated the process by applying to the guardianship authority (s 113[1] MFC). Adoption required the consent of an adoptive child who was older than ten, except when the child was living in the adoptive family and did not know that they were not the biological child of the family. The institution where the child was placed and the legal guardian of the child also had to consent (ss 117–20 MFC).

Adoption required written consent of the biological parents, who had the right to withdraw their consent until adoption took effect. It was possible to adopt the child without such consent when: the court had removed the parental rights of the biological parent(s); parents lacked legal capacity or their whereabouts were unknown; or a parent had not lived together with the child for more than one year and did not raise the child or participate in providing maintenance for them (ss 111, 115–16 MFC).

An administrative body of the local government (which was under the political control of the Communist Party) made adoption decisions (s 113[1] MFC). Only courts had the right to annul the adoption in the interests of the child. Among other reasons, it was possible to annul the adoption on the request of the biological parents when their consent had not been properly received (ss 128–34 MFC).

Most of the children who were voluntarily or involuntarily removed from their parents were placed in residential care. Single mothers had the right to place their children voluntarily into residential care without termination of parental rights, provided that they kept contact and regularly visited their children (Supreme Soviet Presidium of USSR, 1944). When the mother failed to visit the child, she was declared a parent whose whereabouts were unknown and her parental rights were terminated, allowing the adoption of the children without her consent (ss 9, 74 MFC). As an example, in March 1988, 44 per cent of children in Tallinn I Children's Home had single mothers. In 1987, only four single mothers out of 39 regularly visited their children and seven did not wish to raise their children but did not agree to give up parental rights (Rahnu, 1988). Similarly, parents of children with disabilities were strongly recommended to place their children into special institutions; these children were not available for adoption (Tobis, 2000; Linno and Strömpl, forthcoming).

From 1986, adoptions were coordinated and decided by the education departments of local governments, who also had information about children in care and persons wishing to adopt; local vital statistics offices registered such decisions (Rahnu, 1988, 22; Laas, 1991). The focus of the process was on establishing the health of the adoptive parent and the child.

Secrecy was a central requirement of adoptions at that time; adoptive parents were registered on the child's birth certificate if they so wished (s 123[1] MFC). Adoption terminated all contact between the child and the birth parents as the child became a full member of the adoptive family. Secrecy of adoption was deemed essential in cases of small children, who could not remember their life before adoption.

Furthermore, an adoptive mother could avoid social stigma by imitating pregnancy and birth in a maternity clinic (Rahnu, 1988: 26). Adoptive parents could change both the first and family name of the adoptive child and the date of birth of the child (which had to be around three months of the actual birth date). All adoption information was kept in a sealed envelope in a safe at the local education department.

Present status of adoption from care

The Estonian child protection system is risk-oriented (Gilbert et al, 2011) and focuses on supporting the child in the family setting (Linno and Strömpl, forthcoming) and retaining the connection between the child and the family (s 26 of the Constitution of the Republic of Estonia). Research shows that accountability systems for adoptions from care are very limited in Estonia (Burns et al, 2019). The Estonian adoption system has its roots firmly in the Soviet regulation of adoptions, and while the regulation itself has remained relatively similar to the regulation of the USSR, the practice and especially the adoption counselling process have developed substantively in recent years.

International and national legal framework

After 1991, adoptions in Estonia have been regulated by two legal acts: the 1969 MFC (in force until 1994); and the Family Law Act 1995 (FLA), which was revised in 2010. General principles included in the Child Protection Act 2016 (CPA), such as the child's best interests and hearing the child, also apply for adoptions.

International treaties regulating adoptions create binding legal obligations on Estonia and, among other things, guide the implementation of national law (Luhamaa, 2015, 2020). Estonia is a member of the following human rights treaties regulating adoption:

- Convention on the Rights of the Child (CRC) – ratification and entry into force 1991;
- European Convention on Human Rights (ECHR) – ratification and entry into force 1996; and
- Hague Convention on Protection of Children and Co-operation in Respect of Intercountry Adoption – ratification and entry into force 2002.

These instruments, in particular, the CRC, are used by the national courts when interpreting child protection and adoption laws and regulation (see Supreme Court, Administrative Law Chamber [2012] No. 3-3-1-53-12). Until 1995, adoptions were purely administrative matters decided by the local governments (Bernstein, 1997). From 1995 to 2017, adoptions were prepared and coordinated by the county boards, while the courts had decision-making powers and duties. Child welfare services (CWS) of counties registered prospective adoptive parents, analysed their background, prepared them for adoption, helped to find a suitable child for them and prepared necessary documentation. This segregation of the pre-adoption work was criticised by the CRC Committee in 2003 and 2017. The CRC Committee pointed out inconsistencies in monitoring foster and adoptive parents, and recommended that Estonia establish comprehensive national policy and guidelines, as well as a central monitoring mechanism, governing foster care and adoption (CRC Committee, 2003: para 37; 2017: para

51). This system was fully reformed in 2017, and activities specifically connected to adoption were centralised and managed by the national Social Insurance Board (SIB) (s 158 FLA).

The work of the SIB is supported by the CWS of the local governments as they are typically guardians of children without parental care. Today, the CWS of local governments are responsible for social work with the child and organisation of family foster care or residential care. The CWS of the local governments also participate in the adoption process. However, the SIB has the central responsibility for the process: it evaluates adoptive parents, collects necessary documentation, connects the child with prospective adoptive parents, presents documents in court and develops family evaluation guides. Alongside the state and local governments, non-governmental organisations (NGOs) provide supportive activities to families that care for non-biological children (for example, consultation, training of adoptive and foster families, and supervision).

Adoption statistics

Estonian adoption statistics reflect changes connected to territorial reform. From 1995 to 2017, Estonia was divided into 15 counties that represented the central government. Adoption management was the responsibility of county boards, while child protection was the responsibility of local governments.[4] There was no uniform collection of statistics as they were collected by both counties and local governments.[5] Since 2017, adoption activities have been concentrated in a department of the SIB. Table 3.1 summarises the Estonian adoptions statistics for 2010–18 and previous placements of the children adopted from care.

Children in public care in Estonia are divided into two groups: children under the guardianship of an individual (typically family kinship placement); and children under the guardianship of the local government (Linno and Strömpl, forthcoming), who are placed in a foster family, family house or residential care.[6] The number of children taken into public care is decreasing, and their placement generally follows the aim of family placement, with the number of children under the guardianship of the local governments slowly decreasing.

In the late 1980s, there were around 400 adoptions in Estonia annually; two thirds of them were typically adoptions by the kinship family or the spouse of the biological parent (Rahnu, 1988: 2). Recent data show that adoptions from care are less frequent than in earlier years. The number of children adopted from residential care is decreasing, while the number of children adopted from foster care is slowly

Table 3.1: General child protection statistics (age 0–17) and previous placements of children adopted to a new family, 2010–18 (total *N* and per 100,000 children)

	2010	2014	2018
Child population on 1 January[d]	245,360	243,640	252,117
Children in public care[a, d]	2,852 (1,162)	2,556 (1,049)	2,451 (972)
From which children under guardianship[b, d]	1,348 (549)	1,331 (546)	1284 (509)
Total adoptions from care[e]	101 (41)	53 (22)	22 (9)
Inter-country adoptions[c, e]	28 (11)	5 (2)	0
In-country adoptions[e]	73 (30)	48 (20)	22 (9)

Note: [a] Public care: placement in guardianship, residential care or foster care; *N* children in public care is a total number of children in substitute homes, in foster care and kinship care at the end of the year. [b] Guardianship: placement with a person who is the court-appointed guardian for the child (typically kinship placement); responsibility for the child is transferred to the guardian. [c] Adoption of a child from public care in Estonia to parents living in a foreign country. [d] Stock number, 1 January; [e] flow number, cases during a year.

Source: Statistics Estonia and Estonian Ministry of Social Affairs (2010–18)

increasing. This shift seems to reflect the fact that while adoption did not previously follow on from foster care, there is a new trend where successful foster placement can develop into adoption. There are no aggregated data on numbers where parental rights have been removed in relation to children who are in state care; thus, the statistics do not show the number of children who are available to be adopted.

Main principles and ethos

Estonian courts typically only limit parents' rights and see full removal of parental rights as the last resort measure (see, for example, Supreme Court, Civil Law Chamber [2019] No. 2-18-3298). The legislation and practice of the Estonian child protection system rest on needs-based assumptions, where the law focuses on 'children in need of help' or 'in danger', and the aim of protection is the interests of the child[7] (s 1[1] CPA; see also Petoffer, 2011; Riisalo, 2011).

Terminating parental rights and adoption are typically separate proceedings: first, the child is taken into public care and the parents' rights are terminated; and, second, when suitable adopters are found, the adoption process is initiated. Adoption legislation stresses the interests of the child and the child-centric focus of the process (s 147 FLA). In practice, due to a limited number of prospective adoptive parents, the adoption process focuses on connecting the right child with the prospective adopters. There are cases where adoption (including inter-country adoption) is decided before the child has lived with the family as the specialists try to avoid a situation where the child lives in multiple settings before the adoption is confirmed.

The main aim of adoption is to provide a healthy family environment for the growth of every child (s 147 FLA). This principle is the starting point in every child protection intervention in every case where children are in any way involved.

Estonia's child and family policy does not substantively or systematically focus on the issue of adoption. The *Strategy of Children and Families for 2012–2020* does include adoptions from care as a child protection measure, though statements on adoption are potentially conflicting. First, the strategy stresses the need to increase placement of children in family-based substitute care, such as foster care, guardianship and adoption (Ministry of Social Affairs, 2011: 30, 46), instead of residential care. Second, the strategy points out that adoption should only be considered in cases where the ties between a child and their biological family have been fully severed or threaten the child's well-being (Ministry of Social Affairs, 2011: 47). However, the stress on family values can undermine the child's interests as the child is placed in residential care for an extended period in the hope that reunification with the biological parents is possible.[8]

Pre-adoption practices

The adoption process consists of two phases: preparation of the adopter family and the adoptee; and the decision-making process in court. The description of the pre-court adoption procedure is based on several interviews with the head of the substitute care unit of the SIB[9] that were conducted especially to collect information for this chapter.

Adoption register

The SIB coordinates the state's general register of adoptions, which includes information about persons wishing to adopt, as well as the results of the finalised adoptions. This data set is confidential and is only accessible to adoption specialists from the SIB. This centralisation ended the duplication of information about potential adoptive parents and local inconsistencies in adoption practice. Family evaluations and preparation for adoption were also centralised and standardised. Behind this consolidation was the aim to treat all families equally and arrange evaluations free of charge and in a unified system.

Pre-adoption work with the adoptive family

The SIB, in cooperation with local CWS and other specialists (for example, university researchers, officials from the Ministry of Social Affairs and members of interested NGOs), developed the system for a family study. All the preparation of the adoptive families is standardised (see SIB, 2018[10]). Central to the process is working together with families. As the SIB works in four regional centres, its specialists are familiar with local arrangements; adoption also requires good collegial cooperation with the local CWS.

During the first meeting with the family, the potential adopters receive information on different types of substitute care (guardianship, foster care and adoption) and the preparation process (evaluation and support system). As a rule, prospective adopters then have time to think, and they are encouraged to come back if their wish to adopt remains. When necessary, adoptive parents can meet other experienced adoptive parents before making their decision.

The prospective adopters fill in an application and write motivation letters (spouses write them separately). All these documents are registered at the start of adoption preparations and are the basis for family evaluation.

A SIB specialist then conducts a family study, during which they visit the home of prospective adoptive parents and talk with all family members who live together. Families can prepare for these conversations as they receive the discussion topics beforehand. The SIB regards it as essential to assess the motivation of every family member before adoption as there can be underlying motivations or the family might need support or therapy.

Prospective adopters can participate in pre-training through Parent Resources for Information, Development and Education (PRIDE) (a training programme for foster, adoptive and kinship parents), which generally targets foster families but through which adoptive families can also receive support and counselling; the SIB has discretion to make participation in the training obligatory (s 158[5] FLA). Practice shows that some prospective adoptive parents leave the training because the topics of discussion are too personal. During PRIDE pre-training, adoptive families can change their mind and choose to foster instead of adoption. However, if they do not change their mind, general PRIDE training is not obligatory for adoptive parents.

When the family study concludes that the adoptive parents are suitable, they are registered as qualified adoptive parents, and the process of finding a suitable child starts (for 2019 this included 75 families). When interviewed by the authors, the head of the SIB unit stressed that it would be best if the child could be placed with the family when the adoption process is ongoing but adoptive parents are deemed to be suitable. This is often not possible as many adoptive parents oppose a placement that is not already agreed as permanent because they are scared that the child, whose parents' parental rights are not fully terminated, could be returned to their biological parents.

Finding the right child

The SIB collects information about any potential adoptive child and contacts the child and their carers to find the best adoptive family for the particular child, while also taking into account and supporting the feelings and considerations of the adoptive family. The SIB documents all such discussions, advice and processes; the data collected are confidential. The SIB takes into account as far as possible the social context of the child and adoptive parents, for example, ethnic background, culture and religion (s 147[1] FLA).

Estonian legislation stresses the importance of knowing the health conditions of both the child and the adoptive parents (s 158[6] FLA). Adoptive parents receive information on any possible congenital diseases and health problems. This was one of the most frequently mentioned problems noted by experienced adoptive parents (Petoffer, 2017).

When interviewed, an SIB official explained that the wishes of adoptive parents often shift — in earlier years, most adoptive parents were looking for a smaller child; today, some older children are also successfully adopted. For example, one family came with a wish to adopt a small girl but when they looked at children who were waiting for adoption, they found a teenage boy who they later adopted. Also, a second family wanted to adopt one child but met three siblings during the process and adopted them all as they did not want to separate siblings.

Preparing the broader network of the child

Adoption preparations have to be child-centric and consider the needs of the child (ss 151, 158[6] FLA). Children have the right to participate in adoption proceedings according to their maturity. Adoption potentially influences the well-being of other children in the adoptee's network. The SIB stresses the need to know and prepare the broader network of the child — biological relatives, siblings and everyone who is connected to the child. The Register of Social Services and Supports (STAR) includes such information about every child in alternative care in Estonia, with the basic stance that all children have the right to know their life story, which contains all their relations and carers.

An adoption prerequisite is that the biological parents received all possible support and help before the court terminated their parental rights. Biological parents receive information about the planned adoption of their child; they are also informed of the legal and practical implications of adoption (see Supreme Court, Civil Law Chamber [2013] No. 3-2-1-154-13). It is at the discretion of the adoptive family whether and how they wish to keep post-adoption contacts with biological parents. For example, some biological parents leave their photos with adoptive parents so that children can retain an image of their birth parents. The head of the SIB Substitute Care Unit also pointed out in the interview that while they can link up with adoptive families before the court decision, they have no right to intervene in their family life after adoption. At the same time, it could help the adoptive family if they can turn to the SIB with their questions.

Procedure in the court

The prospective adoptive parents initiate the adoption procedure in court by submitting their application (s 159 FLA; s 564 Code of Civil Procedure [CCP]). The SIB then provides the court with relevant background information, including a written report on the health, financial situation and housing of the applicants, and provides an opinion on whether the applicants are capable of raising the child, caring for the child and maintaining the child (s 567 CCP). The SIB participates in the court proceedings together with the court-appointed legal guardian (an individual or the local government) of the child (s 158 FLA). The court also assesses the suitability of the adoptive parents and their bond with the child.

The following consents are necessary for adoption: the person wishing to adopt, the child's guardian (s 153 FLA) and the spouse of an adoptive parent (s 154 FLA). The consent of the biological parent(s) is required when their right to custody is not fully terminated (s 152 FLA). The written consent of the child is obligatory when the child is at least ten years of age (s 151 FLA)[11]; the court should also consider the wishes of a younger child if the child's maturity so permits.

The court holds one or several hearings to establish the facts of the case and check the required consents. The court informs and hears biological parents separately from the other parties to hear any of their concerns and, when necessary, fully terminate their parental rights. Whether all parties meet simultaneously or separately depends on the discretion of the judge but the court has to hear the adoptive parents and the child who is older than ten years. In most cases, the adoptive parents, guardian of the child (usually the local government) and SIB would be simultaneously present at the hearing; the court typically hears the child before the general court hearing. According to the SIB, the court proceedings do not take long, but are concluded within a few weeks.

A single judge in a generalist district court decides the adoption following the CCP and the proceedings are investigative. The court sitting can be declared closed (s 38[1]4 CCP).

Adoption decision

The court formalises adoption in a substantiated written order (ss 478[2], 568 CCP), which sets out the information to be entered into the population register, as well as shows the legal basis for the adoption. It also indicates whether the parents consent to the adoption. The ruling enters into force once the adoptive parents receive it (s 268[2] CCP). If adoption is granted, the order cannot be appealed or amended (s 568 CCP), unless one required consent is missing.

Similarly to the Soviet system, modern Estonian law emphasises adoption secrecy (s 164 FLA). The objective of adoption secrecy is to guarantee the protection of the private life of children, biological parents and adoptive parents, and to prevent undesired interference or possible discrimination. Thus, access to the court order and the case file is limited to the adoptive parents, the child and officials who need to enter the information into the public databases (s 164 FLA; s 59[4] CCP).

Biological parents cannot get information about the adoptive family; it is in the discretion of the adoptive family to establish such contact if they so wish. To resolve this situation, the SIB consults adults who were adopted as children and who want to find their biological relatives.

Costs relating to adoption

Adoption preparation is free of charge. The costs of the parties in the court proceedings are typically covered by themselves; state legal aid covers the costs of the child's legal representative. Section 23 of the Family Benefits Act 2017 provides for the right of adoptive families to a one-off payment of adoption allowance (€320 on 1 January 2020). Otherwise, adoptive families receive universal child support benefits and the time for adoptive leave is equal to maternity leave.

Consequences of adoption and post-adoption care

Adoption terminates all prior family relationships of the child with and the rights and obligations arising from them (s 162 FLA). The court can, however, require the relationship between siblings to be maintained.[12] In order to protect the child's right to identity, specialists in the SIB advise adoptive parents to think about the opportunity to tell the child about the adoption. Such an approach is supported by evidence that factual information can prevent some traumatic effects of adoption; the precise approach depends on the adoptive child's maturity and interest in their life story.

Per 2020 the Estonian adoption system does not have an aftercare service for either inter-country or national adoptions. Often, the child is not living with the adoptive family before the adoptive process, and moves to the family only after the adoption process is completed. Pre-adoption contact between the adoptive family and the child is also often limited; however, once the adoption process is completed, these families are effectively left alone. There are no special support services, nor is the child's adaptation or well-being evaluated after adoption.

Inter-country adoptions

Inter-country adoption appeared during the first years of independence (Valkama, 1993; Vetik, 1995), when Estonia started adopting its children in care to suitable families abroad. After ratification of the Hague Convention on inter-country adoption in 2002, Estonia limited the extent of inter-country adoptions, and in 2020, it allows inter-country adoptions (mainly to Sweden) to a minimal extent. These adoptions are coordinated by the SIB and require cooperation from the CWS of the receiving state, which prepare the documentation relating to adoptive parents. Otherwise, such cases are decided by Estonian courts and follow the same procedure. Whether these families receive aftercare depends on the national system for adoptive parents.

Reflections from adoptive parents

Adoption from care has received scarce attention in academic research in Estonia. A few master's theses have been published on this topic (Bonder, 2012; Petoffer, 2017); some focus on inter-country adoptions (Amberg, 2014; Karu, 2015).

In 2020, a small inquiry, 'It's my story', was carried out, where 107 respondents answered a questionnaire, followed up with some personal face-to-face interviews (MTÜ Oma Pere et al, 2019). Most adopters in this study had experiences with the unreformed adoption system. Respondents typically mentioned the long waiting time as problematic. As an example, one adoptive mother waited for three years for her child who was placed in residential care from birth, even though the child was born after she had already been positively evaluated and prepared for adoption, and the child's biological mother had not opposed the adoption. A total of 68 of 107 respondents mentioned that they received insufficient information about the health condition of the child. Some adoptive parents continued to gather information about the biological parents in order to prepare for the child's possible questions (MTÜ Oma Pere et al, 2019).

Conclusion

Estonia has moved a long way during its independence and has, in recent years, aimed at providing family-based care for all children. This has not yet been a full success story. The number of children in guardianship is increasing as the state has been able to mobilise kinship placements. This approach is in harmony with Estonia's general concept of family protection, whereby children brought up by relatives are seen to have a better chance for reunification with biological parents compared to those who are adopted. Adoption statistics show a decrease, which is partly due to the decrease in the number of inter-country adoptions but also indicates that it is difficult to find suitable adoptive families.

Services provided to adoptive families follow the earlier understanding: they are equal to biological families that have to cope with bringing up children alone. Adoption places the child back under family care and ends all types of state intervention. This approach is evident in the focus on adoption secrecy and the limited obligatory training for adoptive parents. Redefining adoption secrecy in Estonia is not an easy process. Instead, it requires changes in understandings of the child as a subject of their own life. Pre-adoption work with the child's wider network and attempts to secure relationships with siblings despite the adoption is a positive feature of the Estonian system. Whether these contacts are, in practice, retained requires further research.

Acknowledgements

This project has received funding from the European Research Council under the European Union's Horizon 2020 research and innovation programme (grant agreement No 724460). Disclaimer: This chapter reflects only the authors' views and the funding agency is not responsible for any use that may be made of the information contained therein.

Notes

[1]   Kinship adoption or adoption by the step-parent.

[2]   The authors are grateful to the Head of the Substitute Unit of the Social Insurance Board, Ms Nadezhda Leosk, for detailed data and explanations of the pre-court procedures and practices.

[3]   See generally, for example, Taagepera (1993).

[4]   A total of 213 until 2017 and 79 since 2017 under the Territory of Estonia Administrative Division Act 1995.

[5]   Adopters wishing to adopt a child registered themselves in different counties and were matched with the first suitable child available for adoption from wherever.

[6]   Estonian legislation refers to residential care units as 'substitute homes'.

[7]   Estonian legislation has omitted 'best' and uses the term 'interests of the child' (Luhamaa, 2015: 148–51).

[8]   Services for biological parents whose children are removed are limited; their focus is on providing visitation opportunities, provided the interactions are relatively good. There are no specific services that could improve parents' parental capacity (Ministry of Social Affairs, 2011; Osila et al, 2016).

[9]   See: www.sotsiaalkindlustusamet.ee/et/lapsed-pered/lastekaitse/lastekaitse-osakonna-kontaktid (accessed 1 April 2020). The interviews were conducted in August 2019 by Judit Strömpl.

[10] Lapsendamise ettevalmistamise käigus läbiviidavad kohustuslikud toimingud ja nende sisu, lapsendamise sooviavalduses esitatavate andmete loetelu ja Sotsiaalkindlustusameti kogutavate dokumentide loetelu' ['Obligatory steps to be taken during the preparation of adoption and their content, list of information to be provided in the application for adoption and list of documents to be collected by the Social Insurance Board'] (2018) RT I, 31.01.2018, 3.

[11] Interestingly, the FLA 1995 initially had the age for consent at seven years. Furthermore, the FLA 1995 included the Soviet-era principle that when the child had lived in a family and did not know their past, they could be adopted without the consent of the child. The FLA 2010 did not include this possibility.

[12] Estonia, adoption judgment AEST-01-XX, Discretion Project (ERC Consolidator grant). Available at: www.discretion.uib.no/projects/discretion-and-the-childs-best-interest-in-child-protection (accessed 1 April 2020).

References

Amberg, A. (2014) 'Rahvusvahelise lapsendamisprotsessi kogemuste kirjeldused' ['Experiences in the international adoption process'], master's thesis, University of Tartu.

Bernstein, L. (1997) 'The evolution of Soviet adoption law', *Journal of Family History*, 22(2): 204–26.

Bonder, R. (2012) 'Lapsendamissaladuse avaldamine avalikes huvides' ['Disclosure of the confidentiality of adoption deriving from the public interest'], master's thesis, University of Tartu.

Burns, K., Križ, K., Krutzinna, J., Luhamaa, K., Meysen, T., Pösö, T., Sánchez-Cabezudo, S.S., Skivenes, M. and Thoburn, J. (2019) 'The hidden proceedings – an analysis of accountability of child protection adoption proceedings in eight European jurisdictions', *European Journal of Comparative Law and Governance*, 6(1): 1–35.

Commission of Laws (1817) *Sistematicheskiy svod sushchestvuyushchikh zakonov Rossiyskoy Imperii, s osnovaniyami izdavayemyy Komissiyeyu sostavleniya Zakonov* [*A Systematic Collection of Laws of Russian Empire Published by Commission of Laws*], V Sanktpeterburge: Pechatano Tipografii Pravitel'stvuyushchego Senata.

CRC Committee (2003) 'Concluding observations: Estonia (initial report)', CRC/C/15/Add.196.

CRC Committee (2017) 'Concluding observations: Estonia (second to forth report)', CRC/C/EST/CO/2–4.

Gilbert, N., Parton, N. and Skivenes, M. (eds) (2011) *Child Protection Systems: International Trends and Orientations*, New York: Oxford University Press.

Junkur, E. (1940) 'Lapsendamine' ['Adoption'], thesis, University of Tartu.

Karu, H. (2015) 'Rahvusvaheline lapsendamine Eestist Rootsi: lapsendajate ja spetsialisti vaatenurk' ['Inter-country adoption from Estonia to Sweden – adopters' and specialists' points of view'], master's thesis, University of Tartu.

Laas, A. (1991) 'Lapsendamine' ['Adoption'], thesis, University of Tartu.

Linno, M. and Strömpl, J. (forthcoming) 'Child protection systems in Estonia and Latvia', in J.D. Berrick, N. Gilbert and M. Skivenes (eds) *Oxford International Handbook of Child Protection Systems*, Oxford: Oxford University Press.

Luhamaa, K. (2015) *Universal Human Rights in National Contexts: Application of International Rights of the Child in Estonia, Finland and Russia*, Tartu: University of Tartu. Available at: https://dspace.ut.ee/handle/10062/47885 (accessed 1 April 2020).

Luhamaa, K. (2020) 'International human-rights supervision triggering change in child-protection systems? The effectiveness of the recommendations of the CRC Committee in Estonia', *Juridica International*, 29: 108–23.

Ministry of Social Affairs (2010–18) 'Population statistics: Statistics Estonia. Table RV0241: Population by sex, age and administrative unit or type of settlement', 1 January.

Ministry of Social Affairs (2011) *Strategy of Children and Families for 2012–2020. Smart Parents, Great Children, Strong Society*, Tallinn: Ministry of Social Affairs.

MTÜ Oma Pere, MTÜ Eesti Asenduskodu Töötajate Liit, MTÜ SEB Heategevusfond and Tartu Ülikool Tallinna Ülikool (2019) 'Asendushooldusele paigutatud laste õigus identiteedile' ['The right to identity of children placed in substitute care'], unpublished research report.

Osila, L., Turk, P., Piirits, M., Biin, H., Anniste, K. and Masso, M. (2016) *Young People Aging Out of Care*, Tallinn: Praxis.

Petoffer, S. (2011) 'Oma Pere peab tähtsaks seda, mis eelneb ja järgneb lapsendamisele' ['Own family deems important what happens before and after adoption'], *Sotsiaaltöö* [*Social Work*], 4: 33–4.

Petoffer, S. (2017) 'Perekonna hindamine lapsendamist ettevalmistavas protsessis' ['Family assessment in the adoption preparation process'], master's thesis, University of Tallinn.

Rahnu, T. (1988) 'Lapsendamine' ['Adoption'], master's thesis, University of Tartu.

Riisalo, S. (2011) 'Kaasaegne lapse parimaid huve arvestav lapsendamine' ['Contemporary adoption of children considering the best interest of the child'], *Sotsiaaltöö* [*Social Work*], 4: 31–2.

Roosaare, E. (1944) 'Adoptsioon' ['Adoption'], thesis, University of Tartu.

Supreme Soviet Presidium of USSR (1944) 'Riikliku abi suurendamisest rasedatele naistele, lasterikastele ja vallasemadele, emade- ja lastekaitse tugevdamisest, aunime "Sangar-ema" sisseseadmisest ja ordeni "Ema au" ning medali "Emamedal" asutamisest' ['Decree on increasing state support to pregnant women, women with many children, single mothers, increasing protection of mothers and children'], ENSV Teataja 1945, 4.

Taagepera, R. (1993) *Estonia. Return to Independence*, New York: Routledge.

Tobis, D. (2000) *Moving from Residential Institutions to Community-Based Social Services in Central and Eastern Europe and the Former Soviet Union*, Washington, DC: World Bank Publication.

Valkama, L. (1993) 'Rahvusvahelise lapsendamise korraldamise õiguslikke probleeme Eestis' ['Legal problems relating to international adoptions in Estonia'], master's thesis, University of Tartu.

Vetik, S. (1995) 'Laste adopteerimine ja sellega seoses toimunud muutused' ['Adoption of children and related changes'], master's thesis, University of Tartu.

4

Adoption of children from state care in Ireland: in whose best interests?

Kenneth Burns and Simone McCaughren

Introduction

The Irish adoption model is transforming from an adult-centric, closed and secretive system towards a system where all children – irrespective of their parents' marital status – are treated equally, children have rights independent of their parents and children's best interest are now the paramount principle in decision-making. Ireland has a significant history of its children being adopted to other countries. This practice of sending children overseas, particularly to the US, continued for some time after adoption was legalised in 1952 (Milotte, 2012). Ireland later became a receiving country with the adoption of children from overseas. In the last decade, most Irish adoptions are now step-parent adoptions (AAI, 2014-19). However, this is likely to change with the recent enactment of the Children and Families Relationship Act 2015, which significantly broadens who can be recognised as a child's guardian and, for some, may obviate the need to apply for adoption. Ireland's history of adoption and sending children abroad for adoptions outside of the state was influenced by an enmeshed and insalubrious relationship between church and state (see Whyte, 1971; Milotte, 2012). While significant progress has been made in modernising the adoption system, this reform process is progressing against a backdrop of ongoing criticism regarding how the state has treated those affected by historical adoptions (see the Mother and Baby Homes Commission of Investigation [Murphy, 2019]). The state is also considering if the practice of open adoption should now be placed on a legal footing given the significance of recent legislative developments affecting children in the care system (Department of Children and Youth Affairs, 2019). Up until now, open adoption in Ireland has been a practice almost exclusively for children voluntarily placed for adoption from birth.

Over the last decade, Ireland has invested significant energy and resources in reforming its children's services (see Burns and McGregor, 2019; Burns et al, forthcoming). For example, during this period, the Oireachtas (Parliament) has accelerated the publication and enactment of policies and legislation specific to children's protection and welfare, Ireland established a dedicated Minister for Children, Equality, Disability, Integration and Youth position and, in 2014, a unified child protection agency. As part of this transformation agenda, significant work was also undertaken to reform Ireland's adoption system. In 2010, the Adoption Authority of Ireland (AAI) was established and adoption services were streamlined, a constitutional amendment was passed to enable the Oireachtas to implement a different approach to adoption – including facilitating the adoption of children from state care – and new enabling adoption legislation was introduced that widened the range of individuals and couples that can apply to adopt (McCaughren and McGregor, 2018).

Ireland has transformed into a relatively progressive, secular and liberal country, with marriage equality, openly gay government leaders (including a former Taoiseach [prime minister]), divorce, improved reproductive rights (including abortion in certain circumstances), a strong acceptance of a diverse range of family types and an acceptance of parenting outside of marriage (Connolly, 2015; Central Statistics Office, 2017). It is against this political and social context that this chapter examines the reforms in Irish social policy, legislation and assessment practices in the adoption of children from state care. We argue that the shift towards a more child-centric and rights-based model has been welcome but Ireland is still working out how systems and professionals can meaningfully actualise these changes in front-line practice. The chapter examines systemic reforms in adoption, particularly over the last decade, and considers the implications of the new adoption system for children, parents, child protection, fostering and adoption social workers. While recent legislation paves the way for a greater number of children to be eligible for adoption from the care system, there is little evidence, as of yet, of an increase in the numbers of children in care being adopted by their foster parents. Adoption orders are mostly granted for older teenage children in Ireland; however, new legal measures may facilitate children from the care system to transition into an adoptive family at a younger age than has been the norm. Any new approach to adoption will need to be carefully framed against Ireland's commitment to the principle of family reunification, as articulated in Irish social policy (Department of Children and Youth Affairs, 2017), and Ireland's European Convention on Human Rights Article 8 commitments. We conclude the chapter by examining the inherent complexities of using adoption to achieve the goal of stability for children in care.

This chapter's focus is limited to an analysis of the adoption of children from state care, particularly from long-term foster care. Readers interested in a broader reading on adoption in Ireland are referred to the following sources and themes, which are not comprehensively examined in this chapter: research on adoption in Ireland (O'Brien and Mitra, 2018a); a comprehensive analysis of adoption policy and legislative changes in Ireland (McCaughren and Ní Raghallaigh, 2015; O'Brien and Mitra, 2018b); mother and baby homes (Powell and Scanlon, 2015; Garrett, 2017); and access to adoption records and birth certificates (Irish Association of Social Workers and Council of Irish Adoption Agencies, 2020).

A brief history of adoption in Ireland

Ireland legislated for adoption in 1952, at a time when there were only eight countries in the Western world that had no legislative provisions for adoption (Kornitzer, 1952). The Adoption Act 1952 was based on a closed model of adoption and Catholic principles filtered throughout the Act. During the 1900s, Ireland's social policies, norms and laws were strongly influenced by an oppressively conservative Roman Catholic ethos, with a wafer-thin separation between church and state. Women and their partners who became pregnant outside of marriage were often socially and morally shunned by their family and community. The registration of marital children as 'legitimate' and non-marital children as 'illegitimate' from 1923 until the abolition of this category in 1987 had profound consequences for children and their parents. A total of 125,701 children were recorded as 'illegitimate' between 1923 and 1984 (Ferriter, 2019). Ireland's welfare state did not provide supports for one-parent families, reproductive rights and technologies were intensely curtailed, and abortion services were not available.

Adoption, largely facilitated through religious orders, was one available pathway for citizens who found themselves pregnant outside of marriage. The alternatives were parenting alone while being ostracised from your community, living with your child in a mother and baby home in which infant mortality rates were up to six times higher than for 'legitimate' children (see Milotte, 2012; Garrett, 2017; McCaughren and Powell, 2017), emigration or accessing abortion services in the UK. The Irish state was a hostile and punitive place to be pregnant if you were not in a church- and state-approved marital union. No financial support was in place for single parenthood until 1973 and many women had little or no choice but to consider adoption. With little foresight and forbearance, and no social policies in place to cater for single parenthood, adoption was regarded as the 'solution' for all parties. The child would be placed in a marital family – quite often with a childless couple – thus removing the stigma of 'illegitimacy'. The mother could 'move on' with her life, leave her past perceived 'mistakes' behind her and be accepted back by her family and community. When adoption was legalised in 1952, it was a closed model of adoption: women were encouraged to 'get on' with their lives and forget about their 'moral lapse'. This dehumanising and coercive system of punishment for pregnancy outside of marriage through adoption has left indelible scars on all those involved and is a stain on the nation. We now know that for some women, their full, free and informed consent was not sought for the adoption of their children (Adoption Rights Alliance et al, 2014; Lee, 2014).

From a high point of 1,400 adoptions per year in the late 1960s/early 1970s, adoption in Ireland has been in steady decline. The adoption statistics presented in the next section are not a true reflection of the volume of 'adoptions' of children in Ireland as there is evidence to suggest that private and informal adoptions also took place. These took the form of children being 'boarded-out' from institutions to foster parents and were often referred to as de facto adoptions (Milotte, 2012). It is also known that a number of illegal adoptions of Irish children took place, where children were illegally registered as the natural children of 'adoptive' parents. Some of these informal adoptions took place within the wider family and some under the aegis of the Catholic Church or other voluntary sector adoption agencies (see McConnell, 2019).

Statistics on adoption and children in state care, 1958–2018

At the last census in 2016, Ireland had a total population of 4.76 million people, of which 1,190,502 were children aged 0–17. Figure 4.1 charts the numbers of adoptions (including step-parent adoptions) in Ireland over the last 60 years using data presented in five-yearly intervals. There were over 1,000 adoptions in Ireland every year between 1964 and 1984 (except in 1979) (AAI, 2014–19). The highest number of adoptions were made in 1967 ($n = 1,493$). When calculated as a percentage of all 'non-marital births', this figure for 1967 represented an astonishing 97 per cent of 'non-marital births', a figure that had dropped to 0.8 per cent by 2008 (The Adoption Board, 2009). Between 1978 ($n = 1,223$

Figure 4.1: Adoption orders, 1958–2018

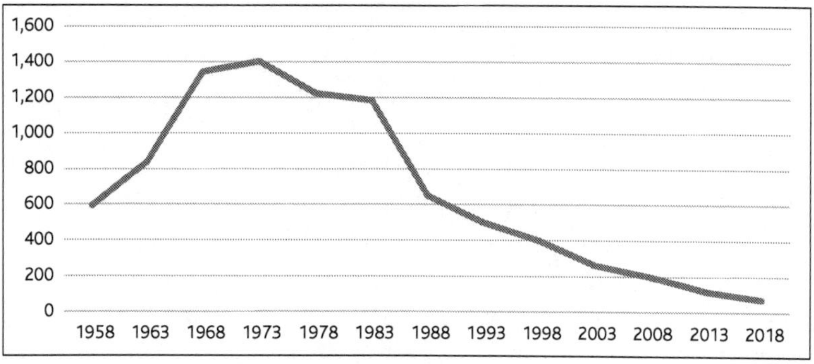

Source: Adoption Authority of Ireland (2014–19)

adoptions) and 2018 (n = 72 adoption orders), there was a 17-fold decrease in adoptions.

Social and political reforms and developments in the Irish welfare state during the 1980s and, in particular, 1990s led to a rapid reduction in the numbers of children being adopted. This decline is largely due to changing demographics, as well as legal and social reforms that diluted the traditional reasons for parents to 'choose' adoption. The introduction of contraception and developments in reproductive rights, declining birth rates, social liberalisation, the growing separation of church and state, the Roman Catholic Church's significantly diminished role in social policy formation and the setting of moral 'standards', and the weakening of the social stigma that was once attached to 'non-marital' parenthood have all contributed to a dramatic diminution in the use of adoption. With more couples wanting to adopt than children available domestically for adoption, the 1990s saw a sharp increase in the number of children adopted from overseas. From January 1991 to October 2010, there were 4,382 inter-country adoptions in Ireland. The numbers of inter-country adoptions reduced with the enactment of the Adoption Act 2010, which introduced more stringent regulations for inter-country adoptions. From November 2010 to September 2019, there were 707 inter-country adoptions (AAI, 2020). Therefore, the pattern of Irish couples adopting infants within Ireland was, to a large extent, replaced by international adoption.

Table 4.1 presents data on the total numbers of adoption orders made by the AAI and the total numbers of children in foster care adopted. The total numbers of adoptions declined by 38 per cent between 2013 and 2018. However, the total numbers of children adopted from state care, while small, has remained steady despite the

Table 4.1: Adoption orders and children in state care, 2013–18

Year	Adoption orders (all)	Adoption orders (stepfamily adoptions)	Children adopted from care (and % of total adoptions)	Children in state care at year end
2018	**72**	35	25 (35%)	5,974
2017	**72**	37	21 (29%)	6,189
2016	**95**	65	19 (20%)	6,267
2015	**94**	66	13 (14%)	6,384
2014	**112**	74	23 (20.5%)	6,454
2013	**116**	86	17 (15%)	6,469

Source: AAI (2014–19) and the Child and Family Agency (2014–19)

drop in total adoptions. For comparison purposes, in 1973, there were 1,402 adoption orders made, of which ten were adoptions of children from care (0.7 per cent). In 1987, there were 1,223 adoptions and 52 of these were children in state care (4 per cent – this figure is likely to contain infant adoptions also). In 2001, there were 293 adoptions orders made, with 18 orders (6 per cent) being made for the adoption of children in long-term foster placements (The Adoption Board, 2003; AAI, 2014–19). Ireland has a long-term pattern of few adoptions of children from long-term foster care for reasons that will be considered in a later section.

Recent legal changes to facilitate the adoption of children in care are not yet reflected in the data presented in Table 4.1. In 2018, there were 212 applications for assessment of eligibility and suitability as adopters to the Child and Family Agency. Of these applications, 27 (13 per cent) were for domestic adoptions, 68 (32 per cent) for step-parent adoptions, and 76 (36 per cent) for inter-country adoption. Of the 151 adoption assessments presented to local adoption committees in the same year, 32 (21 per cent) were for fostering to adoption. However, of the 177 children referred for adoption in 2018, 45 (23 per cent) were for fostering to adoption, down 31 per cent from 2017 (Child and Family Agency, 2020a). If the predicted increase in adoptions of children from state care materialises, it will be another few years before this will become evident in the data due to the length of time it can take from making an application to the granting of an adoption order.

The numbers of children adopted from state care continues to be very low, with 25 children being adopted in 2018, representing 0.42 per cent of all children in care at year end. The 5,974 children in care at year end in 2018 represents 502 children per 100,000 of all children aged 0–17 in Ireland (Child and Family Agency, 2020a), which is one of the lowest rates in Europe. The 72 adoptions in 2018 represents 6.05 children per 100,000, and the 25 adoptions of children from state care represents 2.1 children per 100,000. There were 61,016 births in Ireland in 2018 (Central Statistics Office, 2019). We do not provide a births relative to adoption orders calculation as, in recent years, the largest portion of adoptions in Ireland are of teenage children rather than infants and young children. In 2018, there were 30 adoption orders in total granted for children aged 17, 23 for children aged 12–16, seven for children aged 7–11, nine for children aged 2–6 and three for children aged one (AAI, 2014–19).

Finally, as outlined in Figure 4.2, it is open to the Child and Family Agency (Tusla) or an adoption applicant to apply to the High Court to set aside the consent of a parent who does not agree to an adoption. In 2018, the High Court 'resolved' 22 applications 'made under the Adoption Act 2010 for the making of adoption orders and challenges thereto' (Courts Service, 2019: 65). However, no further breakdown is provided in the annual report of the Courts Service and it is not possible to say how many of these cases related to parents opposing the adoption of their children from long-term foster care.

Adoption process for children in state care

Ireland has a single agency for and specialist approach to adoption decision-making. The AAI was established on 1 November 2010. It is an independent body that was formed under the Adoption Act 2010. Formerly known as the Adoption Board (An Bord Uchtála), the AAI is a quasi-judicial specialist body with full-time staff. The members of the board of the AAI – who are not full-time staff members of the AAI – have backgrounds in law, social work, psychiatry and psychology. Board members are appointed through the independent Public Appointments Service for a set term of office. While the preparatory assessment and documentary work is undertaken by the Child and Family Agency or accredited adoption agencies, the adoption hearings and the final adoption order decision are *only* made by the AAI. Each Child and Family Agency area has an adoption committee that provides governance on adoption services and independently reviews the assessing social worker's recommendation on the eligibility and suitability of the applicant(s) and their recommendation to progress a case on to the AAI. While cases are recommended to the AAI, the AAI is an independent decision-making body and it is not obliged to follow the recommendation to the local Child and Family Agency adoption committee (see Figure 4.2).

Figure 4.2: Adoption application, assessment and decision-making process (Ireland)

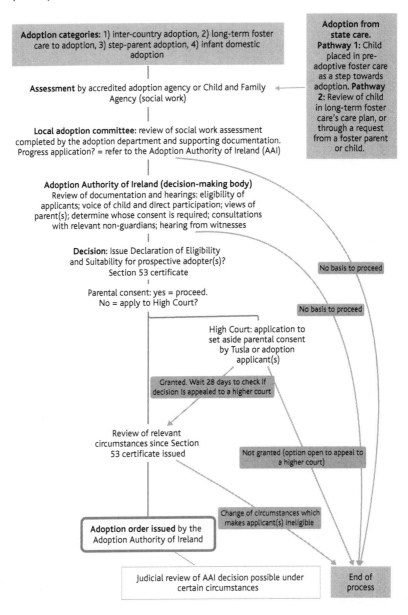

There are five adoption categories in Ireland: inter-country adoption, long-term foster care to adoption, relative foster care, step-parent adoption and infant domestic adoptions. This section exclusively examines the process of adoption from long-term foster care.

A total of 93 per cent of children in state care in Ireland in 2018 were in foster care (n = 5,551), most of whom were supported by the state's Child and Family Agency in general foster care (n = 3,957 [66.2 per cent]) or relative foster care (n = 1,594 [26.7 per cent]). There is a relatively small, though slowly increasing, portion of children in private foster care arrangements (n = 388) (Child and Family Agency, 2020a). Foster parents in Ireland are exclusively assessed as foster parents and not as dual foster carers and adopters. However, front-line practitioners advised that, recently, 'traditional' foster carers are applying to adopt children in their care under the new adoption legalisation. In these circumstances, foster carers who are already assessed as foster carers are being further assessed as adopters. There are very few children placed in state foster care at birth with the explicit goal of being adopted. This has been an infrequently used care option due to the heretofore absence of a concurrent care planning policy and a significant emphasis on reunification in the Irish child protection system, which reflects the strong family-centric influence of the Irish constitution and a strong social policy and practice orientation to favour reunifications, or, at least, not to sever parental rights through adoption. The Child Care (Amendment) Act 2007 brought into law Section 43A of the Child Care Act 1991, which grants long-term foster carers enhanced rights. This allows foster carers more autonomy in relation to many day-to-day issues, such as providing consent for medical treatment and issuing passports. Foster carers can apply for enhanced rights if the child has been living with them for a period of five years, and the Child and Family Agency must consent in advance to the order being granted. The process map in Figure 4.2 describes the adoption application and assessment process in Ireland. There are two pathways for children in state care to be adopted.

In the first pathway, a parent can request and consent to their infant being placed in pre-adoptive foster care with the express purpose of being adopted. The pre-adoptive foster carers' role is to care for the child, who will either return home to their birth parent(s) or move into an adoptive placement. Up until now, children placed in pre-adoptive foster care could not be placed for adoption with their foster carers. Children would spend time in pre-adoptive foster care until such time as the birth parent(s) consented to adoption. Under Irish law, consent cannot be sought from the birth parent(s) until at least six weeks after the baby's birth. The birth parent(s) would be involved in choosing the couple with whom the child would be placed. The child would then move to their adoptive placement – known as the trial adoption period – until such time as the final consent is signed and an adoption order is made by the AAI.

The second pathway for children in state care to be adopted is via non-consensual adoption. This process begins either with a request by the foster parent, child or child protection social work department to pursue adoption once it is clear that family reunification is not feasible. Prior to the constitutional amendment on children in 2012, and the publication and enactment of related enabling legislation, it was legally difficult to pursue an adoption of a child from state care, especially if the child's parents were married. It was not the norm to consider the severing of parental rights through adoption; reunification was always considered as part of the child's childcare review (care planning) process and long-term care was preferred to adoption.

Some of the reasons for child protection and welfare social work departments in Ireland not pursing the adoption of children from long-term foster care included: family reunification being the default goal for social work departments and government policy; it being legally and procedurally difficult to pursue the adoption of children in long-term care, especially for the children of married parents; professional and community discomfort with severing parental rights in a closed adoption model; the severing of support and payments for foster parents once an adoption had been made (the child protection department would close the case); the normative culture set by a family-focused constitution; and the lack of a policy framework and guidance to systematically pursue adoption, or at least to routinely consider adoption as a feasible care option at children's childcare reviews. Decision-making on what was in a child's best interests was framed according to the aforementioned considerations.

Why are so few children adopted from state care in Ireland?

As described earlier, Ireland has not traditionally used the care system as a pathway to adoption. Prior to the enactment of the Adoption (Amendment) Act 2017, 'the threshold for abandonment in Ireland was set up to the age of 18 years and adoption was only legally available to children born outside marriage' (Palmer and O'Brien, 2019: 399). It has been argued that the criteria were both too high and impractical to prove, which, in turn, led to many children remaining in state care (McCaughren and McGregor, 2018). Therefore, much of Ireland's adoptions were 'voluntary', meaning that parents consented and there were few non-consensual adoptions. While the Adoption Act

1988 made adoption by foster carers possible, the criteria were almost impossible to satisfy.

In practice, children in long-term state care (and their foster carers), before reaching the age of 18 years, apply for an adoption order to be made. An adoption order can only be made in Ireland if the child is under 18 years of age at the date of the adoption order. The statistics therefore reflect the older age of children who tend to be adopted from Irish state care. However, recent constitutional and legislative changes have now opened the way for potentially more children in state care to be adopted. Article 42A states that 'Provision shall be made by law that in the resolution of all proceedings ... concerning the adoption ... of any child, the best interests of the child shall be given paramount consideration.' The legislation also includes provision for children of married parents who have been in long-term foster care to be eligible for adoption after a certain period of time. The Adoption (Amendment) Act 2017 provides for the adoption of a child who has been in the care of the state for a continuous 'specific period of time' of 36 months and where there are no reasonable prospects that the birth parents will be able to care for the child. The Adoption (Amendment) Act 2017 states that an adoption order will only be granted if the child has resided with the applicants for a continuous period of not less than 18 months. The Act also states that in respect of any child who is capable of forming their own views, the AAI or the court 'shall ascertain those views and such views shall be given due weight having regard to the age and maturity of the child', and in making adoption order decisions, 'the best interests of the child shall be the paramount consideration'.

Moving towards a new model of assessment

Ireland's earlier adoption legislation was drafted as a response to the high number of Irish children being adopted overseas, and at a time when adoption involved the placement of young babies with adoptive couples. Ireland has changed quite considerably, not only in terms of the changed demographics of children placed for adoption, but also in terms of the much wider range of people who can now become guardians for children, which, for some, obviates the need to pursue adoption (for information on eligibility, see the Children and Family Relationships Act 2015). The new Act opens up the possibility of children becoming legal members of their foster families through adoption along a clearer and less onerous pathway. To date, Ireland has not operated a system of dually assessing carers: couples or individuals were either assessed as foster carers *or* adoptive parents. The assessment criteria were different depending on whether it was a foster care assessment or adoption assessment. The child was either going to be fostered (and perhaps reunified with their birth family) or adopted, and there was limited possibility for the child to be considered for adoption by their foster carers.

From closed to more open adoptions

While the Adoption Act 2010 made a number of significant changes, from a legal perspective, adoption is still based on the closed model of adoption, even though front-line adoption social work practice has embraced a far more open approach. Indeed, older adoption legislation was written at a time when it was unthinkable that adopted children would continue to have contact with their birth parents. Open adoption within the broader remit of post-adoption support is now being given real consideration in Ireland (Department of Children and Youth Affairs, 2019).

A recent review of open or semi-open adoption in Ireland (Department of Children and Youth Affairs, 2019) found that while voluntary open adoption arrangements were common practice in Ireland, there are no formal support systems in place. It also found that there was a lack of consistency in relation to the types of open adoption arrangements being practised. The report made a number of recommendations about how open adoption can be practised in Ireland in the future. Among its recommendations is that there should be 'a statutory basis for service to support voluntary forms of post-adoption contact, including the exchange of information' (Department of Children and Youth Affairs, 2019: 3). It further recommends that guidelines should be drafted in relation to the provision of services to support post-adoption contact where such support is requested. It also suggests that the perspectives of children who have direct experience of open adoption should be sought and that an online resource for birth parents and relatives, adoptive parents, and adopted children should be developed. Up until now, it has been common practice for the placing agency to provide post-adoption support to adoptive families and this included support for those children in open adoptions. However, as the report notes, while the Child and Family Agency (Tusla) 'operates an "open door policy", practice needs to evolve in such a way that it is responsive to the needs of families living with open adoptions' (Department of Children and Youth Affairs, 2019: 52).

Unlike traditional infant adoptions, children in long-term foster care are likely to have established links to their birth families through contact/access arrangements (see Section 37 of the Child Care Act 1991). If a child's relationship with their natural family is legally severed, the state ensures that their rights under the United Nations Convention on the Rights of the Child can be protected. *The National Standards for Foster Care* (Department of Health and Children, 2003: 12) also stipulate that children in foster care must be 'encouraged and facilitated to maintain and develop family relationships and friendships', and that children's wishes in relation to contact must be facilitated. Children entering the care system often have complex additional needs for which foster parents who adopt, especially if they adopt children in their foster care much younger than is currently the case, will need ongoing and sometimes intensive support post-adoption. The state ought to have an ongoing responsibility to these children, which adoption from foster care should not extinguish.

Conclusion

A substantial cultural shift and amount of work will be required to understand, support and navigate a new and reconstituted form of adoption, which could facilitate a greater number of children to be adopted from state care. However, such a transition will need to be implemented against a backdrop to the processing of a history of a formerly punitive, oftentimes hurtful and disorganised system of adoption in Ireland in the 20th century. For those seeking to promote a greater number of children being adopted from state care, trusting an adoption system that has not yet been able to address fundamental issues, such as the rights of adopted persons to identifying birth information, may prove to be challenging. Adoption was historically a response to unmarried parenthood, and creating an association between adoption and children in care may not always be positive in the minds of parents, children, foster carers and professionals. It is unclear if there is a consensus about whether adoption will be, or ought to be, prioritised over other forms of care, such as long-term fostering. The Child and Family Agency (2020b) is imminently due to publish their new *Pathways to Permanency Handbook*. This policy is expected to provide practitioners with guidelines on a new model of permanency and concurrent planning, including guidance on the adoption of children in long-term care.

The issue of resources has long been cited as a reason for long-term drift and a fear on the part of foster carers that they and their foster children would not be supported financially by the state if an adoption order was made. Cregan (forthcoming) has argued that finances may be a barrier for some foster carers to pursue adoption for children in their care; however, it is very likely that foster carers who adopt a child in state care will soon be eligible to receive a support payment. Traditional perceptions of adoption representing a 'clean break' may no longer be relevant when children in state care are likely to have ongoing relationships with members of their birth family, something that, in practice, will continue into their adoptive placement. Indeed, the profile of foster carers might also change. Foster care has traditionally been seen as either a short-term or long-term *loco parentis*-type arrangement, and mostly not as a starting point to adoption.

Ireland's new adoption model repositions children's rights and their best interests as central to any permanency planning and decision-making. It changes the way in which children have historically been viewed; children now have a voice and are independent rights holders. All decisions regarding the long-term care of children and young people must be based on their best interests and should be assessed on a case-by-case basis, rather than decisions being made in the interests of adults or institutional systems.

We argue that attention must be given to the lifelong impact of adoption and how the adoption system can best support the ongoing needs of all parties. However, it is hoped that Ireland is moving towards a more inclusive and coherent system focused on decision-making, adoption assessment practices and care models based on the best interests of the child. It is now necessary for the Child and Family Agency to develop a dedicated post-adoption support unit that delivers a coordinated and streamlined service.

Acknowledgements

The authors would like to thank Triona Hall, Principal Social Worker, for her comments on earlier drafts of this chapter.

References

AAI (Adoption Authority of Ireland) (2014–19) 'Annual reports 2013–2018'. Available at: aai.gov.ie/en/what-we-do/further-information/publications.html (accessed 25 July 2019).

AAI (2020) 'Intercountry adoptions by parents habitually resident in Ireland: 1991–date'. Available at: aai.gov.ie/images/ICA_by_parents_habitually_resident_in_Ireland_Report_111219_FINAL.pdf (accessed 12 March 2020).

Adoption Rights Alliance, Parkes, A. and McCaughren, S. (2014) 'Time to reform adoption laws has arrived', *Irish Examiner*, 5 November. Available at: www.irishexaminer.com/viewpoints/analysis/time-to-reform-adoption-laws-has-arrived-296344.html (accessed 12 March 2020).

Burns, K. and McGregor, C. (2019) 'Child protection and welfare systems in Ireland: continuities and discontinuities of the present', in L. Merkel-Holguin, J.D. Fluke and R. Krugman (eds) *National Systems of Child Protection: Understanding the International Variability and Context for Developing Policy and Practice*, Dordrecht: Springer International/Palgrave Macmillan, pp 115–38.

Burns, K., Devaney, J., Holt, S. and Marshall, G. (forthcoming) 'Child protection and welfare on the island of Ireland: Irish issues, global relevance', in N. Gilbert, J. Duerr Berrick and M. Skivenes (eds) *International Handbook of Child Protection Systems*, London: Oxford University Press.

Central Statistics Office (2017) *Census of Population 2016 – Profile 4 Households and Families*, Cork: CSO.

Central Statistics Office (2019) 'Vital statistics yearly summary 2018'. Available at: www.cso.ie/en/releasesandpublications/ep/p-vsys/vitalstatisticsyearlysummary2018/ (accessed 25 July 2019).

Child and Family Agency (2014–19) 'Review of adequacy reports 2007–2017'. Available at: www.tusla.ie/publications/review-of-adequacy-reports/ (accessed 3 October 2019).

Child and Family Agency (2020a) *Annual Review on the Adequacy of Child Care and Family Support Services Available 2018*, Dublin: Tusla, Child and Family Agency. Available at: www.tusla.ie/uploads/content/Review_of_Adequacy_Report_2018_Final_for_Publication_V2.pdf (accessed 23 January 2020).

Child and Family Agency (2020b) *Pathway to Permanency Handbook (Draft Edition)*, Dublin: Tusla, Child and Family Agency.

Connolly, L. (2015) 'Locating the Irish family: towards a plurality of family forms', in L. Connolly (ed) *The 'Irish' Family*, New York: Routledge, pp 10–38.

Courts Service (2019) 'Annual report 2018'. Available at: www.courts.ie/annual-report (accessed 15 December 2020).

Cregan, M. (forthcoming) 'PhD research dissertation', School of Applied Social Studies, University College Cork.

Department of Children and Youth Affairs (2017) *Children First: National Guidance for the Protection and Welfare of Children*, Dublin: Government Publications.

Department of Children and Youth Affairs (2019) 'Review and consultation in respect of the potential introduction of open or semi-open adoption in Ireland. Report produced in accordance with Section 42 of the Adoption (Amendment) Act 2017 (November 2019)'. Available at: https://assets.gov.ie/38717/3defc42d3e84425e a00e621d1610f800.pdf (accessed 7 November 2019).

Department of Health and Children (2003) *The National Standards for Foster Care*, Dublin: Government Publications.

Ferriter, D. (2019) '"I was not a human being": a history of Irish childhood', *Irish Times No Child 2020*, 19 January. Available at: www. irishtimes.com/news/social-affairs/i-was-not-a-human-being-a-history-of-irish-childhood-1.3758896 (accessed 1 January 2020).

Garrett, P.M. (2017) 'Excavating the past: mother and baby homes in the Republic of Ireland', *British Journal of Social Work*, 47(2): 358–74.

Irish Association of Social Workers and Council of Irish Adoption Agencies (2020) 'Rights to birth certificates is still an option', press release, 16 January. Available at: www.iasw.ie/page/503 (accessed 14 February 2020).

Kornitzer, M. (1952) *Child Adoption in the Modern World*, London: Putnam.

Lee, P. (2014) 'Her story in her own words', keynote address at the 'Redefining Adoption in a New Era: Opportunities and Challenges for Law and Practice Conference', University College Cork.

McCaughren, S. and McGregor, C. (2018) 'Reimagining adoption in Ireland: a viable option for children in care?', *Child Care in Practice*, 24(3): 229–44.

McCaughren, S. and Ní Raghallaigh, M. (2015) 'Adoption in Ireland: exploring the changing context', in A. Christie, B. Featherstone, S. Quin and T. Walsh (eds) *Social Work in Ireland: Changes and Continuities*, London: Palgrave Macmillan, pp 71–87.

McCaughren, S. and Powell, F. (2017) 'The fate of the illegitimate child', in N. Howlin and K. Costello (eds) *Law and the Family in Ireland 1800–1950*, London: Palgrave Macmillan, pp 195–213.

McConnell, D. (2019) 'Bill to restore birth certs for illegally adopted', *Irish Examiner*, 29 January. Available at: www.irishexaminer.com/ breakingnews/ireland/bill-to-restore-birth-certs-for-illegally-adopted-899929.html (accessed 14 February 2020).

Milotte, M. (2012) *Banished Babies* (2nd edn), Dublin: New Island.

Murphy, Y. (2019) 'Mother and Baby Homes Commission of Investigation. Fifth interim report'. Available at: www.mbhcoi.ie/ MBH.nsf/page/Latest%20News-en (accessed 24 May 2019).

O'Brien, V. and Mitra, S. (2018a) *An Audit of Research on Adoption in Ireland 1952–2017*, Dublin: The Adoption Authority of Ireland.

O'Brien, V. and Mitra, S. (2018b) *An Overview of Adoption Policy and Legislative Changes in Ireland 1952–2017*, Dublin: The Adoption Authority of Ireland.

Palmer, A. and O'Brien, V. (2019) 'The changing landscape of Irish adoption: an analysis of trends (1999–2016)', *Child Care in Practice*, 25(4): 399–418.

Powell, F. and Scanlon, M. (2015) *Dark Secrets of Childhood: Media Power, Child Abuse and Public Scandals*, Bristol: Policy Press.

The Adoption Board (2003) *Report of a Board Uchtála (The Adoption Board)*, Dublin: The Stationery Office.

The Adoption Board (2009) *The Adoption Board Annual Report 2008*, Dublin: The Stationery Office.

Whyte, J.H. (1971) *Church and State in Modern Ireland 1923–1970*, Dublin: Gill and Macmillan.

5

Adoption from care: policy and practice in the United States

Jill Duerr Berrick

Introduction

Adoption was practised in the US before the founding of the country and it has been legally codified since the mid-1800s. Layers of state and federal laws have since expanded the practice and, today, the US stands out among nations for both the number of children adopted overall and the number of children adopted from care. This chapter provides a brief history of adoption practice and policy in the US, followed by an examination of current philosophical and practical aspects of adoption from care, and concludes with an assessment of future issues in the field.

A brief review of US adoption history

During the colonial period, adoption was used by the new European-American immigrants to secure legal heredity so that property or wealth could be passed from one individual to another (Carp, 2005). These were 'private adoptions', whereby the care and custody of a child was transferred from one (or two) parent(s) to another adult. Older children (typically boys) were the usual candidates for adoption (Freundlich, 2001); some boys were also adopted to secure their labour since the family was the primary economic engine of the developing country (Mintz, 2004). In 1851, the state legislature passed the Massachusetts Adoption Act, the first law to codify appropriate legal procedures surrounding private adoption. That law attended to the rights of birth parents and adoptive parents. It also targeted the needs of children as unique constituents of the legal transaction (Carp, 2005).

Fast-forward to the 20th century and the phenomenon of private adoption flourished. During and after the Second World War, out-of-wedlock pregnancy rates rose significantly and the stigma associated with these births was high. At the same time, the infant mortality rate – which had been alarmingly high for centuries – began to fall. With the discovery of infant formula, infants could survive in settings separated from the birth mother (Carp and Leon-Guerero, 2005). These factors provided the main impetus for the supply side of the adoption equation. At the same time, private individuals, eager to start or expand their families, provided ample demand for healthy, white infants who needed a home. Adoption as part of child welfare became a practice specialism within social work to serve the interests of both couples seeking adoption and babies needing new homes. Child welfare staff were trained to serve as mediators in these private adoptions to facilitate the legal exchange of young children between families. Their job was to assess the appropriateness of prospective adoptive parents, and they focused many of their efforts on 'matching', that is, they assessed children as 'normal' or 'defective', and they carefully matched parents to children using categories of race, ethnicity, physical features and religion (Gil, 2005).

These 'matching' practices ensured that, for example, white children would live with white families, black children would live with black families and Protestant children would live with Protestant families. The only group that experienced intentional race mismatching was Native American/Alaska Native children. Adoption of tribal children into white homes was considered one strategy to deal with the 'Indian problem' in the US. That is, if Native American children could 'pass as' white, the hope was they would assimilate into the dominant culture and long-standing issues of cultural difference and tribal sovereignty would decline. The federal government launched the Indian Adoption Project to promote adoption of Native American children into white homes, and from 1958 to 1967, hundreds of tribal children were adopted out of their communities. In the 1960s and 1970s, some estimates suggest that well over four fifths of all tribal children in foster or adoptive homes were living with non-indigenous families (Unger, 1977).

With the advent and greater use of effective birth control methods, along with reductions in the stigma associated with single parenthood, the supply of healthy babies available in the private adoption market declined. At about the same time, child welfare caseloads and public awareness about out-of-home care grew. By the 1970s, several factors drew public attention to the child welfare system and to adoption from care. Numbers in care were rising and emerging research showed the disquieting effects of lengthy stays in the out-of-home care system. Research showed that children who lingered in care often experienced instability, moving from one home to another; some child welfare agencies lost track of children's whereabouts altogether (Fanshel and Shinn, 1978).

African American children were especially likely to be placed in out-of-home care, yet the odds of adoption for African American children were low (Barth, 1997). Transracial placement – matching African American children with white families – grew modestly throughout the 1960s; yet, by the early 1970s, the practice grew increasingly contested. In 1972, the National Association of Black Social Workers demanded a halt to transracial placements for African American children (NABSW, 1972). In their statement, transracial placement was equated with cultural genocide and white adoptive parents were cautioned that they would not be able to adequately prepare black children to live with the racism prevalent in the US.

These tensions – associated with race, foster care and adoption – gained political urgency and were finally expressed in 1978, with federal legislation governing the adoption of Native American children. The Indian Child Welfare Act (ICWA) set requirements for foster care placements, privileging placement with extended family, with the child's tribe or with a different tribe (in order of preference); the law only allowed foster care placement with a non-relative non-tribal member if the privileged options were exhausted. During a child's stay in foster care, social workers were required to make active efforts to reunify the family. The ICWA also set the standard for adoption very high, requiring courts to prove parents unfit 'beyond a reasonable doubt', which is a very high legal bar.

Two years later, Congress passed and the President signed the Adoption Assistance and Child Welfare Act 1980 (AACWA), a parallel law designed for all children in the US, except tribal children, with some of the same intentions but somewhat different features from the ICWA. The AACWA required states to make 'reasonable efforts' (rather than 'active efforts') to prevent foster care placement. Like its predecessor law, it also required states to pursue reunification with parents if out-of-home placement was required. Placement preferences were more diffusely defined as the 'least restrictive (most family like) and most appropriate setting available and in close proximity to the parent's home, consistent with the best interests and special needs of the child' (US Social Security Act, s 475 [42 U.S.C. 675] 5[A]).

With the advent of the AACWA, there were over 200,000 children in out-of-home care in the US. Many of these children had been in care for several years, with little done to secure their long-term living arrangements. 'Permanence' became a central focus of the new law, imposing on public child welfare agencies an obligation to establish case plans for all children in care, and to prioritise efforts towards reunification with the birth family wherever possible. The law established limits on the amount of time parents were offered services to help secure their children's return; thereafter, adoption was considered the second-best permanency option, though the legal bar of proof to terminate parental rights and pursue adoption was set as a 'preponderance of the evidence', a much lower standard than the bar set for tribal children.

Estimates from the early years following the AACWA suggest that about 17,000 children were in 'adoptive placements' in 1982 (though there are no reliable data on the number of these children whose adoptions were ultimately finalised). A decade later, about 20,000 children were adopted per year, and by the mid-1990s, almost 30,000 children were annually adopted from care (Maza, 1984; Flango and Flango, 1994; Testa, 2004).

Some congressional leaders were impatient with the gradual increase in public adoptions. They also expressed frustration that public child welfare officials too often favoured family preservation efforts over expedited permanency for children (see D'Andrade and Berrick, 2006). Legislators' efforts to tilt the balance in favour of children's rights to permanency, over parents' rights to their children, resulted in the Adoption and Safe Families Act 1997 (ASFA). That law: further limited the amount of time parents would be offered services to promote reunification; created a list of 'exceptional circumstances' that, if present, would allow child welfare agencies to bypass offering services to parents and expedite adoption; and provided annual adoption 'incentive payments' to states that increased the number of finalised adoptions above an established base rate (D'Andrade and Berrick, 2006).

The number of adoptions from out-of-home care rose. In 2000, approximately 50,000 children were adopted in the US from the public child welfare system. A decade later, public adoptions rose another 16 per cent to almost 60,000 children per year (Shuman and Flango, 2013) (for details, see Table 5.1). Today, the US is referred to as an 'adoption nation'; according to some estimates, the US has a higher rate of adoption than any other country (Pertman, 2011). Recent estimates suggest that the annual number of adoptions has stabilised at close to 60,000 per year (US DHHS, 2019), accounting for about 40 per cent of all adoptions nationwide (the other 60 per cent are accounted for by international and private adoptions) (Vandivere et al, 2009).

Table 5.1: Trends in adoption in the US[a]

Year	Children in out-of-home care[b] (rate per 100,000 children)	Number of public adoptions from out-of-home care[c]	Rate of adoptions from public care per 100,000 children[d]	Number of inter-country adoptions	Rate of inter-country adoptions per 100,000 children
2003	510,000 (697)	50,355	68.8	19,237[e]	26.0
2005	513,000 (697)	51,323	69.8	20,679[f]	28.1
2010	408,525 (551)	52,340	70.6	12,149	16.4
2015	427,910 (581)	53,549	72.7	8,650[g]	11.75
2018	437,283 (595)	63,123	85.9	4,059[h]	5.5

Notes and sources: [a] Data on the number of children adopted privately in the US are not available. [b] Data are derived from Adoption and Foster Care Analysis and Reporting System (AFCARS) reports #10–#26 (US Department of Health and Human Services). The denominator is derived from the US census and includes all children aged 0–17. The numerator is derived from AFCARS and, since 2009, includes all children aged 0–20 (0–17 prior to 2009). Youth aged 18 and older typically represent less than 10 per cent of the total out-of-home care population. [c] Data are derived from AFCARS reports #10–#26 (US Department of Health and Human Services). [d] Data are derived from: www.census.gov/programs-surveys/popest/data/tables.2010.html. [e] Data noted here are from 2001. Data shown from 2001 to 2010 are derived from Selman (2009). [f] Data noted here are from 2006. [g] Data noted here are from 2012 and are derived from the Child Welfare Information Gateway, 'Trends in U.S. adoptions'. Available at: www.childwelfare.gov/pubPDFs/adopted0812.pdf (accessed 21 December 2019). [h] Data are derived from the National Council for Adoptions, see: www.adoptioncouncil.org/blog/2019/03/fy2018-intercountry-adoption-report-released (accessed 21 December 2019).

Adoption today

Adoption is considered an essential permanency option for children who cannot return home, in part, because the alternative of long-term foster care with non-relatives is generally considered detrimental to children's well-being. Too many children experience impermanence in foster care, where they endure sequential relationships that are neither enduring nor legally enforceable (Testa, 2005). Adoption, by contrast, confers considerable benefits to children, including rights to inheritance and, in some instances, greater financial security during childhood. Some evidence also indicates that adoption offers children a sense of stability and belonging that is different from the experience of foster care (Brodzinsky et al, 1998). Adoption is also a relatively stable phenomenon; the disruption rate is very low. Some estimates indicate that about 8 per cent of adoptions disrupt (Rolock, 2015), though others suggest that the figure is closer to 5 per cent (Rolock et al, 2019). Foster care, in contrast, is a relatively impermanent setting for children, which can be especially consequential when young children are placed in care. The large majority of entries to care in the US are for children under the age of five (US DHHS, 2019). Given the tender age of so many children in foster care, the prospect of long-term foster care is considered highly problematic. As a result of the age distribution of children in care, and a generally accepted view that children should not be raised in care long-term, the majority of children adopted are quite young. One study of a nationally representative sample of adoptive families found that only 20 per cent of children were older than age six at placement into the adoptive home; almost half (45 per cent) were under one year of age (Malm et al, 2011). According to the most recent data available: the mean age of adopted children in 2018 was 6.1 years; 49 per cent were male; and approximately half of children adopted in 2018 (49 per cent) were white, 21 per cent were Hispanic and 17 per cent were black or African American (US DHHS, 2019). Although over 100,000 children are typically available for adoption from foster care every year (US DHHS, 2019), some children have a lower likelihood of being adopted. African American children are about 38 per cent less likely to be adopted compared to white children, and children with mental health problems are less likely to be adopted; children with other disabling conditions, however, are more likely to be adopted (Akin, 2011).

Adoption is not the only permanency option for children in foster care. For children placed with relatives, adoption may not be an appropriate outcome, in part, because relatives may be reluctant to see the termination of parental rights for another family member. Instead, legal guardianship is increasingly used as an appropriate permanency option. Under guardianship, a judge transfers the care and custody of the child but the birth parent retains their legal rights of parenthood. Under these arrangements, a parent can petition the court for the child's return, should safety conditions at home substantially improve. As adoption is considered more legally binding than guardianship, it is preferred as a permanency opportunity, particularly for children living with non-relatives, though an older child's wishes would likely be considered if guardianship were strongly preferred. Although there is growing interest in legal guardianship for children placed with kin, adoption is still pursued for many. In one study of adoptive families, 17 per cent of adoptive parents were relatives previously known to the child and an additional 6 per cent were relatives unknown to the child (Malm et al, 2011).

Despite the positive regard and philosophical orientation towards adoption, a number of legal barriers exist to guard against its excesses. Adoption policies vary considerably in each of the 50 states but some general parameters shape the process. Typically, parents are offered services from child welfare agencies, along with time to use these services to improve the safety of their home and parenting following a child's removal and placement in care. Once the time frame and services end, a social worker recommends to the judge a permanent plan for the child. This preferred plan is reunification, but if a return home is not possible, adoption may be recommended. Prior to an adoption decision, a number of court hearings may occur, including the determination to terminate parental rights for each of the parents. The legal threshold for this decision was changed in 1997 under the Adoption and Safe Families Act and is now based on 'clear and convincing evidence'. (As described earlier, the standard for tribal children is higher. A decision that 'continued custody of the child by the parent or Indian custodian is likely to result in serious emotional or physical damage to the child' must be established 'beyond a reasonable doubt' [National Indian Law Library, 2019].) Throughout the entire process, parents are provided free legal counsel if they have a low income, or they can secure legal counsel on their own. In several states, children are also assigned a lawyer, and the public agency also argues its case through legal counsel.

Parents have rights to appeal each decision, including the determination to terminate parental rights. Depending on the age of the child and the state in which the child lives, the child may be invited to share their view about adoption as well. Appeals by one or more parties can be frequent, usually resulting in delays to the adoption process. The right to appeal, however, is designed to ensure equal protection for parents and children against capricious actions by the state. Once the time period for all legal appeals has elapsed, a child is considered legally free for adoption.

Across states, some other general principles apply, though there is great variability in policy and practice. The 'best interests of the child' is the standard used to determine if adoption is appropriate. As adoption is not possible until after termination of parental rights has occurred, the focus of judicial proceedings is not on the birth parent(s), but solely on the child. One way to make a relevant best interest determination is to ask the child about their wishes. Depending on the state, children aged ten or older are typically asked to express their views and are asked for their consent. Finally, adoption decisions are usually confidential. Unless there is agreement among the parties, the birth parent may not know the identities of the adoptive parents, the child's name and birth certificate are usually changed, and related documentation is reissued by the state (Hollinger, 2012).

Following adoption finalisation, adoptive parents typically receive an initial tax credit; thereafter, they usually receive a monthly subsidy, similar to the foster care subsidy, until the child turns 18. These federal subsidies are available to children who are categorised as 'special needs' or 'hard to place' (NACAC, 2019). Given that the large majority of children in foster care come from disadvantaged backgrounds or have one or more health, developmental or mental health conditions (Burns et al, 2004), most children are considered eligible (federal data indicate that 93 per cent of adoptive parents receive an adoption subsidy [US DHHS, 2019]). In fact, one study showed that about half of children adopted from care had a special healthcare need (Malm et al, 2011), and approximately half of boys adopted from care utilised mental health services, as did almost two fifths of girls (Tan and Marn, 2013). Adopted children are entitled to publicly funded medical and mental healthcare (Medicaid) until age 21, some are covered up to age 26 through the Affordable Care Act, and others may be covered by their adoptive parents' employer-sponsored health insurance (CWIG, 2015). Some evidence suggests that the economic supports offered to families are an important incentive promoting adoption for children who would otherwise remain in foster care (Argys and Duncan, 2007). Other evidence shows that public expenditures for adoption are less than foster care due to reduced court costs, social worker costs and other service needs (Zill, 2011).

Future issues in adoption

Some aspects of adoption practice are changing rapidly and dramatically in the US, in part, as a response to the changing composition of adoptive families and in response to changes in the social environment. Adoption from care evolved in parallel with private, independent adoptions based on many assumptions of privacy, confidentiality and secrecy (Carp, 2004). Today, however, the majority of children adopted from care are adopted by their foster parents (52 per cent) or by a relative (36 per cent) (US DHHS, 2019). As such, children, foster/adoptive parents and birth parents are typically known to one another before adoption proceedings begin.

When all members of the adoption triad (birth parent, adoptive parent and child) are known to one another, open adoption is often pursued. Open adoption may involve a variety of strategies to maintain contact between children and birth parents, including annual cards or letters, phone contact, or regular meetings. Grotevant and McRoy (1998) have referred to open adoption as a 'continuum of openness' given the variety of family preferences. Many states have allowed open adoption agreements to be instated at the point of adoption. These are typically non-binding agreements that set the parameters for parties' hopes and expectations more than requirements. Sometimes, arrangements for openness are mediated by the state; other families make arrangements informally. Evidence from one study indicates that about two fifths of adopted children have had contact with their birth family following adoption (Malm et al, 2011). Research on open adoption suggests that the agreement guidelines are usually followed during the early years after the adoption but that the frequency of contact between birth parents and children usually declines over time (Berry et al, 1998). In general, the research on outcomes for children experiencing open adoption are neither positive nor negative (Grotevant et al, 1999); one national study of children adopted from care found no differences between children whose adoption was open compared to children whose adoption was closed (Vandiviere and McKlindon, 2010).

Adoption contact agreements may be between birth parents and children, as well as between siblings who are separated. Some evidence suggests that sibling relationships are especially meaningful and important to children in care (Herrick and Piccus, 2005), so their separations through foster care or adoption require especially thoughtful consideration, and open adoption agreements can help in that regard. Increasingly, however, siblings are often placed together in the same adoptive home, either simultaneously or sequentially. In one national study, over four fifths of adopted children from foster care also had a sibling placed in foster care; about two fifths saw their sibling adopted into their adoptive home with them (Malm et al, 2011).

Just as attitudes about privacy and secrecy in adoption are changing, so are cultural mores about who is an appropriate adoptive parent. Over two thirds of adoptive parents (68 per cent) are married or unmarried (3 per cent) couples, though the number of single adoptive parents is rapidly rising and well over one quarter of adoptive parents are single (25 per cent female; 3 per cent male) (US DHHS, 2019). In some states, efforts to recruit adoptive parents from the lesbian, gay, bisexual, trans and queer (LGBTQ) community are also robust. Training and support for social workers has expanded significantly in the US to address prejudices and stigma (Mallon, 2008). Nevertheless, in some states, adults who are LGBTQ are discouraged from pursuing adoption, and another handful allow private, non-profit agencies to deny opportunities for public adoption to members of the LGBTQ community (Agosto, 2012).[1]

Discussions about sexual orientation and its appropriateness for care mirror historical debates about the role of race and transracial placement in the field of adoption (for a discussion, see Bartholet, 1991) and, before that, the role of religion in trans-religious placements (for a discussion, see Pfeffer, 2002). However, Congress effectively ended the debate when they passed the Multi-Ethnic Placement Act 1996, prohibiting states from denying or delaying foster or adoptive placements based on the race or ethnicity of the child or of the prospective foster or adoptive parent. In the most recent national study, about one quarter (28 per cent) of children adopted from care were living in transracial, transethnic or transcultural households (Malm et al, 2011), and the research evidence on outcomes for children in transracial adoptive homes is generally positive (Vandiviere and McKlindon, 2010). The Multi-Ethnic Placement Act was passed, in part, based on the argument that denial of transracial placements was racially discriminatory and therefore illegal under the equal protection clause of the US constitution.

Ten states currently allow state-licensed child welfare agencies to refuse to work with LGBTQ individuals or couples if such work conflicts with their religious views (Movement Advancement Project, 2019). Whether Congress will pass similar legislation to ban discrimination against the sexual orientation of adoptive parents is unlikely in the near future. Advocates of the ban on LGBTQ families argue that forcing private agencies to serve LGBTQ families is antithetical to their religious convictions; efforts to force agencies to work with LGBTQ parents thus violate the first amendment right to freedom of religion. Critics of the ban, however, refer to the equal protection clause of the constitution and argue that their right to publicly funded adoption services cannot be abridged.

Other topics likely to garner significant attention relate to the needs of children following the adoption decision. A good deal of research suggests that raising children who hail from foster care can be challenging for many families (Hill and Moore, 2015; Good, 2016). The large majority of children in foster care have health, mental health or developmental challenges that require a highly effective caregiving environment (Berrick and Skivenes, 2012). As such, demand for post-adoption services is high. Unfortunately, many adoptive parents who need services indicate that services are unavailable, or services do not meet their needs (Barth and Miller, 2004). As such, demand for post-adoption services is likely to continue to be an important issue in adoption policy discussions; determining whether federal, state or local jurisdictions are responsible for financing these services, and for how long, will be contested.

The most difficult adoption issue likely to shape policy and practice in future years relates to the ICWA, the 1978 law described earlier that set strict conditions under which tribal children could be adopted. The ICWA was designed to:

> protect the best interests of Indian children and promote the stability and security of Indian tribes and families by the establishment of minimum Federal standards for the removal of Indian children from their families and the placement of such children in foster or adoptive homes which [will] reflect the unique values of Indian culture. (s 1902 ICWA)

It placed significant restrictions on state and local governments to limit the separation of children from their parents; it created placement preferences so that if children were separated into foster care, they would remain with their extended family, in their own tribe or in another tribe; and it set a very high bar for terminating parental rights. The goals of the ICWA were to cede to the tribes authority to care for their own children, as well as to limit the likelihood that children would be separated from their family, their tribe and their cultural heritage.

Advocates for the law point to the importance of tribal bonds and suggest that the best interests of the child can only be considered when children have the opportunity to grow and develop within their tribal identity (Cross, 2014). In short, cultural continuity, it is argued, is always in the best interests of the child (Weaver and White, 1999). Critics, however, suggest that the ICWA places the tribe's interests over the interests of individual parents, particularly if or when individual parents' tribal affiliation has no personal meaning. As such, the ICWA has the potential to pit parents' rights against tribal community rights, with the law favouring tribal community rights.

The law has been tested before the US Supreme Court in a 2013 decision (see Adoptive couple v Baby girl – 570 U.S. 637, 133 S. Ct. 2552 [2013]). In that case, a toddler was ultimately allowed to remain with her non-tribal parents but the judges demurred on the merits of the ICWA's preferential restrictions. A new case, much debated in child welfare circles, is likely to make its way to the US Supreme Court as well. In that case (Brackeen v Bernhardt 942 F. 3d 287 – Court of Appeals, 5th Circuit 2019), critics argue that the ICWA hinges on racial preferences that should be viewed as unconstitutional under the equal protection clause of the 14th amendment. Advocates for the ICWA argue that the placement preferences in the ICWA are based on the rights of tribal sovereign nations and that race is not a factor. If the ICWA is overturned, the decision would have far-reaching implications for adoption and many unrelated issues relating to tribal sovereignty in the US.

Conclusion

Adoption has long been used in the US as a strategy to secure legally binding and lasting relationships for children who have been separated from or who have lost their parents. Today, large numbers of children are adopted from care, though over 115,000 remain in care with an ultimate 'goal' of adoption (US DHHS, 2019). Some of these children will eventually be adopted; others may transition to guardianship and some may be reunified. The notion of 'permanency' for children has been taken quite seriously in the US. Some states have aggressively pursued permanency opportunities, dramatically reducing the proportion of children who remain in care long-term (see Magruder, 2010).

A number of federal policies have been developed to incentivise and support adoption in the US. Today, adoptive parents receive financial support through tax credits and direct payments, and states can receive financial benefits from the federal government when the numbers of annual adoptions rise. There is no sign in the US that enthusiasm for adoption is in decline; quite the contrary. Both the demand for children among adults hoping to start or grow their family, or to make a difference for others, and the supply of children with little prospect of returning to their original family suggest that adoption is likely to continue to be viewed as a viable strategy for securing children's futures.

Recent debates about the ICWA have exposed some of the challenges associated with privileging community/tribal rights over the rights of individual parents or individual children; however, that debate has not been considered relevant to non-tribal children, who represent the vast majority of all adopted children in the US. In the larger US community, children's rights to permanency prevail in most adoption discussions, ensuring that the practice will likely continue for some time to come.

Acknowledgements

This project has received funding from the Research Council of Norway under the Independent Projects – Humanities and Social Science program (grant no. 262773). Disclaimer: This chapter reflects only the authors' views and the funding agency is not responsible for any use that may be made of the information contained therein.

Note

[1] Public child welfare agencies may not discriminate based on race, national origin, religion or sexual orientation. Private agencies (usually religiously affiliated) are not held to the same standards relating to discrimination, though many provide adoption services to children in foster care. On 1 November 2019, the Trump administration announced a new federal rule that would allow discrimination against LGBTQ prospective adoptive parents.

References

Agosto, A. (2012) 'Is there a relationship between LGBT couple adoption laws and change in adoption rates?', doctoral dissertation. Available at: http://hdl.handle.net/10211.3/10211.13_310 (accessed 12 December 2020).

Akin, B. (2011) 'Predictors of foster care exits to permanency: a competing risks analysis of reunification, guardianship, and adoption', *Children and Youth Services Review*, 33: 999–1011.

Argys, L. and Duncan, B. (2007) 'Economic incentives and foster child adoption', *Southern Economic Journal*, 74(1): 114–42.

Barth, R.P. (1997) 'Effects of age and race on the odds of adoption versus remaining in long-term out-of-home care', *Child Welfare*, 76(2): 285.

Barth, R.P. and Miller, J.M. (2004) 'Building effective post-adoption services: what is the empirical foundation?' *Family Relations*, 49(4): 447–55.

Bartholet, E. (1991) 'Where do black children belong? The politics of race matching in adoption', *University of Pennsylvania Law Review*, 139(5): 1163–254.

Berrick, J.D. and Skivenes, M. (2012) 'Dimensions of high-quality foster care: parenting plus', *Children and Youth Services Review*, 34(9): 1956–65.

Berry, M., Dylla, D.C., Barth, R.P. and Needell, B. (1998) 'The role of open adoption in the adjustment of adopted children and their families', *Children and Youth Services Review*, 20(1–2): 151–71.

Brodzinsky, D.M., Smith, D.W. and Brodzinsky, A.B. (1998) *Children's Adjustment to Adoption: Developmental and Clinical Issues*, Thousand Oaks, CA: Sage.

Burns, B.J., Phillips, S.D., Wagner, H.R., Barth, R.P., Kolko, D.J., Campbell, Y. and Landsverk, J. (2004) 'Mental health need and access to mental health services by youth involved with child welfare', *Journal of the American Academy of Child and Adolescent Psychiatry*, 43: 960–73.

Carp, W. (2004) *Adoption Politics: Bastard Nation and Ballot Initiative 58*, Lawrence, KS: University of Kansas Press.

Carp, W. (ed) (2005) *Adoption in America*, Ann Arbor, MI: University of Michigan Press.

Carp, W. and Leon-Guerero, A. (2005) 'When in doubt, count: World War II as a watershed in the history of adoption', in W. Carp (ed) *Adoption in America*, Ann Arbor, MI: University of Michigan Press.

Cross, T.L. (2014) 'Child welfare in Indian country: a story of painful removals', *Health Affairs*, 33(12): 2256–9.

CWIG (Child Welfare Information Gateway) (2015) *Healthcare Coverage for Youth in Foster Care and after*, Washington, DC: US Department of Health and Human Services, Children's Bureau.

D'Andrade, A. and Berrick, J.D. (2006) 'When policy meets practice: the untested effects of permanency reforms in child welfare', *Journal of Sociology and Social Welfare*, 33(1): 31–52.

Fanshel, D. and Shinn, E.G. (1978) *Children in Foster Care: A Longitudinal Investigation*, New York: Columbia University Press.

Flango, V. and Flango, C. (1994) *The Flow of Adoption Information from the States*, Williamsburg, VA: National Center for State Courts.

Freundlich, M. (2001) *Adoption and Ethics: The Impact of Adoption on Members of the Triad*, Washington, DC: Child Welfare League of America.

Gil, B. (2005) 'Adoption agencies and the search for the ideal family: 1918–1965', in W. Carp (ed) *Adoption in America*, Ann Arbor, MI: University of Michigan Press.

Good, G.A. (2016) 'Adoption of children with disabilities: an exploration of the issues for adoptive families', *Early Child Development and Care*, 186: 1–20.

Grotevant, H.D. and McRoy, R. (1998) *Openness in Adoption: Exploring family Connections*, Thousand Oaks, CA: Sage.

Grotevant, H.D., Ross, N.M., Marchel, M.A. and McRoy, R.G. (1999) 'Adaptive behavior in adopted children: predictors from early risk, collaboration in relationships within the adoptive kinship network, and openness arrangements', *Journal of Adolescent Research*, 14(2): 231–47.

Herrick, A.M. and Piccus, W. (2005) 'Sibling connections: the importance of nurturing sibling bonds in the foster care system', *Children and Youth Services Review*, 27: 845–61.

Hill, K. and Moore, F. (2015) 'The postadoption needs of adoptive parents of children with disabilities', *Journal of Family Social Work*, 118: 64–182.

Hollinger, J. (2012) *Adoption Policy and Practice*, Neward, NJ: Matthew Bender Press.

Magruder, J. (2010) 'A comparison of near-term outcomes of foster children who reunified, were adopted, or were in guardianship', dissertation, University of California, Berkeley.

Mallon, G. (2008) *Social Work Practice with Lesbian, Gay, Bisexual, and Transgender People*, New York: Routledge Press.

Malm, K., Vandiviere, S. and McKlindon, A. (2011) 'Children adopted from foster care: child and family characteristics, adoption motivation, and well-being', Office of the Assistant Secretary for Planning and Evaluation, US Department of Health and Human Services.

Maza, P. (1984) 'Adoption trends: 1944–1975. Child welfare research notes #9', US Children's Bureau.

Mintz, S. (2004) *Huck's Raft: A History of American Childhood*, Cambridge, MA: Harvard University Press.

Movement Advancement Project (2019) 'Foster and adoption laws', LGBT Map. Available at: www.lgbtmap.org/equality-maps/foster_and_adoption_laws (accessed 19 July 2019).

NABSW (National Association of Black Social Workers) (1972) 'Position statement on transracial adoptions', National Association of Black Social Workers. Available at: https://cdn.ymaws.com/www.nabsw.org/resource/collection/E1582D77-E4CD-4104-996A-D42D08F9CA7D/NABSW_Trans-Racial_Adoption_1972_Position_(b).pdf (accessed 19 June 2019).

NACAC (North American Council on Adoptable Children) (2019) 'Eligibility and benefits for federal Title IV-E adoption assistance', North American Council on Adoptable Children. Available at: www.nacac.org/resource/eligibility-benefits-federal-assistance/ (accessed 3 June 2019).

National Indian Law Library (2019) 'Topic 18: adoption', National Indian Law Library. Available at: https://narf.org/nill/documents/icwa/faq/adoption.html (accessed 3 June 2019).

Pertman, A. (2011) *Adoption Nation: How the Adoption Revolution Is Transforming Our Families – and America*, Boston, MA: Harvard Common Press.

Pfeffer, P.F. (2002) 'A historical comparison of Catholic and Jewish adoption practices in Chicago, 1833–1933', in E.W. Carp (ed) *Adoption in America: Historical Perspectives*, Ann Arbor, MI: University of Michigan Press.

Rolock, N. (2015) 'Post-permanency continuity: what happens after adoption and guardianship from foster care?', *Journal of Public Child Welfare*, 9: 153–73.

Rolock, N., White, K., Ocasio, K., Zhang, L., MacKenzie, M. and Fong, R. (2019) 'A comparison of foster care reentry after adoption in two large U.S. states', *Research on Social Work Practice*, 29(2): 153–64.

Selman, P. (2009). 'The rise and fall of intercountry adoption in the 21st century', *International Social Work*, 52(5): 575–94.

Shuman, M. and Flango, V.E. (2013) 'Trends in U.S. adoptions: 2000–2009', *Journal of Public Child Welfare*, 7(3): 329–49.

Tan, T.X. and Marn, T. (2013) 'Mental health service utilization in children adopted from US foster care, US private agencies and foreign countries: data from 2007 National Survey of Adoption Parents', *Children and Youth Services Review*, 35: 1050–4.

Testa, M. (2004) 'When children cannot return home: adoption and guardianship', *The Future of Children*, 14(1): 115–29.

Testa, M. (2005) 'The quality of permanence: lasting or binding? Subsidized guardianship and kinship foster care as alternatives to adoption', *Virginia Journal of Social Policy and Law*, 12(3): 499–534.

Unger, S. (ed) (1977) *The Destruction of American Indian Families*, New York: Association on American Indian Affairs.

US DHHS (US Department of Health and Human Services) (2019) 'Adoption foster care analysis reporting system (2008–2018) #26', Administration for Children and Families, Administration on Children, Youth, and Families, Children's Bureau. Available at: www.acf.hhs.gov/cb/resource/trends-in-foster-care-and-adoption (accessed 3 June 2019).

Vandiviere, S. and McKlindon, A. (2010) 'The well-being of U.S. children adopted from foster care, privately from the United States and internationally', *Adoption Quarterly*, 13(3/4): 157–84.

Vandivere, S., Malm, K. and Radel, L. (2009) 'Adoption USA: a chartbook based on the 2007 National Survey of Adoptive Parents', US Department of Health and Human Services, Office of the Assistant Secretary for Planning and Evaluation. Available at: http://aspe.hhs.gov/hsp/09/NSAP/chartbook/ (accessed 3 June 2019).

Weaver, H. and White, B. (1999) 'Protecting the future of indigenous children and nations', *Journal of Health and Social Policy*, 10(4): 35–50.

Zill, N. (2011) *Adoption from Foster Care: Aiding Children While Saving Public Money*, Washington, DC: Brookings Institute.

PART II

Adoption from care in family service-oriented child protection systems

---

6

Adoption from care in Austria

Jenny Krutzinna and Katrin Križ

Introduction

> The child has already been living in the household of the now adoptive parents for several years, thus adapting the legal status to the social status. The adoption therefore had to be approved. (Case AAUT05-17 from 2017 court judgment)

Austria is a federal republic, consisting of nine states, with a child population of 1,535,958 as of 1 January 2019 (Statistik Austria, 2019a, 2019b). Austrian federalism is limited, in that only few legislative powers remain with the regional states ('*Länder*'). The domain of child welfare and protection is one of them and thus falls under the responsibility of the states. The federal 1989 child welfare law constitutes the basis of child welfare services (CWS) but the nine states have their own laws. Austria's decentralised and regionalised system, with no nationwide quality criteria, a lack of many standardised and comparable statistics, and large variation in local practices, met with harsh criticism in the past (Reinprecht, 2015). The 2013 Federal Child Welfare Services Law (B-KJHG) introduced uniform criteria for service providers and standardised statistics across the regions; however, it did not change the systemic division of competencies between the federal state and the regions as the implementation of child protection legislation and responsibilities remained at the district and regional levels (Reinprecht, 2015). The local and regional variation in services may be further exacerbated following the devolution of child welfare from the federal level to the nine states after the repeal of the first part of the 2013 Child Welfare Services Law.

Legislation and organisations

Adoption is regulated by Articles 191–203 of the Austrian Civil Code, which set out the conditions for adoption: 'The adoption of a minor child shall be granted if it serves the child's well-being, and if a relationship [between the child and their adoptive parents] has been established or should be established' (Art 194 Austrian Civil Code).[1] While the law seems to promote adoption in cases where children have developed a parent–child relationship with their prospective adoptive parents, it is rare that children in foster care are adopted by their foster carers. Based on our own inquiries with the states' public CWS for the years 2016 and 2017, there are only a few of these adoptions in each of the nine regional states per year. No national statistics on children who are adopted from care are available. We have relied on interviews with several key informants and experts in the field of child welfare to fill the knowledge gaps. The adoptions of children in care by their foster families include: children whose birth parents wish them to be adopted, for example, if they have started a new family and the child is doing well in the foster family; children whose foster parents approach the CWS when the children have not had contact with their parents for a long time to ask the CWS to approach the court regarding adoption of the child; and foster children seeking to be adopted by their current foster parents.

Most children adopted domestically are adopted shortly after birth, either because their parents (mostly mothers) decided that they want the child to be adopted, or because their mothers gave birth 'anonymously' at the hospital, that is, without revealing their identifying personal details to the hospital staff. In both cases, the CWS will have custody of the baby and will choose prospective adopters from a long list of adoption applicants. There are currently approximately ten adoption applicants per child, some of whom will have been waiting for up to five years to adopt a child (Braunisch et al, 2018). These children will be placed with adoptive rather than foster families and adoptive parents can already visit the baby in hospital. The baby will stay with their future adoptive parents for six months before an adoption can occur. During this period, the birth mother can withdraw her consent to the adoption without the need for specific reasons.

Unlike many other countries, Austria allows foster parents to apply for full custody of a child they are caring for, provided that this is in the child's interests, that a parent–child relationship has developed with the foster parents and that reunification with the biological family has been ruled out (Art 184 Austrian Civil Code). This allows foster carers to make decisions concerning the child's life without intervention by biological parents or the CWS, and without having to first adopt the child. Previously, foster carers retained their right to receive foster child allowance payments following the transferral of full custodial rights to them; however, this is now only possible where exceptional personal and financial circumstances of the foster carers necessitate such payments (Art 44 Child Welfare Services Law of Vienna). In practice, this loss of financial support provides a disincentive to applications for full custody by foster families. The level of foster allowance is set by the states and depends on the age and needs of the child (for example, Vienna grants a basic monthly allowance for a child under six years of age of €510 (Stadt Wien, 2020b)). From the child's perspective, adoption could be seen as preferable because it gives the child more rights in terms of financial support as adoptive parents are financially responsible for the child by law whereas foster parents are not (and, most commonly, biological parents lack the funds to support their children who are placed in care).

Trends and statistics

The Austrian statistics available to the public do not capture the exact ages when children are adopted, nor do they allow a distinction between different types of adoptions.[2] Therefore, we do not have any data on the children adopted from care, as defined in this volume. The adoption statistics by the Austrian Office of Statistics are based on the court decisions about adoptions (Statistik Austria, 2019a). The Federal Child Welfare Services Law requires nationwide data to be collected at the federal level, while previously the states produced their own reports. Since 2015, national numbers have been published in an annual report, which includes numbers on domestic adoptions.

We know that the number of domestic adoptions has declined somewhat from approximately 11 per 100,000 children in 2002 to around six per 100,000 in recent years (Federal Ministry of Labour, Family and Youth, 2019a; Statistik Austria, 2019a). Table 6.1 provides an overview of the number of children who have contact with the Austrian child welfare system; Table 6.2 shows the number of children in out-of-home care; and Table 6.3 shows the number of domestic and inter-country adoptions. A comparison of the tables illustrates how rare child protection adoptions are in comparison to out-of-home care.

While fostering can, in theory, be an entry point to adoption, it is the exception, with children more likely to return to their biological parents or stay with foster parents until the age of legal maturity (18 years in Austria) (*Die Presse*, 2016a). In Graz, for instance, only one child is adopted by their foster parents every three to four years. This highlights the child welfare system's clear focus on family reunification or, where this proves impossible, on long-term foster

Table 6.1: Statistics about the child welfare system's responses, 2018

Child welfare in Austria	Statistics	Per 100,000 children
Child welfare statistics		
Number of children receiving child welfare services, including care support services and out-of-home care provision	49,580	3,228
Number of children receiving care support measures	36,255	2,360
Number of children receiving out-of-home care provision	13,325	867
– in residential care[a]	8,110	528
– in foster homes[a]	5,325	347
Number of court-ordered measures	5,413	352
– as out-of-home care	4,784	311
– as other support services	629	41

Note: [a] These numbers are only partially adjusted for those cases where a child received support under both categories.
Source: Bundeskanzleramt (2019)

Table 6.2: Children receiving out-of-home care

Year	Number of children	Per 100,000 children
2018	13,325	868
2015	13,126	868
2010	11,088	719
2005	10,043	622

Source: Federal Ministry of Labour, Family and Youth (2019b)

Table 6.3: Adoptions in Austria (excluding stepchild adoptions)

Year	Number of adoptions		Per 100,000 children (domestic adoptions only)	Child population[b]
	Domestic	Inter-country		
2018	99	11	6.4	1,535,958
2017	82	20	5.3	1,533,569
2016	93	28	6.1	1,525,337
2015[a]	104	30	6.9	1,512,787
2010	110	–	7.2	1,541,669
2005	156	–	9.7	1,614,076

Note: [a] Inter-country adoptions were not reported prior to 2015. Adoption numbers prior to 2002 not available. [b] As of 1 January of the relevant year, that is, 2018 data are from 1 January 2019.
Source: Bundeskanzleramt (2019) and Statistik Austria (2019b)

placements until the child reaches maturity, with contact with the birth parent(s). Our own inquiries with the CWS in the nine Austrian states indicate that there are between zero and two adoptions of children living with foster parents per state per year (approximately ten per year in the entire country). In addition, the official statistics indicate that there were 36 anonymous births in Austria in 2018 and five babies placed in baby boxes (Bundeskanzleramt, 2019). These would be infants who, if not 'claimed' by their parents within six months, might have been adopted.

Principles and systemic factors underpinning child protection adoptions in Austria

The principles of family preservation and subsidiarity are strongly embedded in child welfare legislation and policy in Austria. According to the subsidiarity principle, the state, including the CWS, will provide social assistance only when the family cannot provide it (Reinprecht, 2015). Where adoption is considered the best option for children, it is governed by the principle of permanency for the child – the law supports adoptions of children by caregivers with whom they have established a strong bond. Furthermore, it is governed by the biological principle (parental consent to adoption, retaining legal ties between the child and the birth parents post-adoption, and the child maintaining contact with birth parents), as well as the participation of older children in the adoption process.

The typical approach to permanency for children in care is foster care, not adoption. This is illustrated by the low number of adoptions in comparison to the overall number of children in care. As the quote at the beginning of this chapter indicates, a justification for adoptions of foster children by their foster families typically used by the courts is that the children have already developed an attachment to their foster carers and view them as their social parents. Foster care may be the preferred permanency option over adoption because the CWS work under the assumption that children can eventually be reunified with their family given the provision of enough support to the birth parents by the CWS, as one of our social worker interviewees revealed. In practice, very few children are reunified with their families, with approximately 90 per cent of all children staying in long-term care; also, the CWS will usually not support children's move back to their biological parents if they have already spent significant time with their foster carers (Braunisch et al, 2018). Unfortunately, the Austrian statistics do not provide any longitudinal information about children in care, so we do not know at what age children typically enter care and how long they remain in care.

The strength of the principle of family preservation is related to the strength of the biological principle, which is reflected in Austrian law. A peculiarity of the Austrian system is that: adopted children retain limited legal ties to their biological parents; they have the right to inherit from their biological parents after adoption (Art 199 Austrian Civil Code); and birth parents remain the child's parents within the construct of the subsidiarity principle. This means that birth parents' liability to pay child support persists but ranks behind the adoptive parents' obligation. Thus, birth parents must only financially support the adopted child if the adoptive parents become unable to do so (Art 198 Austrian Civil Code). A peculiarity of the Austrian adoption system is that it allows only for *Vertragsadoption* (contractual adoption), rather than *Volladoption* (full adoption), which prevents the adoptive child's legal integration into the wider adoptive family (Bundeskanzleramt, 2020a). The biological principle also means that strong emphasis is put on the biological parents' consent to the adoption. Adoptions without parental consent are extremely rare in Austria due to a high legal threshold for dispensing with parental consent (Burns et al, 2019) and a social work culture of hesitance towards cutting all ties between the child and birth family.

Pre- and post-adoption practices and decision-making regarding adoption

Practices with children, birth parents and future adoptive parents

Prospective adoptive parents are required to attend a preparatory course for adoption applicants. These are typically outsourced by the states to charities or non-governmental organisations (NGOs). In Vienna, the association Eltern für Kinder Österreich (Parents for Children Austria) has been commissioned to prepare applicants for adoption (Eltern für Kinder Österreich, 2020a). Special modules are offered depending on the type of adoption, and some elective modules are also offered. The preparatory course consists of lectures, group work, exercises and reflection, and its completion is a prerequisite for the official suitability assessment. In Vienna, the suitability of the adoptive parents is assessed by two professionals of the child welfare services agency (Art 52[1] Child Welfare Services Law of Vienna; see also MAG ELF, 2015).

The CWS emphasise children's right to know their biological heritage. Thus, the prospective adopters' understanding of children's ancestry as important to children's development is underscored, and adoptive parents are expected to be honest and open with children (Stadt Wien, 2020a). The child welfare agencies are under a legal obligation to keep documentation about the child's biological parents for 50 years after the date of approval of the adoption. The child's custodians may request information for particularly important medical or social reasons, as long as the adopted child has not yet reached the age of 14, after which point the child has this right (Art 49 Child Welfare Services Law of Vienna).

After the CWS agency has found adoptive parents for the child, the birth parents need to grant permission. Birth parents' declarations of consent must be delivered to the court in person; however, if this causes disproportionate difficulties or costs, or the proceedings have not yet started, parental declaration can be given via a notarised document (Art 86[4] Non-Contentious Proceedings Act 2003). The birth parents can decide to revoke their consent in person or writing until the court decision (Art 87 Non-Contentious Proceedings Act 2003).

Section 6 of the Austrian Civil Code (Arts 191ff) sets out the formal criteria for adoption. Adoptive parents must have legal capacity and be over 25 years of age. Married couples can only adopt jointly unless one parent is the biological parent of the child to be adopted. If the adoption applicants are currently acting as trustees for the child, they must first be released of their responsibilities and prove the discharge of their duties before they can adopt the child. In addition, the consent requirements outlined earlier must be fulfilled.

Decision-making regarding adoption

Decision-making body and consent

Adoptions in Austria typically only occur with parental agreement. They are based on a written contract between the biological parent and the child protection agency (closed adoptions), or the biological and adoptive parents (open adoptions). Adoptive children themselves sign this contract if they have sufficient decision-making capacity. Consent to the adoption must be given by the biological parents, the married adoptive parents or the spouse of the adopting adult, and the legal guardian of the adoptive child. Until mid-2018, a child of 14 years or older also had to consent to the adoption; however, under the current law, only the child's guardian must give consent. The law imposes a positive presumption of decision-making capacity (Art 192[2] Austrian Civil Code); in practice, some states have set this at age 14

(Kinder- und Jugendhilfe Oberösterreich, 2019). Where a child is found to lack decision-making capacity, the child's legal representative will sign the adoption contract on the child's behalf and in line with the child's best interests (Art 192 Austrian Civil Code).

Adoptions only become valid if approved by a court (Bundeskanzleramt, 2020b). Adoption proceedings are held at district courts and are presided over by a judge with expertise in family law. These hearings are typically not open to the public. The courts will always ask the CWS for a *Stellungnahme* (statement of opinion) when making a decision and will typically assess whether there are significant arguments against the adoption, as reported by one of our interviewees. The approval of the adoption by the court renders the adoption official. The adoption contract can be drafted by an attorney, a notary public and the CWS (Land Salzburg, 2019). Strict consent requirements apply: the court can only grant permission for an adoption if the child's parents, the spouse or domestic partner of the adoptive parent, and the child who has reached maturity but who lacks legal capacity or the legal representative of the minor child consent to the adoption (Art 195 Austrian Civil Code). Although adoption requires parental consent, an exception applies where the location of the parents is unknown for at least six months, or where the parents are incapacitated for longer than a temporary period (Art 195[2] Austrian Civil Code). The court must deny permission to the adoption if a biological child's care or subsistence is endangered by the adoption (Art 194[2] Austrian Civil Code).

Children have a right to be heard, which may be waived where children are unable to be heard for longer than merely temporarily (for example, due to young age), or where it may endanger the child's well-being (Art 196 Austrian Civil Code). Typically, children are heard directly by the judge; however, they may also be heard by the youth welfare agency, the family court services, the juvenile court services or by other appropriate means, such as by experts, if they have not reached the age of ten years, if required by their development or state of health, or if it is otherwise unlikely that children will express their sincere and uninfluenced opinion (Art 105 Non-Contentious Proceedings Act 2003).

Other parties with a right to be heard are children's current foster parents or the manager of the residential home where the child resides, as well as the CWS. This right does not apply to a person who has previously acted as legal guardian for the child in signing the adoption contract on the child's behalf, or where a hearing could only be arranged with disproportionate difficulties.

The role of different parties

The preparation for the adoption is done by the child welfare agencies, which: advise and guide the birth parents during the adoption; advise, prepare, assess and train the adoptive parents; and choose suitable adoptive parents based on the child's needs (see, for example, Article 50 Child Welfare Services Law of Vienna). Until 2020, the legal provisions setting out pre- and post-adoption practices and procedures were found in the Federal Child Welfare Services Law (B-KJHG) but they are now regulated by state laws.

The CWS with district offices (in the eight states) and the CWS Unit of the Social Work Department of the City of Vienna are responsible for drawing up the adoption contract, filing an application with the court and providing an assessment to the court (Bundeskanzleramt, 2020b). There is no legal minimum period that a child has to spend in pre-adoptive care in Austria (Sapinski, 2016a), but children usually live with their prospective adoptive parents for at least six months before an application to court for adoption is made by the CWS. (Unlike foster parents, the prospective adoptive parents do not get paid.)

The CWS meet with the parents to explain the legal consequences of the adoption. The adoptive parents and the biological parents will sign a contract (Bundeskanzleramt, 2020b). The CWS then complete an *Adoptionsantrag* (application for adoption), which they send to the court. In the case of an adoption from foster care, this application includes a *Pflegeaufsichtsbericht* (report about the foster carers), which contains: the history of the foster carers; their partnership history and professional status; the child's history and how well the child has done with the foster parents; the parents' background; and the fact that everyone agrees to the adoption, that there exists a child–parent relationship between the child and the foster carers, and that this is why the CWS are applying for an adoption. The judge can call a meeting with the parents and/or the adoptive parents and hear older children; typically, the court will rely on the CWS report rather than arrange a hearing with the parents, as reported by one of our key informants. Once an adoption has been approved, there are no further checks by the CWS of the adoptive family. However, post-adoption services, typically in the form of seminars or support group meetings, are sometimes available through NGOs that provide support to adoptive families. In international adoptions, depending on the child's country of origin (for example, South Africa), the CWS may be obliged to provide post-placement reports to the authorities over a period of several years (see Eltern für Kinder Österreich, 2020b).

The decision, which is written by the judge, is sent to the involved parties in a document that is typically three to four pages long. It contains the name of the court and judge, the date of the decision and the type of decision made by the judge (adoption granted or not), followed by information about the adoptive parents, the child and the birth parents, the date when the decision goes into effect, and the reasoning behind the decision (as specified in Article 89 Non-Contentious Proceedings Act 2003). The section on the judge's reasoning provides some brief background information about the child's care trajectory leading to the adoption and explains the reasoning in reference to the law. The decision can be appealed within 14 days but only for very significant legal reasons, for example, when the court that decided the appeal deviated from the case law of the Supreme Court, or the case law is missing or inconsistent (Bundeskanzleramt, 2020b). The appeal is then decided by the next higher-instance court, up to the Supreme Court. District court decisions about adoptions are not publicly available; discretionary approval may be granted by the Ministry of Justice for access for research purposes. The Supreme Court publishes decisions about appeals on the *Rechtsinformationssystem des Bundes* (RIS) (the legal information system of the federal government) (Bundeskanzleramt, 2020c).

Arrangements for post-adoption birth parent and sibling contact

Austrian law does not grant any rights for contact to birth parents or other family members after an adoption has been approved by the court. Contact rights with regard to children taken into care were extended through the 2013 Law Amending Child Custody and Right to a Name (KindNamRÄG), with the effect that third parties, including siblings, now have a right to contact where there is a close personal or familial relationship between the child and the third party (Art 188[2] Austrian Civil Code). Where contact is deemed to be in the child's best interests, the court can make the necessary order. Such a third-party contact application may also be filed by the CWS, and contact orders must be made if the child's well-being would otherwise be endangered. In practice, upon successful application to the court, children may thus continue to have contact with their birth family under the previous contact arrangements post-adoption. We do not know how common such contact applications are or how often the court will grant a right to contact post-adoption. Typically, any arrangements for post-adoption contact with birth parents may be agreed upon in the adoption contract between the parties, though this does not give rise to a legal claim and the agreement is non-binding on the parties.

Contact arrangements will also depend on the type of adoption. In Austria, there are three types: incognito, open and semi-open adoptions (Bundeskanzleramt, 2020d). In the case of incognito adoptions, the CWS will try to accommodate the preferences of the birth parents with regard to some characteristics of the adoptive parents (for instance, regarding cultural and religious background), and the birth parents will only receive limited information about the adoptive family, such as age, profession, duration of the marriage and number of children. The names and address will be kept secret, and birth parents will not be able to contact the adoptive family. In semi-open adoptions, the birth parents do not know where their child lives but may contact the child and their adoptive family through their local child welfare agency or the magistrate's office. They may send letters and photographs, and they can also arrange meetings in neutral locations. Open adoption means that birth parents know where the child and the adoptive family live and can make contact directly without the involvement of the CWS (Bundeskanzleramt, 2020d). From the age of 14, adopted children may request access to their adoption files (Art 49 Child Welfare Services Law of Vienna) and may then choose to contact their birth family. We do not know the prevalence of these different types of adoptions in Austria; however, in Vienna, approximately one third of adoptions are now open (Winroither and Weiser, 2014).

Conclusion

As in many other countries, the Austrian adoption system is currently under-studied and under-reported. The lack of specific data on the various types of adoptions, their numbers and the outcomes of different interventions is met by a research gap on adoptions from care in the scholarly literature. Almost no commentary on the challenges of the adoption system exists, at least not from recent years. Media reporting is mostly limited to the child removal stage of the CWS; adoptions rarely feature independently. As we have argued elsewhere, systematic research would be of critical importance in assessing existing CWS policies and programmes, especially now that the devolution of the CWS has become a reality cemented in law (Križ et al, forthcoming). To our knowledge, there are no empirical studies systematically assessing which child welfare policies appear to be most effective across the country.

In Austria, adoption from care continues to be a 'niche' measure when it comes to long-term out-of-home care for children, with foster and residential placements being much more prominent measures. A growing popularity of fostering in comparison to adoption may have several reasons. First, the extremely small number of children available for adoption means that waiting times are long, at around two to three years (Bundeskanzleramt, 2020b) and even longer for babies (Graz, for example, has waiting times for adopting a baby of about five years [*Die Presse*, 2016a]). The ratio of prospective adopters to children available for adoption is approximately ten to one (Braunisch et al, 2018). For instance, in Lower Austria, there were 123 qualified adoption applicants in 2014, resulting in 16 domestic and 17 international adoptions (*Die Presse*, 2016b). Second, the regional child welfare agencies have started to promote fostering proactively to meet the constant high demand for foster families (Kraus, 2011); however, some children are very difficult to place, such as children over the age of three years or children with developmental challenges (Tragler, 2018).

There is some empirical evidence from other jurisdictions that adoption may lead to better life outcomes for some children in care than long-term foster care (see Triseliotis, 2002). We do not have outcome data like these for Austria, so it would be impossible to offer evidence-based recommendations here. That said, the failure to actively pursue adoption for children for whom reunification has been effectively ruled out may deprive children in care of the type of legal permanency only adoption can grant, especially those children who enter care as infants or who establish secure attachments with long-term foster carers and do not have positive contact with birth family members. It therefore seems sensible to consider adoption as a route for permanency for these children. However, the strength of the principle of family preservation and the biological principle mean that long-term foster care may remain the welfare measure of choice in Austria for the time being. Another argument in favour of long-term foster care concerns the practical difficulties for children in securing post-adoption contact with birth parents, grandparents and siblings. The CWS also sometimes have very important practical reasons for not promoting adoption; for instance, when birth parents of a child in care decide to give up their child for adoption but the child's foster carers do not wish to adopt, the CWS will not pursue this further because it may not be in the best interests of the child to experience another change in caregiver, as one of our interviewees made clear.

Future adoption policy outlook

We do not anticipate any major policy changes in the area of adoptions in the foreseeable future. First, adoption from care has not been on the political agenda in recent years, nor does it receive much attention from the media or in public debate. The most significant recent change in adoption is related to a 2015 decision by the Austrian Constitutional Court that granted same-sex couples the same right to adoption as heterosexual couples. Before 2016, same-sex couples could be step- and foster parents but could not adopt (Pickert, 2015). Despite much resistance from political conservatives, the new law came into effect on 1 January 2016 (Ettinger and Aichinger, 2015; Sapinski, 2016b). Second, the challenges arising as a result of the recent steps towards the devolution of child welfare policy from the federal to the regional states are likely to dominate the child protection domain in the short term. In the longer term, the question related to adoption from care arises as to whether calls for greater focus on preventive measures will be heard. Recently, some organisations, including SOS Children's Villages and the Austrian Kinder- und Jugendanwaltschaft (Children's and Youth Ombuds-Office), have called for the government to provide more support for families to prevent children being removed from their homes in the first place (Austrian Ombudsman Board, 2020).

Acknowledgements

This project has received funding from the European Research Council under the European Union's Horizon 2020 research and innovation programme (grant agreement No 724460). Disclaimer: This chapter reflects only the authors' views and the funding agency is not responsible for any use that may be made of the information contained therein.

Notes

[1] An exception applies where there is an overriding concern for a biological child of an adopting parent, in particular, regarding the maintenance or upbringing of that child (Art 194[2] Austrian Civil Code).

[2] Although excluded for present purposes, it should be noted that adoption of a person over 18 years is possible in Austria, provided that a close (parent–child-like) relationship has existed for at least five years (Art 194 Austrian Civil Code).

References

Austrian Ombudsman Board (2020) 'Mehr Unterstützung, dass Kinder bei ihren Familien leben können' ['More support, so that children can live with their families'], Austrian Ombudsman Board. Available at: http://volksanwaltschaft.gv.at/artikel/mehr-unterstuetzung-dass-kinder-bei-ihren-familien-leben-koennen (accessed 10 March 2020).

Braunisch, S., Janik, R., Hardy, J. and Pfneisl, E. (2018) 'Krisenpflegefamilien: Eltern auf Zeit' ['Emergency care families: temporary parents'], *Addendum*, 7 August. Available at: www.addendum.org/jugendamt/pflegefamilien/ (accessed 10 March 2020).

Bundeskanzleramt (2019) *Kinder- und Jugendhilfestatistik 2018* [*Children and Youth Welfare Statistics 2018*], Vienna: Bundesanstalt Statistik Österreich.

Bundeskanzleramt (2020a) 'Rechte des Adoptivkindes' ['Rights of the adopted child'], Federal Chancellery. Available at: www.oesterreich.gv.at/themen/familie_und_partnerschaft/adoption/1/Seite.720010.html (accessed 10 March 2020).

Bundeskanzleramt (2020b) 'Ablauf der Adoption' ['Adoption process'], Federal Chancellery. Available at: www.oesterreich.gv.at/themen/familie_und_partnerschaft/adoption/Seite.720003.html (accessed 10 March 2020).

Bundeskanzleramt (2020c) 'Rechtsmittel und Rechtsmittelklagen' ['Appeals'], Federal Chancellery. Available at: www.oesterreich.gv.at/themen/dokumente_und_recht/zivilrecht/2/Seite.1010340.html (accessed 10 March 2020).

Bundeskanzleramt (2020d) 'Arten der Adoption' ['Types of adoption'], Federal Chancellery. Available at: www.oesterreich.gv.at/themen/familie_und_partnerschaft/adoption/Seite.720002.html#offen (accessed 10 March 2020).

Burns, K., Križ, K., Krutzinna, J., Luhamaa, K., Meysen, T., Pösö, T., Sánchez-Cabezudo, S.S., Skivenes, M. and Thoburn, J. (2019) 'The hidden proceedings – an analysis of accountability of child protection adoption proceedings in eight European jurisdictions', *European Journal of Comparative Law and Governance*, 6: 1–35.

Die Presse (2016a) 'Fünf Jahre Wartezeit in Graz' ['Five years' waiting period in Graz'], 23 February. Available at: www.diepresse.com/4931475/funf-jahre-wartezeit-in-graz (accessed 10 March 2020).

Die Presse (2016b) 'Bisher kein Interesse in Oberösterreich' ['So far no interest in Upper Austria'], 23 February. Available at: www.diepresse.com/4931461/bisher-kein-interesse-in-oberosterreich (accessed 10 March 2020).

Eltern für Kinder Österreich (2020a) 'Ausbildung' ['Training']. Available at: www.efk.at/de/ausbildung/ (accessed 10 March 2020).

Eltern für Kinder Österreich (2020b) 'Ablauf chronologisch/Wartezeit/ Ausbildung' ['Process/waiting period/training']. Available at: www. efk.at/de/ablauf-suedafrika/ (accessed 10 March 2020).

Ettinger and Aichinger (2015) 'ÖVP-Frauen: Nein zu neuem Adoptionsrecht' ['ÖVP-women: no to the new adoption law'], *Die Presse*, 15 January. Available at: www.diepresse.com/4639414/ovp-frauen-nein-zu-neuem-adoptionsrecht (accessed 10 March 2020).

Federal Ministry of Labour, Family and Youth (2019a) 'Adoption', Factbook 'Kinder in Österreich' ['Children in Austria']. Available at: www.kinderrechte.gv.at/factbook/adoptionsverfahren/ (accessed 10 March 2020).

Federal Ministry of Labour, Family and Youth (2019b) 'Fremduntergebrachte Kinder', 'Adoption', Factbook 'Kinder in Österreich' ['Children in Austria']. Available at: www.kinderrechte. gv.at/factbook/fremduntergebrachte-kinder/ (accessed 10 March 2020).

Kinder- und Jugendhilfe Oberösterreich (2019) 'Informationsblatt für Adoptivwerberinnen' ['Information sheet for adoptive applicants']. Available at: www.kinder-jugendhilfe-ooe.at/Mediendateien/dl_ adoption_infoblatt.pdf (accessed 10 March 2020).

Kraus, D. (2011) 'Der Trend zum Pflegekind: Immer mehr trauen sich' ['The trend towards a foster child: more and more dare'], *Die Presse*, 28 May. Available at: www.diepresse.com/666070/der-trend-zum-pflegekind-immer-mehr-trauen-sich (accessed 10 March 2020).

Križ, K., Krutzinna, J. and Pantuček-Eisenbacher, P. (forthcoming) 'The Austrian child welfare system. Moving towards professionalization and participation', in J. Berrick, N. Gilbert and M. Skivenes (eds) *International Handbook of Child Protection Systems*, Oxford: Oxford University Press.

Land Salzburg (2019) 'Zur Adoption freigeben' ['Placing for adoption']. Available at: www.salzburg.gv.at/soziales_/Seiten/zur_adoption_ freigeben.aspx (accessed 10 March 2020).

MAG ELF (Wiener Kinder- und Jugendhilfe) (2015) *Qualitätshandbuch – Soziale Arbeit mit Familien [Quality Handbook – Social Work with Families]*, Vienna: Stadt Wien.

Pickert, N. (2015) 'Adoption? Das ist doch voll schwul!' ['Adoption? That's totally gay!], *Der Standard*, 25 January. Available at: www. derstandard.at/story/2000010985308/adoption-das-ist-doch-voll-schwul (accessed 10 March 2020).

Reinprecht, C. (2015) 'Immigrant children and families in the child welfare system in Austria', in M. Skivenes, R. Barn, K. Križ and T. Pösö (eds) *Child Welfare Systems and Migrant Children: A Cross Country Study of Policies and Practice*, Oxford: Oxford University Press, pp 82–105.

Sapinski, H. (2016a) 'Kurzes Familienglück: (Adoptiv-)Eltern für ein Wochenende' ['Short family happiness: (adoptive) parents for a weekend'], *Die Presse*, 25 May. Available at: www.diepresse.com/ 4993569/kurzes-familiengluck-adoptiv-eltern-fur-ein-wochenende (accessed 10 March 2020).

Sapinski, H. (2016b) 'Das Gesetz hinter dem Kinderwunsch' ['The law behind the desire to have children'], *Die Presse*, 21 May. Available at: www.diepresse.com/4993570/das-gesetz-hinter-dem-kinderwunsch (accessed 10 March 2020).

Stadt Wien (2020a) 'Ein Kind adoptieren' ['Adopting a child'], City of Vienna. Available at: www.wien.gv.at/menschen/kind-familie/ adoption/adoptieren.html (accessed 10 March 2020).

Stadt Wien (2020b) 'Pflegekindergeld – Sozialinfo Wien' ['Foster child allowance – social information Vienna'], City of Vienna. Available at: www.wien.gv.at/sozialinfo/content/de/10/SearchResults. do?keyword=Pflegekindergeld (accessed 10 March 2020).

Statistik Austria (2019a) 'Age in single years by time section', STATcube. Available at: https://statcube.at/statistik.at/ext/statcube/ jsf/tableView/tableView.xhtml# (accessed 10 March 2020).

Statistik Austria (2019b) 'Bevölkerung nach Alter und Geschlecht' ['Population by age and sex']. Available at: www.statistik.at/ web_de/statistiken/menschen_und_gesellschaft/bevoelkerung/ bevoelkerungsstruktur/bevoelkerung_nach_alter_geschlecht/index. html (accessed 10 March 2020).

Tragler, C. (2018) 'Pflegekinder: Aufwachsen mit zwei Familien' ['Foster children: growing up with two families'], *Der Standard*, 18 June. Available at: www.derstandard.at/story/2000081157854/ pflegekinder-aufwachsen-mit-zwei-familien (accessed 10 March 2020).

Triseliotis, J. (2002) 'Long-term foster care or adoption? The evidence examined', *Child and Family Social Work*, 7: 23–33.

Winroither, E. and Weiser, U. (2014) 'Adoption: Der lange Weg zum Kind' ['Adoption: the long way to a child'], *Die Presse*, 15 March. Available at: www.diepresse.com/1575457/adoption-der-lange-weg-zum-kind (accessed 10 March 2020).

7

Adoption from care in Finland: currently an uncommon alternative to foster care

Pia Eriksson and Tarja Pösö

Introduction

In Finland, inter-country and domestic adoptions are guided by the Adoption Act. A few children are adopted from care but most domestic adoptions are step-parent adoptions in reconstituted families. It is thus hardly surprising that the concept of 'adoptions from care' does not exist in Finnish legislation, policy or practice.

The history of adoption legislation is longer in Finland than that of child welfare legislation. Ever since the first Adoption Act in 1925, adoption and child welfare legislation and practice have been organised as two separate and different types of interventions into family life. Throughout the history of adoptions, their profile has changed considerably. Domestic adoptions were common up until the 1970s (Kauppi and Rautanen, 1997). In the post-war period, many children were placed with new families through adoption or adopted abroad (Kauppi and Rautanen, 1997; Pösö, 2009). In fact, immediately after the Second World War, more children were adopted than placed in foster families by care order decisions. During the war, approximately 70,000 children were transferred to Sweden and Denmark as 'war children' for their safety (Korppi-Tommola, 2008). The volume of adoptions and 'war children' had an impact on later generations as many experienced the separation of children from their parents as part of the country's history and, perhaps, their own family history. In the 1970s, the profile of adoption slowly changed towards inter-country adoptions with Finland as a receiving country. The numbers of inter-country adoptions started to grow when legislation regulating inter-country adoptions was passed in 1985. The peak in inter-country adoptions was reached at the same time as in other Western countries in the early 2000s, with a decline in numbers since (Selman, 2010; Official Statistics Finland, 2019).

The first Child Welfare Act, introduced in 1936, specified for the first time the criteria for removing a child from parental care into public care. According to the second Child Welfare Act in 1983, in-home services should always be prioritised and child removals implemented only as a last resort. Child welfare authorities were – and still are – obliged to support the child and family in their own community by providing in-home services in those situations where universal services and benefits for families are not enough to secure the child's health and development. This emphasis in Finnish child welfare legislation and policy is obviously of a family service orientation, with a focus on children's rights, as described in the comparative child welfare literature (Gilbert et al, 2011). Despite this emphasis on universal, preventive and in-home services in legislation and policy, more than 1 per cent of children under the age of 18 are in out-of-home care each year as a result of the Child Welfare Act. There are three main forms of out-of-home care placement: care orders, emergency placements and supportive voluntary placements. All placements – even care orders, which have the highest thresholds and most severe implications for family life – should always be only temporary as the Child Welfare Act 2007 does not guarantee any permanent placements. Nevertheless, reunifications are rare in child welfare (Pösö et al, 2019).

This brief overview on the history of adoptions and child welfare removals highlights that when exploring adoptions from care in 2020, we can see traces of the complex history regarding the separation of children from their parents and the state's attempts to support families and avoid permanent out-of-home placements as a part of child welfare. The present practice of adoptions from care is understandably influenced by the history and culture regarding separations. In the first half of this chapter, we will describe the legislation, guidelines and statistics regarding adoptions from care in more detail, and then move on to explore the nature of present practice and knowledge about adoptions from care in Finland.

Legislation and guidelines about adoption from care

The Adoption Act 2012 covers all situations of adoption in which a legal relation of a parent and a child is to be ratified between the adoptee and adoptive parent(s). The Act addresses the adoption of minors and adults, and regulates both domestic and inter-country adoptions.

Five principles of the present Adoption Act are of special importance to the topic of adoptions from care. First, the principle of the child's best interests should guide all adoption decisions:

> In all decisions and other measures concerning the adoption of a minor child, the best interests of the child shall be the paramount consideration. Particular attention shall be paid in assessments of the best interests of the child to how a child who cannot grow up in his or her family of origin can best be ensured a permanent family as well as balanced development and wellbeing. (s 2 Adoption Act 2012)

Second, adoption requires consent given by the birth parents and the child if he or she is 12 years or older. Only in exceptional cases may adoption be granted without consent, and then only when the child's best interests strongly support adoption (s 11 Adoption Act 2012). If the parties actively object or withdraw from expressing their view, the nature and intensity of the contact between the child and the parents should be considered when assessing the child's best interests. If the parents have challenges in expressing their view due to their health or disabilities, or if their whereabouts are not known, adoption may be granted only in exceptional situations. Third, adoption counselling for adoptees as well as for the birth and prospective adoptive parents is an essential precondition for any adoption decision (this is explained in more detail in the following section). Fourth, the (district) court makes all decisions regarding adoption. Its decisions may be appealed. All adoptions are handled by authorities as private adoptions are not allowed in Finland. Fifth, the (district) court may grant the right to maintain contact between the adopted child and their birth parents if it has been agreed upon between the parties and is not contrary to the best interests of the child ('open adoption').

Although the Adoption Act does not recognise adoption from care as a distinct category, the guidelines given to practitioners by the Ministry of Social Affairs and Health in 2013 separate adoptions of 'a child not previously known' and adoptions of 'a previously known child' to the prospective adoptive parents. The latter means intra-familial adoptions (for example, reconstituted families) and adoptions from foster care (Sosiaali- ja terveysministeriö, 2013b: 20). Although prospective adoptive parents usually have to apply for a permit from the National Adoption Board at the Supervisory Authority for Welfare and Health in order to adopt, the permit is not needed if the foster parents intend to adopt a child whom they have fostered for at least a year. The child welfare authorities have to assess the adoption option from the point of view of the child's best interests and the relationship between the child and the foster parents. The guidelines also specify adoption counselling, which we will present in the following section.

Adoption is not mentioned in the Child Welfare Act 2007 as a form of removal or placement. Removals by the Child Welfare Act have different criteria, procedures and decision-making bodies from those of adoption (Pösö and Huhtanen, 2017). However, when looking at the government proposals for the Adoption Act and Child Welfare Act, one notes that adoption has been occasionally contrasted with child welfare removals, and its nature as an alternative to such removals has been debated to some extent in the legislative process over the years. The intention to keep adoptions and child welfare removals separate has, however, been consistent throughout the history of adoption and child welfare legislation. For example, when the Child Welfare Act 2007 was prepared, the government proposal included the following statement:

> The child's best interest could be best met in some child welfare situations by adoption decisions even when the parents object. It is not, however, proposed that there would be any regulation about adoption in the Child Welfare Act. Instead the regulations of the Adoption Act should be used in those cases. (Hallituksen esitys eduskunnalle lastensuojelulaiksi ja eräiksi siihen liittyviksi laeiksi, 2006: 91)

In this statement, the legal regulation of adoption was once again separated from the regulation of child welfare removals.

From the perspective of keeping child welfare removals separate from adoption, it is interesting that the web-based 'Handbook of child welfare' by the Finnish Institute for Health and Welfare clearly takes the stance that the possibility of open adoption makes adoption more similar to placements in foster care than previously (Terveyden ja hyvinvoinnin laitos, 2020). The handbook, which is aimed at professionals, describes adoption as one form of family-based foster care, with the difference of being permanent as compared with 'ordinary' (that is, temporary) foster care. The handbook encourages social workers to consider it as an option in situations where the child needs long-term care outside their home. However, neither the handbook nor the national guidelines specify in any detail the criteria for considering adoption as an alternative to foster care placement. It is up to each individual social worker to consider whether adoption is in the best interests of the child.

Decision-making and the preparatory processes

The district courts (numbering 20 in Finland) make all adoption decisions. The adoption process can be initiated by either the birth parent(s) or the prospective adoptive parents by requesting adoption counselling from social services. If foster parents want to adopt a child in their care, they can initiate the decision-making process.

According to Sections 10–11 of the Adoption Act, adoption can be granted only with consent from both the birth parent(s) and the child, if he or she is 12 years or older. Neither can adoption be granted against the will of a child younger than 12 years if the child is so mature that their view can be taken into consideration. Adoption can be granted without this consent only in exceptional circumstances. Consent is acquired in the process of adoption counselling, in which the birth parents, child and prospective adoptive parents are given information about the legal elements of adoptions, as well as advice, assistance and an opportunity to reflect on the impact of the decision. At the end of the counselling process, the parties sign a document in which they express their consent (or objection). As the courts do not necessarily organise oral hearings in all civil court cases (Nylund, 2017), this document may be the main source of information about the parties' views for the court. For several reasons, adoption counselling is an essential part of the decision-making process; hence; it is described in more detail here.

Under the Social Welfare Act 2014 and Adoption Act 2012, municipalities must provide adoption counselling by a registered social worker with a master's degree-level university education. The organisation of provision differs between municipalities. At the moment, approximately 70 per cent of adoption counselling has been outsourced to Save the Children Finland as the only non-municipal agency granted permission to provide adoption counselling (Laine et al, 2018).[1] In the municipalities providing the service themselves, adoption counselling is often placed organisationally within the municipal child welfare agency or family law units (Eriksson et al, 2015).

Pre-adoption counselling is provided to every party in the process, and it is a prerequisite for the decision-making process. According to guidelines by the Ministry of Social Affairs and Health (Sosiaali- ja terveysministeriö 2013b), adoption counselling with the birth parent(s) should include information about the legal aspects of adoption and other options to provide good care for the child, as well as information about the psychosocial aspects of adoption. Counselling should make it possible for the birth parent(s) to also process the matter on an emotional level. The expression of consent (or objection) should always follow a period of reflection. If the child being adopted has reached the age and degree of maturity that enables them to express their view on the adoption, the social worker should work with the child in a holistic manner, informing about and explaining the aims and consequences of adoption. When relevant, efforts should be made to determine the child's attitude towards maintaining contact with their birth parent(s) after the adoption. Then, a child aged 12 years or older is asked to give their view about the adoption. For prospective adoptive parents, adoption counselling should include a thorough process of assessment and preparation for adoptive parenthood (for a description, see Eriksson, 2016).

Adoption counselling results not only in the parties' better understanding of adoption, but also in formal assessments and statements provided by adoption counsellors to the district court. The documents include a report about the suitability and motives of the prospective adopter(s), as well as the assessment of the adoption from the point of view of the child's best interests.

For children adopted from care, the decision-making process is the same as for any type of adoption. However, if foster parents are to become adoptive parents, they do not need a separate permit for adoption, though they should still be provided with adoption counselling. In addition, the child welfare authorities in charge of the child in care provide their own assessment, which is not needed for other types of domestic adoptions. Although there is no research available to highlight the courts' decision-making processes about adoptions, we assume that those processes are more to confirm the outcome of the preparatory process than to question or reinvestigate the motives, circumstances or views as adoption applications typically include the consent of all parties.

Adoptions and children in care: numbers and profiles

In 2018, there were 404 adoptions in total in Finland (Official Statistics Finland, 2019). This number includes 273 adoptions of children (see Table 7.1) and 131 adoptions of adults.[2] Of these adoptions, 65 per cent were intra-familial adoptions. Intra-familial adoptions refer to the process in which a married spouse or the other partner in a registered partnership adopts their spouse's child(ren).

Table 7.1: Children adopted and in care by care order during 2000–18

Year	Total number of adoptions of children[a]	Domestic adoptions of children[a]	Adoptions from care[b]	Children in care by a care order decision (31 December)[c]	Children in care by care order decision per 100,000 children (31 December)[c]	Children in care by care order decision leaving care during the year for reasons other than ageing out of care[c]
2000	338	118	N/A	6,643	585	4.2%
2005	444	108	N/A	8,135	737	4.2%
2010	408	224	N/A	8,925	823	4.1%
2015	317	199	10	9,052	844	4.1%
2018	273	190	N/A	9,295	878	4.3%

Notes and sources: [a] Data from Official Statistics Finland (2019). [b] Data from Laine et al (2018). [c] Data from Finnish Institute for Health and Welfare, provided by request on 9 March 2020 (including children aged 0–17 years, excluding those turning 18 during the year).

As legislation does not recognise adoption from care as a separate category, there are no statistics on these adoptions. The only systematic study highlighting the number of adoptions from care (Laine et al, 2018) is one that analysed all district court judgments of domestic adoptions (N = 623) in 2015 and 2016. Judgments that included information linking the child to the child protection system were selected and studied in more detail. As a result, the researchers estimate that 13 children had been adopted from care: ten children in 2015 and three children in 2016. The court case files were not informative in their details about the child welfare background in every case, so it is important to treat the numbers of adoptions from care as only approximate (Laine et al, 2018). The case files documented the care order decision in only ten cases, though it is very likely that all of them had been taken into care by a care order decision. Nevertheless, the numbers do confirm the message from child protection practice: children are adopted from care but very rarely.

The children adopted from care in 2015 and 2016 were between 2.5 and 14 years old at the moment of adoption, with the average age being 7.6 years. All decisions were based on consent. The birth parents, together or on their own, had initiated the adoption process in 11 cases, whereas the child initiated in one case and the foster family in another case. In all cases, the adoptive family was the foster family in which the child had stayed from 0.5 years to 13.5 years (Laine et al, 2018).

In the same study by Laine et al, there were newborns who had been adopted at birth: 20 in 2015 and 30 in 2016. The parent-to-be had contacted the adoption counselling service during the pregnancy on their own initiative, and child welfare authorities were only involved in organising the placement of the baby during the mother's period of reflection. Thereafter, the children were placed in adoptive families. All decisions were based on the consent of the relevant parties. These numbers may be contrasted with the numbers of infants (aged under one year) taken into care, which were 27 in 2015 and 38 in 2016, suggesting that newborn adoptions are almost as common as infants' care order placements (Flykt et al, 2020).

Regarding children of all ages, there were 9,295 children in care (by a care order decision) on the last day of 2018 (878 children per 100,000 children under the age of 18) (see Table 7.1). In that year, 1,777 children were taken into care by a new care order decision (Terveyden ja hyvinvoinnin laitos, 2019: 8), which is significantly higher than the number of domestic adoptions of children (190). The number of children in care increased over the 2000–18 period. If emergency removals, supportive voluntary placements and aftercare placements are included in the numbers as well, the number of children and young people in out-of-home care is much higher: in 2018, 18,544 children were in out-of-home care. In 2018, 55 per cent of children in care were in foster care (of which 13 per cent were in kinship care), 28 per cent in residential care and 12 per cent in professional family homes (Terveyden ja hyvinvoinnin laitos, 2019: 6). (This does not add up to 100 per cent since 5 per cent lived in supported accommodation or with parents.)

The placements of children in care tend to be long-term. Of the children in care in 2018, 50 per cent had been in some form of out-of-home care for almost half of their lifetime or more (Terveyden ja hyvinvoinnin laitos, 2018). In addition, reunifications of children and families are rare before the child reaches the age of 18. In 2018, 4.3 per cent of children in care exited care for reasons other than ageing out of care (see Table 7.1).

Too many or too few?

Although we only have information about the numbers of adoptions from care for 2015 and 2016, it is reasonable to assume that the overall numbers of adoptions from care are very small. Considering the number of children in care and the fact that most children stay in care for long periods during their childhood, it is relevant to ask whether the number of adoptions from care is *too* small.

As the current Child Welfare Act does not acknowledge permanent placements, reunification with the birth parents must be constantly evaluated. Although permanency is only occasionally and in passing on the agenda in child welfare policy (Sosiaali- ja terveysministeriö, 2013a), the child's right to and need for permanency has been the main argument advocated by some Finnish child welfare experts (for example, Sinkkonen and Tervonen-Arnkil, 2015) in favour of increasing adoptions as an alternative to care order placements. In that view, adoption is seen as being a better basis for permanent relations and overall permanency in childhood, and consequently in the best interests of the child. In a recent survey (Heinonen, 2018), practitioners working with children and families in health and social care ($N = 771$) took a positive view of adoption as an alternative to care order placements since, in their view, adoption could better meet children's needs for permanent relations. However, social workers working in child welfare were more hesitant in their views than their colleagues in other fields of health and social care. These more hesitant opinions emphasised the rights of parents to have a family and the parents' attempts and opportunities to overcome their problems (Heinonen, 2018).

These two perspectives on adoptions from care – the child's need for permanency and the parents' right to be reunified with their child – provide different views on the question of whether the number of adoptions is too low or too high. From the first perspective, the number is obviously very low. It might not, however, look so low if we include the adoptions of newborns in the analysis.

The number of newborn adoptions is higher than the number of children under the age of one year taken into care, as described by the study covering 2015 and 2016 (Laine et al, 2018). As noted earlier, preparations for newborn adoptions start during the pregnancy, and they rest on the parents' initiative. There is no solid research on the motives or situations of parents deciding to voluntarily relinquish their infant for adoption in Finland. However, messages from adoption counselling professionals suggest that the reasons are often related to challenges that the (adult) parent(s)-to-be would experience in their future role as parent(s) as the pregnancy may have been unwanted or poorly timed. When Finnish children were adopted to other countries in the 1950s–1970s, the motives were related to the social stigma attached to being a single mother and the social deprivation of the post-war country (for example, Pösö, 2009). Society has changed since those years, and Finland is now known to have one of the most progressive family policies (Eydal and Kröger, 2010). Single mothers are supported in many ways, and it is possible to terminate pregnancy. Nevertheless, some parents-to-be feel that they cannot or do not want to look after their child with the services and benefits provided, and that their rights and obligations as parents should be given to other adults. The very existence of newborn adoptions is a reminder that parents themselves also organise permanent care for their children without the involvement of the child welfare authorities. The legal, organisational and practical separation of adoptions from child welfare removals makes it possible.

Critical points in present policy and practice regarding adoption from care

The fragmentary nature of psychosocial counselling

As described earlier, adoption counselling is a fundamental precondition for any adoption initiative to proceed. Expertise in delivering adoption counselling requires both legal knowledge and a high level of know-how in terms of the psychosocial and emotional aspects of adoption. Knowledge used in adoption counselling is also important for the adoption process itself as social workers giving adoption counselling function as gatekeepers. If they decide not to give counselling to a certain party or refuse to complete it, the petition will not make it to court.

The requirement for social workers to have adoption expertise in handling pre- and post-adoption services was included in the Adoption Act 2012. However, as adoptions are small in number, the opportunities to acquire such specialised knowledge are limited (Eriksson, 2016). In addition, as adoptions from care are rare and the national guidelines for adoption counselling predominantly focus on other types of adoption, we can assume that there is very little expertise in adoptions from care among social workers. A recent study by Eriksson et al (2015) demonstrates that only half of prospective adoptive parents in inter-country adoptions considered the social worker offering adoption counselling to have enough adoption expertise. This was more common in specialised units offering the service compared to those organisational arrangements in which adoption counselling was integrated within other social work tasks. The same diversity of expertise is likely to exist regarding adoptions from care.

Unfortunately, there is no research that would give us some understanding of the birth parents' position in adoption counselling when the child is already in care. Even anecdotal knowledge is limited. We can only speculate that if adoption counselling is not provided properly and if the child welfare authorities express even a suggestion of pressure towards adoption, the true expression of consent required during the adoption counselling process would be threatened. In the worst-case scenario, the possibility of open adoption could falsely be used to make adoption's legal implications on parental rights obscure and groundlessly similar to those of foster care placement.

The complex issue of consent

Consent is a complex issue in any form of separation of children from their parents. Sections 14–17 of the Adoption Act define the conditions for informed consent. First, the person must have enough time to thoroughly deliberate the adoption decision. This is further specified for newborn adoptions: consent should not be given before eight weeks have passed since the birth of the baby. If the person has not received adoption counselling, there must be other ways to guarantee that they are fully informed of the nature of adoption. Consent should be given in written form, and the person has the right to withdraw their consent before the court has made its decision.

This trust in consent and consensual decisions is typical of Finnish child welfare. Most child welfare removals are also based on consent, including those care order removals that restrict parental rights (Pösö et al, 2018). However, the role of consent in parent–child separations is currently not much questioned in Finnish society. Rather, it is taken for granted that parents (and children of a certain age) can give their consent to adoption (or a care order), there are legitimate procedures to receive consent and the decision-making systems can rely on the expression of consent. For outsiders to Finland, the custom of relying strongly on consent given as part of adoption counselling may be seen in a more critical light. Moreover, the likely differences in the quality of adoption counselling may suggest that consent is not necessarily always based on thorough information.

Low levels of post-adoption support

Both pre- and post-adoption counselling and services should be provided according to the Adoption Act. The present form of post-adoption services is, however, limited to assistance in establishing contact between the adoptee and their birth parents. After an adoption has been granted, the child and the adoptive family rely on the same services as other families, even if the adopted children's needs and experiences are often similar to those in care. Foster carers who become adoptive parents miss out on the psychosocial support they received from child welfare workers to deal with the special needs of the child. This highlights the nature of adoption as being a means of creating a family resembling a biological one and not primarily as a way to answer the needs of a child who cannot be looked after by their birth parents.

The lack of post-adoption support might be a big obstacle for some foster parents to become adoptive parents as they would lose all financial and psychosocial support given by child welfare services as foster carers (Laine et al, 2018). From a service perspective, the status of the adoptee differs from that of a child in care. Children in care are entitled to aftercare services, among other services, which support their independent lives after care, both financially and in other ways. If they are adopted, they no longer have access to aftercare services and they become dependent on the adoptive parents' private support.

Lack of research

Given the infrequency of adoptions from care, it is hardly surprising that the knowledge base and research on the topic is very limited in

Finland (Laine et al, 2018). There have been development projects with related publications carried out by some non-governmental organisations (NGOs) with the ambition of increasing social workers' awareness of adoption – in particular, 'open adoption' – as an alternative to child welfare removals (for example, Partanen et al, 2013; Timonen, 2013; Sinkkonen and Tervonen-Arnkil, 2015). There is some Finnish research on the inter-country adoption process from different perspectives (for example, Sukula, 2009; Eriksson, 2016; Högbacka, 2017) and on the adjustment and belonging of inter-country adoptees (for example, Raaska, 2015; Ruohio, 2016); however, there is scarce current knowledge on the domestic adoption process. Due to the lack of research, little can be said about the present processes and outcomes of adoption from care, as well as its possible strengths and weaknesses. It would be important to learn more about those children who were adopted from care, the reasoning and motives of the adults involved (foster parents, birth parents and social workers), and the position of the siblings in those cases. Self-evidently, the decision-making system and adoption counselling in these cases need to be studied as well.

Conclusion

Currently, adoption in Finland is seen as a means of creating families through legal bonds rather than a method of permanent placement for children in care. Adoption policy and practice has mainly concerned inter-country adoptions and services for prospective adoptive parents. At the same time, domestic newborn adoptions are granted every year without much attention, and issues related to adoptions from care and the rights and needs of children in long-term care have been on the margins of child welfare policy.

However, some researchers anticipate that the focus of adoption policy may shift from the prospective adoptive parents more to the rights of the child in the future (Eriksson, 2016). This shift may bridge adoptions and child welfare removals in a new way, and eventually increase adoptions from care. Three tendencies support this scenario. First, there is an obvious need to rethink how the rights and needs of children in long-term care are best met as children are rarely reunified with their parents. Positive views on adoption by some practitioners as an alternative to foster care might slowly start to influence practice (Heinonen, 2018). Second, the present system of child welfare removals has been criticised as being costly and insufficient in its outcomes, requiring new approaches to providing care for children who are not looked after by their parents. Third, as inter-country adoptions are decreasing due to a lack of children available for adoption, thus suggesting a change in the 'adoption market' (Högbacka, 2008), domestic adoptions could become more of an option for 'creating a family' for those who want to adopt a child. Nevertheless, we find it unlikely that there would be a fundamental change in favour of non-consensual adoptions in the future.

Self-evidently, the challenge will be how to effectively integrate these tendencies to safeguard the best interests of the child while making decisions that treat all parties fairly. The alternatives of permanent foster care and adoption should be wisely balanced.

Acknowledgements

Tarja Pösö's contribution to this chapter has been supported by the project 'Consent and Objection in Child Welfare Decision-Making', funded by the Academy of Finland (decision 308 402).

This project has received funding from the Research Council of Norway under the Independent Projects – Humanities and Social Science program (grant no. 262773). Disclaimer: This chapter reflects only the authors' views and the funding agency is not responsible for any use that may be made of the information contained therein.

Notes

[1] Save the Children Finland plays an important role in adoption practice, with adoptions being an important part of the organisation's work since the 1920s (Garrett and Sinkkonen, 2003; Kauppi and Rautanen, 1997).
[2] Adoptions of adults may include adoptions in which foster parents adopt a foster child when the child becomes an adult.

References

Eriksson, P.K. (2016) *Prospective Adoptive Parents within Pre-Adoption Services: An Interplay of Emotions and Power in Social Interaction*, Report 4, Helsinki: Mathilda Wrede-Institutet.

Eriksson, P.K., Elovainio, M., Mäkipää, S., Raaska, H., Sinkkonen, J. and Lapinleimu, H. (2015) 'The satisfaction of Finnish adoptive parents with statutory pre-adoption counselling in inter-country adoptions', *European Journal of Social Work*, 18(3): 412–29.

Eydal, G. and Kröger, T. (2010) 'Nordic family policies: constructing contexts for social work with families', in H. Forsberg and T. Kröger (eds) *Social Work and Child Welfare Politics Through the Nordic Lenses*, Bristol: Policy Press, pp 29–46.

Flykt, M., Punamäki, R. and Pösö, T. (2020) 'Vauvojen huostaanotto kehityksellisenä ja tutkimusperustaisena kysymyksenä' ['Care orders of infants as a developmental and research-based topic'], *Yhteiskuntapolitiikka*, 85(3): 293–300.

Garrett, P. and Sinkkonen, J. (2003) 'Putting children first? A comparison of child adoption policy and practice in Britain and Finland', *European Journal of Social Work*, 6(2): 19–32.

Gilbert, N., Parton, N. and Skivenes, M. (eds) (2011) *Child Protection Systems: International Trends and Orientations*, New York: Oxford University Press.

Hallituksen esitys Eduskunnalle lastensuojelulaiksi ja eräiksi siihen liittyviksi laeiksi (2006) ['Government proposal to the Parliament for the Child Welfare Act and some other acts relating to it'], HE 252/ 2006vp. Available at: www.finlex.fi/fi/esitykset/he/2006/20060252 (accessed 6 February 2020).

Heinonen, E. (2018) *Adoption asema lastensuojelussa* [*The Position of Adoption in Child Protection*] (Verkkojulkaisu 2), Helsinki: Lastensuojelun keskusliitto. Available at: www.lskl.fi/materiaali/lastensuojelun-keskusliitto/LSKL_adoptio_julk_0499_LR-2.pdf (accessed 6 February 2020).

Högbacka, R. (2008) 'The quest for the child of one's own: parents, markets and transnational adoption', *Journal of Comparative Family Studies*, 39(3): 311–30.

Högbacka, R. (2017) *Global Families, Inequality and Transnational Adoption: The De-kinning of First Mothers*, Basingstoke: Palgrave Macmillan.

Kauppi, M. and Rautanen, E. (1997) *Oikeus hyvään kotiin. Pelastakaa Lapset ry ja suomalainen lastensuojelutyö 1922–1997* [*The Right to Have a Good Home. Save the Children and Finnish Child Welfare in 1922–1997*], Helsinki: Pelastakaa lapset ry.

Korppi-Tommola, A. (2008) 'War and children in Finland during the Second World War', *Pedagogica Historica*, 44(4): 445–55.

Laine, S., Pösö, T. and Ujula, T. (2018) 'Adoptio lastensuojelussa: lukumääristä ja ominaispiirteistä' ['Adoption in child welfare: some numbers and features'], *Yhteiskuntapolitiikka*, 2(83): 199–207.

Nylund, A. (2017) 'Introduction to Finnish legal culture', in S. Koch, K. Skodvin and J. Sunde (eds) *Comparing Legal Cultures*, Bergen: Fagbokforlaget, pp 285–316.

Official Statistics Finland (2019) 'Adoptions', Statistics Finland. Available at: www.stat.fi/til/adopt/2018/adopt_2018_2019-08-21_tie_001_en.html (accessed 3 March 2020).

Partanen, P., Pasanen, K., Reinikainen, H. and Tervonen-Arnkil, K. (2013) *Avoimuutta ja yhteyksiä – Kotimainen adoptio muutoksessa* [*Openness and Contacts. Domestic Adoption under Change*], Helsinki: Pelastakaa Lapset ry.

Pösö, T. (2009) 'Memories about inter-country adoptions of Finnish children: deciding about the child's best interest', *Adoption and Fostering*, 33(4): 53–63.

Pösö, T. and Huhtanen, R. (2017) 'Removals of children in Finland: a mix of voluntary and involuntary decisions', in K. Burns, T. Pösö and M. Skivenes (eds) *Child Welfare Removals by the State: A Cross-Country Analysis of Decision-Making System*, New York: Oxford University Press, pp 18–39.

Pösö, T., Pekkarinen, E., Helavirta, S. and Laakso, R. (2018) ' "Voluntary" and "involuntary" child welfare: challenging the distinction', *Journal of Social Work*, 18(3): 253–72.

Pösö, T., Toivonen, V.-M. and Kalliomaa-Puha, L. (2019) 'Haluaa kotiin äidin luo. Erimielisyydet ja lapsen etu huostaanoton jatkamista koskevissa valituksissa ja hallinto-oikeuden ratkaisuissa' ['Want to be at home with mother. Disagreements and child's best interest in the appeals against care order continuation and in the judgments by administrative courts'], *Oikeus*, 3: 226–43.

Raaska, H. (2015) 'International adoption: symptoms of attachment disorders and their associations with the child's background and developmental outcome', dissertation, University of Turku.

Ruohio, H. (2016) *Suomalaiset kansainvälisesti adoptoidut. Perheeseen ja kansaan kuuluminen* [*Finnish Adoptees of Inter-country Adoption. Belonging to the Family and Nation*], Report 181, Helsinki: Nuorisotutkimusverkosto, Nuorisotutkimusseura.

Selman, P. (2010) 'The rise and fall of intercountry adoptions in the 21st century', *International Social Work*, 52(5): 575–94.

Sinkkonen, J. and Tervonen-Arnkil, K. (eds) (2015) *Lapsi uusissa olosuhteissa* [*Child in New Conditions*], Helsinki: Duodecim.

Sosiaali- ja terveysministeriö (2013a) *Toimiva lastensuojelu* [*Functioning Child Welfare*], Report 19, Helsinki: Ministry of Social Affairs and Health.

Sosiaali- ja terveysministeriö (2013b) *Adoptioneuvonta. Opas adoptioneuvonnan antajille* [*Adoption Counselling. A Handbook for Providers of Adoption Counselling*], Report 21, Helsinki: Ministry of Social Affairs and Health. Available at: http://urn.fi/URN:ISBN:978-952-00-3357-6 (accessed 6 October 2019).

Sukula, S. (2009) *Matka äidiksi – tarinoita adoptiosta ja yksinvanhemmuudesta* [*Journey into Being a Mother – Stories on Adoption and Single Parenthood*], Tampere: Tampere University Press.

Terveyden ja hyvinvoinnin laitos (2018) 'Kodin ulkopuolelle sijoitettujen lasten sijoitusten kestot 2016. Tilastoraportti 9' ['The length of placements of children placed in out-of-home care. Statistical report 9']. Available at: http://urn.fi/URN:NBN:fi-fe2018042318219 (accessed 6 February 2020).

Terveyden ja hyvinvoinnin laitos (2019) 'Lastensuojelu 2018. Tilastoraportti 23/2019' ['Child welfare 2018. Statistical report 23/2019']. Available at: www.julkari.fi/bitstream/handle/10024/138211/Tr23_19_LASU.pdf?sequence=5&isAllowed=y (accessed 3 March 2020).

Terveyden ja hyvinvoinnin laitos (2020) 'Avoimen adoption merkitys lastensuojelussa' ['The relevance of open adoption in child welfare']. Available at: https://thl.fi/fi/web/lastensuojelun-kasikirja/tyoprosessi/erityiskysymykset/avoimen-adoption-merkitys-lastensuojelussa (accessed 19 February 2020).

Timonen, P. (eds) (2013) *Adoptio – lapsen etu?* [*Adoption – In the Best Interest of the Child?*], Helsinki: Lastensuojelun Keskusliitto.

8

Adoption from care in Germany: inconclusive policy and poorly coordinated practice

Thomas Meysen and Ina Bovenschen

Introduction

As in most other countries, the principle of the child's best interests is the legal foundation for all adoption decisions. In Germany, apart from step-parent adoptions, which account for around 60 per cent of all adoptions (Federal Statistical Office, 2019), adoption mainly represents a legal option for children whose birth mothers have decided – mostly before giving birth – that they cannot care for their children. Hence, in the majority of cases, birth parents relinquish their children for adoption immediately after birth, often because of their highly burdened life circumstances. Most of the children placed with parental agreement move to an adoptive home within the first days, weeks or months of life. In contrast, only a small number of children are adopted from out-of-home care (foster or residential care). Adoptions (from care) without parental consent are even rarer due to legal restrictions on non-consensual termination of parental rights. Although adoptions from care are rare in Germany, and adoption is not primarily viewed as a permanency option that must be considered for children in care who cannot return home, this chapter aims to shed light on the current status of adoption from care in Germany.

Legal framework of adoption and organisations involved in adoption

The legal framework

Although adoption services are embedded in the child and youth welfare system, they have a separate place in family law and in child protection as well as child and youth welfare law, resulting in the legal framework for adoptions in Germany presenting an inconclusive picture. First, the roots of adoption as a legal option to found a family in Roman law are still present. Regulations within family law are to be found within an entirely separate chapter of the Civil Code (CC) as well as of the Act on Proceedings in Family Matters. Responsibility for the civil law provisions on adoption lies with a division of the Federal Ministry of Justice and Consumer Protection, alongside the law on guardianship for minors and legal custodianship for adults (Federal Ministry of Justice and Consumer Protection, 2019). This makes for a distinction from other family law matters, such as child protection, parental custody, access and family relations.

Second, in terms of service provision and assessment, adoption services have their core legal base in a '*special part*' of the Social Code – the Adoption Placement Act – which, on the one hand, embeds them in the child and youth welfare system and, on the other, provides for a special status. Responsibilities for policy and legislation referring to the Adoption Placement Act lie within the Federal Ministry for Family Affairs, Senior Citizens, Women and Youth (2020).

Although adoption is regulated by federal law, its legal bases are scattered and complex. The provisions for domestic adoptions are as follows:

- legal requirements and legal effects of adoption are in the German CC (ss 1741–1772);
- court proceedings are in the Act on Proceedings in Family Matters (ss 186–199);
- adoption services are in the Adoption Placement Act, as well as the Act on the Prevention and Coping of Pregnancy Conflicts; and
- adoption as a permanency option for children in out-of-home-care (as well as the required counselling and '*cautioning*' before finalising adoption without parental consent) are part of the Social Code Book VIII on child and youth welfare (ss 36[1] or 51).

Concerning placements in out-of-home care (both foster care and residential care), German law mainly differentiates according to the systems it addresses. A withdrawal of parental rights to enable a placement is within the sole responsibility of the family courts and therefore regulated in the CC (ss 1666, 1666a). The placement itself is regulated in the Social Code regulating the child and youth welfare system.

Organisations involved in adoption services

Federalism plays out strongly in the field of adoption services as the federal constitution guarantees communities a right to self-government within the legal framework. In contrast to the low number of adoptions in Germany (for details, see later), there are many adoption agencies, the large majority being part of the youth welfare offices (*Jugendamt*) in the cities and counties. However, due to a constitutionally guaranteed tradition of the principle of subsidiarity (Daly, 2000), in some regions, (Christian) non-governmental organisations (NGOs) provide adoption services instead of the youth welfare offices.[1] All NGOs are supervised and monitored by regional youth welfare offices at the state level (*Landesjugendämter*). Regional youth welfare offices are required to cooperate with adoption agencies in their region and to be involved in cases of hard-to-place children (that is, children with special needs). As with in-care placements, placements for adoption fall within the responsibility of the child and youth welfare services; therefore, the organisational structures vary between states (*Länder*) and even between municipalities within a state. Usually, three different units are involved in domestic adoptions:

- Adoption agencies, which are responsible for: assessment and training of (prospective) adoptive parents; preparing and supporting birth parents who are considering placing their children for adoption; matching between a child and prospective adoptive parents; and providing post-adoption support.
- General social services, which work with the families of origin prior to and during out-of-home care and are responsible for assessing the children's needs, deciding on the provision of support services and child protection. With respect to adoption, they are only involved in adoptions from care.
- Foster care services, which are responsible for assessment and preparation of potential foster parents, as well as supervision and support of the foster family. They too are only involved in adoptions that are from care.

Although the assignment of tasks and the extent of integration between the units vary, adoption agencies and foster care services are sometimes combined in one unit. This can be traced back to the critique of institutional care during the 1968 movement that led to a systematic placement of younger children in foster care (Ristau-Grzebelko, 2011;

Berth, 2019). Further, the fundamental reform in 1976 introduced a probationary period, called 'adoption care' (*Adoptionspflege*), and also created a lingual closeness to 'foster care' (*Vollzeitpflege*). Until today, child protection matters remain in the separate units of adoption and foster care services (Helming, 2011). Cooperation between the different services or units varies extremely and coordination struggles because after placing a child in out-of-home care, the general social services continue working with the family of origin whereas the foster care services work with the foster family. Adoption services are often not involved at all when children are placed in foster care or residential care.

Section 3 of the Adoption Placement Act explicitly addresses securing quality and professionalism in adoption services. An adoption agency has to be staffed by at least two full-time equivalents; part-time workers are not allowed to predominantly have other tasks. However, this regulation is frequently circumvented as only 57 per cent of adoption agencies are staffed accordingly (Bovenschen et al, 2017b). There are requirements with respect to case workers including at least one year's experience in the field of adoption or foster care (Reinhardt et al, 2019). In practice, 91 per cent are social workers, the others are mainly *pedagogues*; they have an average of 12.5 years of professional experience (Bovenschen et al, 2017b). In sum, the legal/organisational positioning of adoptions can be characterised as having an insular existence, with a mixture of federal policy influence and different systemic cultures of practice.

Main principles and ethos of adoption

Adoption legislation and practice

Section 1741 of the German CC requires that 'the adoption of a minor child shall be granted if it serves the child's best interests, and if a parent–child-relationship is to be expected'. Both the child and the legal parents have to consent; from the age of 14, the child has to give consent themselves (ss 1746, 1747 CC). Adoption terminates all parental rights and legal family relationships to the family of origin (s 1755 CC) (exceptions are made for adoptions by relatives). At the same time, adoptive parents gain the legal position of parents in every respect (s 1754 CC). The legal concept starts from the premise that not only all legal ties, but also all actual ties, to the family of origin are ended. Called '*incognito adoption*', German adoption law forbids the disclosure of an adoptive family's name or address (ss 1747 [2]2, 1758 CC; see also Helms and Botthof, 2017).

Legislators' reasoning in the 1970s was that 'it is essential for the child's unimpaired development that the old family which has not been able to take on the up-bringing of the child does not disturb the adoptive family' (Deutscher Bundestag, 1975: 9, 46). This initial conceptualisation is deeply rooted in a practice of confidentiality as professional ethos, usually leading to working with the birth family and adoptive family separately (Bovenschen et al, 2017b).

In contrast to the legislation, adoption practice has changed during recent decades, and an increasing number of adoptions are now 'semi-open/mediated' or 'open/fully disclosed'. The form of contact in open adoptions is manifold and may include phone calls, visiting with each other and sharing photos and letters (Bovenschen et al, 2017a). However, as confidential adoption remains the legal norm, neither birth parents nor other members of the family of origin have a right to contact or a right to receive information about the child after consenting to adoption (s 1751 CC). Despite this, some adoptive families[2] do decide upon contact with birth family and/or exchange of information at their own discretion. However, contact after adoption remains fairly unusual in Germany. A recent study found that in 36 per cent of the cases, the child had personal contact with members of the family of origin at least once. In another 38 per cent, there was information shared at least once, mostly letters via adoption agencies. Regular contact or information exchange took place at a lower rate with around 25 per cent. The majority of this subgroup are children adopted from care (Bovenschen et al, 2017b).

Confidential birth

In 2014, 'confidential birth' was legally established by the Act for the Expansion of Support for Pregnancy and to Regulate the Confidential Birth. The legal framework offers an opportunity for a pregnant woman to get the medical help she needs and give birth in a hospital or with a midwife without having to reveal her identity. The baby is usually placed into state care and freed for adoption. In consideration of the child's right to know their own birth identity, the pregnancy counselling centres are obliged to provide the adoption agencies with messages and items the mother leaves in trust for the child (s 26). When the child turns 16, they are given access to the birth mother's personal details and can contact her unless the birth mother has objected to disclosing her personal data.

The Act aimed to reduce the numbers of children placed in baby hatches and other forms of anonymous births, and to secure information for the children in accordance to their constitutional right to know their own heritage (Art 2[1] Basic Law). However, as a study evaluating the law reported, numbers for the different forms of anonymous births are still high (Sommer et al, 2017), and the Act has been critically discussed.

Parental consent/substitution of parental consent

An adoption requires parental consent, and there is no option to terminate parental rights after a fixed time in care. The family court can decide on a 'substitution' of parental consent but courts are reluctant to grant an application for adoption without parents' consent. In reaction, youth welfare offices rarely advocate substitutions of parental consent. In 2018, there were 225 cases (including step-parent and kinship adoptions) with a substitution of parental consent in Germany (Federal Statistical Office, 2019). The requirements for substitution of parental consent to adoption (s 1748 CC) set a high threshold:

- a particularly serious and persistent violation of parental duties or parental indifference, and a disproportionate disadvantage for the child if the adoption does not take place;
- a serious but not persistent violation of parental duties with the consequence that the child probably cannot return to the parent;
- a permanent incapability of caring for and bringing up the child as the result of a serious mental illness or disability of the parent(s), along with serious harm to the child because they could not grow up in a family without an adoption; and
- the mother and father not being married with the mother having sole custody, a father who does not give consent and a disproportionate disadvantage for the child if the father's consent is not substituted.

Legislation interprets 'serious violation of parental duties' as meaning that parents do not meet the basic physical or psychological needs of the child. In addition to the violation, a balancing is required. If 'disproportionate disadvantage for the child' can be assumed, adoption is preferable 'because adoption provides for a better basis for the integration of the child in a new family' (Federal Constitutional Court, 2002).

Substance or alcohol addiction is not a violation in itself, only if it influences the child's health negatively (Wapler and Frey, 2017). Likewise, the threshold is not met if a parent agrees to placement in a foster family and does not keep (regular) contact (Federal Constitutional

Court, 1987). 'Parental indifference' cannot be assumed in case of ambiguous behaviour since no contact can be an act of deference to the child; therefore, it mostly relies on the statements and expressed interests in the court proceedings (Federal Constitutional Court, 2002). A 'permanent incapability to care' does not allow for an adoption against the parents' will if the child can grow up in a family (including a foster family) without adoption (Federal Supreme Court, 1996).

An expert review published by the German Research Centre on Adoption (EFZA) recommended integration of the section on substitution of parental consent to an adoption as the most intrusive child protection measure within the provisions on withdrawal of parental rights in child protection cases (Wapler and Frey, 2017). This would clearly place adoptions from care in the child protection context, in which it is, to date, scarcely visible. To date, no legislative changes are anticipated.

Adoption from care: the role in child welfare policies

The German CC does not recognise adoption from care as a distinctive category, and German legislation does not pursue a permanent family life situation (in an adoptive home) against parents' wishes. However, the Social Code Book VIII includes an obligation for permanency planning if a sustainable enhancement of parenting in the family of origin cannot be achieved in a time frame that takes the child's development into account (s 37 [2]). General social services in the youth welfare offices are required to assess whether adoption is an option before and during a long-term placement (s 36 [1]2 Social Code Book VIII). However, results show that adoption agencies and general social services mainly work independently from each other, and that adoption agencies are rarely involved in the support and care planning process (Hoffmann, 2011; Bovenschen et al, 2017b).

Statistics on child protection and adoption

Table 8.1 shows that the number of children and youth in out-of-home care (both foster care and residential care) increased steadily during recent years. Specifically, due to the refugee influx in Europe beginning in 2015, the number of children and youth in care (especially children and youth in residential care) increased sharply from 2015 to 2016. In December 2016, 69,401 children and youth below the age of 18 lived in foster care and 77,857 in residential care or other forms of assisted living (a total of 147,258 children and youth aged 0–17 and a rate of

Table 8.1: Children (< 18 years of age) in foster care/residential care and placed for adoption from care

Year	Children in care at year end		Total in care (rate per 100,000 children)	Total placed for adoption care from care (rate per 100,000 children)
	Foster care	Residential care		
2016	69,401	77,857	147,258 (1,082)	269 (2.0)
2015	67,122	68,109	135,231 (1,003)	250 (1.9)
2010	56,726	53,744	110,470 (812)	326 (2.4)
2005	47,517	51,855	99,372 (356)	373 (2.6)

Source: Federal Statistical Office (2011a, 2011b, 2017a, 2017b, 2018a, 2018b). All data referring to 2005 were generated based on statistics provided by the Federal Statistical Office on request.

1,082 per 100,000 children under 18). In international comparison, the number of children and youth in care in Germany has historically been rather high (Thoburn, 2008). In terms of the legal basis of out-of-home care, data show that the majority of children and youth are in voluntary care (56.1 per cent of those in foster care and 73.1 per cent of those in residential care in 2016), and parental rights remain (partially) with the biological parents.

Foster families mainly provide long-term placements, resulting in an average residence time that is, in international comparison, one of the highest (Thoburn, 2008; Küfner et al, 2011). In 2016, children and youth under the age of 18 had lived an average of 29 months in a foster home at the time of leaving care or changing in-care placement. Further results show that 65 per cent of foster care placements were declared as permanent during the first year. After a duration of between one and two years, the rate was at 85 per cent, between two and three years, it was at 88 per cent, and after that, it was at 98 per cent (Kindler, 2011a). Data on residential care reveal that, in 2016, children and youth stayed an average of 17 months before leaving care or changing placement. Referring to residential care, adoptions are highly exceptional, and existing cases may be largely explained by the fact that, in some regions, due to the lack of foster families, children who are intended to be in foster care have to be placed in residential care instead. The majority of children moving from foster care to adoption care (a probationary period during which the child is living with prospective adopters before the adoption may be finalised) are younger than six years of age (ranging between 66 per cent and 78 per cent of all children moving from foster care to adoptive homes in 2005 and 2016).

Table 8.2: Adopted children and youth (< 18 years of age)

Year	Non-kinship adoptions (domestic and inter-country)[a]	Adoptions from foster care[b]	Adoptions from residential care[b]
2018	1,330	421	124
2015	1,362	437	218
2010	1,669	461	385
2005	1,861	537	431

Note: [a] Excluding step-parent and kinship adoptions. [b] Including both domestic and inter-country adoptions. Data include adoptions from foster care and adoptions from residential care but exclude adoptions of children who lived with relatives prior to adoption. Thus, the data presented here differ from those provided in Burns et al (2019).

Source: Data were generated from annual statistics published by the Federal Statistical Office (Federal Statistical Office 2006, 2011c, 2016, 2019).

Federal adoption statistics show that the total number of adoptions in Germany, both domestic and inter-country adoptions, is low compared to the rather high number of children in out-of-home care (see Table 8.2). The number of adoptions (including domestic and inter-country adoptions but excluding step-parent and kinship adoptions) has declined from 1,861 adoptions in 2005 to 1,330 adoptions in 2018 (Federal Statistical Office, 2019) (see Table 8.2).[3] The Federal Statistical Office also publishes information on the number of children moving to adoptive homes from foster care or residential care (see Table 8.2).

Reasons for low numbers of adoption from care

To date, there are no empirical studies investigating the reasons for low numbers of adoptions from care in Germany. However, experts in the field discuss the following reasons:

- Parental consent: most birth parents would not consent as they see themselves as parents and want to maintain a role as caring parents. The threshold for an adoption order without parental consent is high.
- Financial support: the costs of care and services are assumed to be major obstacles to foster parents who would otherwise adopt their foster child. There are an increasing number of foster children with special needs. If foster parents take care of a child with special needs, they not only receive the so-called foster care allowance (*Pflegegeld*), but may also apply for additional funding to cover costs for specific care and services. In contrast, there is no subsidised adoption in Germany. Adoptive parents in Germany are not entitled to financial support to help meet the specific needs of their children.

- Counselling: there is no proactive counselling towards adoption by general social services or foster care services. Since working towards parental consent when placing a child in out-of-home care is of high value in practice (Witte et al, 2019), bringing up the issue of adoption may contradict the efforts. A line is drawn between care placements and adoption, and, as reported earlier, adoption agencies are rarely involved in the care planning according to Section 36 of the Social Code.

Decision-making in adoption proceedings

Prior to the court proceedings, adoption agencies are obliged to counsel all parties (Bovenschen et al, 2017a). The counselling reliably takes place and is usually conducted with all parties (birth parents, potential adoptive parents and child) separately. It gives space for the development of informed consent or for clarification of objections. If the substitution of parental consent is at stake, a formal process is initiated in which the youth welfare office advises the parent(s) about their rights and the legal consequences of an adoption (s 51 Social Code Book VIII).

The process of counselling and assessment can be described as follows (Bovenschen et al, 2017a):

- Birth parents: depending on circumstances, either parents contact the adoption agency or, specifically in case of adoptions from care, the general social services or foster care services bring up the issue. Information is given, and the parents are counselled in a strictly confidential setting. If the parents decide for an adoption of their child, they have to sign their formally witnessed consent to the adoption; such a consent cannot be given before the child is eight weeks old (s 1747 [2]1 CC). After authentication, parental responsibility is suspended, including the obligation to pay child support; personal contact may not be continued (s 1751 CC). However, they sustain a right to receive support by the adoption agency, even after finalisation of the adoption (s 9 Adoption Placement Act).
- Adoptive child: whether an adoption is in the child's best interests has to be thoroughly evaluated (s 1741 [1] CC). An assessment of the individual needs and wishes of the child, as well as their health and developmental status, is seen as an indispensable professional standard (Bovenschen et al, 2017a). The views and interests of the child have to be taken into account according to the child's age.

From the age of 14, the child has to give their own consent. In the adoption mediation process, the child has a right to receive support according to their individual needs (s 9 Adoption Placement Act). Adoption agencies usually offer counselling sessions and home visits, and they play a key role in making referrals, for example, to child guidance clinics, therapists and clinics, and in enabling the adopted child to access the adoption file when they turn 16 (s 9c [2] Adoption Placement Act). Supervision of the child's access to the adoption file is obligatory.

- Adoptive parents: for the adoptive parents, the process begins with the application for adoption (s 1752 CC). The home study represents an assessment of whether they are suited for adopting both a child in general and the particular child (s 7a [1]2 Adoption Placement Act). A recommendation with detailed criteria by the federal association of the regional youth welfare offices at the state level (*Landesjugendämter*) acts as a non-binding and widely followed guideline (Bundesarbeitsgemeinschaft Landesjugendämter, 2019). The process of preparing for the adoption is intensive and unanimously considered as the most important part of a successful adoption (Bovenschen et al, 2017b). By the time the applicants are approved as adopters, they may be matched to a child. After all have consented to initiating the adoption process or the parental consent is substituted, a period of adoptive care begins, which usually takes one year with newborns and infants, and even longer with older children (Bovenschen et al, 2017b: 56). During this time, a guardian is appointed to the child. The period includes regular counselling and home visits. If foster parents apply to adopt their foster child, this process may vary as the parents have already been assessed when they became foster parents. Thus, the home study is usually shorter compared to the regular adoption process. If the child has already lived with the family for a long time, there may be no period of adoptive care. If the requirements for the adoption of the child are met, the youth welfare office and/or the adoption agencies file a report to the family court (s 50 Social Code Book VIII), and may take part in the hearing (s 194 Act on Proceedings in Family Matters). The judgment of the family court brings the adoption into effect. Adoptive parents also have the right to counselling from the adoption services after the adoption (s 9 [2]2 Adoption Placement Act).

After all legal requirements are fulfilled, the family court acts as the decision-making body. Adoption agencies prepare the case and issue a professional report (s 189 Act on Proceedings in Family Matters). The family court judgment is mainly a re-enactment since birth parents, adoptive parents and the child are heard. If no indication of conflict arises, no further assessment is usually initiated. Children have to be heard by the judge from the age of three or four. Exceptions are only permissible if the personal hearing by the judge poses a risk of harm to the child (Federal Constitutional Court, 1980; see also s 192 Act on Proceedings in Family Matters).

Conclusion

In Germany, practice rarely uses adoption as an option if a child stays in long-term foster care. Reasons seem to be multifaceted. Future research may help to understand if and how the role of adoption in permanency planning for children in out-of-home care who cannot return home may be strengthened in the future.

Regulations on adoption can be considered as conservative. Recent amendments in adoption law have mostly been enacted when forced by the Federal Constitutional Court (for example, concerning adoption by same-sex parents or discrimination of children in refused step-parent adoption cases). Hence, adoptions from care have not been touched by federal lawmakers, and neither the Federal Ministry of Justice nor the Ministry for Family Affairs have shown signs that changes are to be anticipated.

However, within its legislative scope, the Federal Ministry for Family Affairs has been pushing for reforms. The Adoption Service Act, in force since April 2021, includes provisions aiming at enhancing the quality of the adoption services. Among others, the cooperation of adoption agencies with other units is to be strengthened. Additionally, contact after adoption – and thereby the birth parents' rights to receive information about their child even after adoption – is encouraged. Counselling for both the members of the family of origin and the adoptive parents on the issue of contact after adoption is mandatory and must be documented. With the consent of both parties, counselling has to be repeated at appropriate intervals. Birth parents are to receive a right to information about the child after adoption. However, the adoptive parents still decide whether and which information is to be shared with the birth parents (Federal Ministry for Family Affairs, Senior Citizens, Women and Youth, 2019).

Nevertheless it seems questionable whether in cases of long-term out-of-home placements, cooperation between adoption services, on the one hand, and foster care services and general social services, on the other, will improve. Along with other professionals, we argue that adoptions from care, especially in long-term placements of children in foster families, should receive more attention in care planning processes. There is the possibility that organisational fragmentation – with general social services working with the family of origin before and after the placement, while foster care placement services work with the foster families (mostly without ever involving the adoption agencies in the care planning) – will be reduced over time. Current reform efforts promote a two-familial systemic approach if children are placed in care. In anticipation of a successful implementation of the proposed legislation, it is expected that adoptions from care will become a real option in the process of permanency planning for children.

Notes

[1]   In addition, a small number of private agencies are approved for services regarding inter-country adoptions.

[2]   Due to the fact that most children are comparably young when adopted, in many cases, the adoptive parents make decisions about contact after adoption.

[3]   Further data reveal that the decline for both domestic and inter-country adoptions started in the early 1990s. For a discussion of possible reasons for this trend, see Bovenschen et al (2017a).

References

Berth, F. (2019) 'Zur Geschichte des Säuglingsheims. Eine vergessene Institution des bundesdeutschen Sozialstaats' ['History of infants homes. A forgotten institution of the West German welfare state'], *Zeitschrift für Pädagogik*, 65(1): 73–93.

Bovenschen, I., Bränzel, P., Heene, S., Hornfeck, F., Kappler, S., Kindler, H. and Ruhfaß, M. (2017a) *Empfehlungen des Expertise- und Forschungszentrum Adoption zur Weiterentwicklung des deutschen Adoptionswesens und zu Reformen des deutschen Adoptionsrechts* [*Recommendations of the German Research Centre on Adoption: Future Perspectives for Adoption Practice and Adoption Legislation*], Munich: German Youth Institute.

Bovenschen, I., Bränzel, P., Dietzsch, F., Zimmermann, J. and Zwönitzer, A. (2017b) *Dossier Adoptionen in Deutschland. Bestandsaufnahme des Expertise- und Forschungszentrums Adoption* [*Adoptions in Germany: Summary of the German Research Centre on Adoption*], Munich: German Youth Institute.

Bundesarbeitsgemeinschaft Landesjugendämter (2019) *Empfehlungen Adoptionsvermittlung* [*Recommendations for Adoption Services*] (8th edn), Mainz: Landesamt für Soziales, Jugend und Versorgung, Landesjugendamt.

Daly, M. (2000) *The Gender Division of Welfare. The Impact of the British and German Welfare States*, Cambridge: Cambridge University Press.

Deutscher Bundestag (1975) 'Entwurf eines Gesetzes über die Annahme als Kind. Gesetzentwurf der Bundesregierung vom 7. Januar 1975, Bundestags-Drucksache 7/3061' ['Draft Law on Adoption. Government Bill of 7 January 1975. Federal Parliament printing 7/3061'], Bonn.

Federal Constitutional Court (1980) 'Judgement of the 1st chamber of the 1st senate of 5 November 1980 – 1 BvR 1 BvR 349/80', Karlsruhe.

Federal Constitutional Court (1987) 'Judgement of the 1st chamber of the 1st senate of 20 January 1987 – 1 BvR 735/86', Karlsruhe.

Federal Constitutional Court (2002) 'Judgement of the 3rd chamber of the 1st senate of 16 January 2002 – 1 BvR 1069/01', Karlsruhe.

Federal Ministry for Family Affairs, Senior Citizens, Women and Youth (2019) 'Organigramm' ['Organisation chart']. Available at: www.bmfsfj.de/bmfsfj/ministerium/organigramm (accessed 28 December 2019).

Federal Ministry for Family Affairs, Senior Citizens, Women and Youth (2020) 'Entwurf eines Gesetzes zur Verbesserung der Hilfen für Familien bei Adoption (Adoptionshilfe-Gesetz). Gesetzententwurf vom 22. Januar 2020' [Draft Law on the Enhancement of Support for Families in Case of Adoption (Adoption Service Act). Government Bill of 22 January 2020], Berlin.

Federal Ministry of Justice and Consumer Protection (2019) 'Organigramm' ['Organisation chart'], Berlin. Available at: www.bmjv.de/SharedDocs/Downloads/DE/Ministerium/Organisationsplan/Organisationsplan_EN_20200915.pdf (accessed 10 December 2020).

Federal Statistical Office (2006) 'Statistiken der Kinder- und Jugendhilfe. Adoptionen 2005'. ['Statistics on children and youth welfare. Adoptions 2005'], Wiesbaden. Available at: www.statistischebibliothek.de/mir/receive/DEHeft_mods_00028553 [Accessed 27 November 2020].

Federal Statistical Office (2011a) 'Statistiken der Kinder- und Jugendhilfe. Erzieherische Hilfe, Eingliederungshilfe für seelisch behinderte junge Menschen, Hilfe für junge Volljährige Vollzeitpflege' ['Statistics on children and youth welfare. Foster care 2010'], Wiesbaden. Available at: www.statistischebibliothek.de/mir/receive/DEHeft_mods_00028353 [Accessed 27 November 2020].

Federal Statistical Office (2011b) 'Statistiken der Kinder- und Jugendhilfe. Erzieherische Hilfe, Eingliederungshilfe für seelisch behinderte junge Menschen, Hilfe für junge Volljährige Heimerziehung, sonstige betreute Wohnform' ['Statistics on children and youth welfare. Residential care 2010'], Wiesbaden. Available at: www.statistischebibliothek.de/mir/receive/DEHeft_mods_00028225 [Accessed 27 November 2020].

Federal Statistical Office (2011c) 'Statistiken der Kinder- und Jugendhilfe. Adoptionen 2010'. ['Statistics on children and youth welfare. Adoptions 2010'], Wiesbaden. Available at: www.statistischebibliothek.de/mir/receive/DEHeft_mods_00027796 [Accessed 27 November 2020].

Federal Statistical Office (2016) 'Statistiken der Kinder- und Jugendhilfe. Adoptionen 2015'. ['Statistics on children and youth welfare. Adoptions 2015'], Wiesbaden. Available at: www.statistischebibliothek.de/mir/receive/DEHeft_mods_00098015 [Accessed 27 November 2020].

Federal Statistical Office (2017a) 'Statistiken der Kinder- und Jugendhilfe. Erzieherische Hilfe, Eingliederungshilfe für seelisch behinderte junge Menschen, Hilfe für junge Volljährige Vollzeitpflege' ['Statistics on children and youth welfare. Foster care 2015'], Wiesbaden. Available at: www.statistischebibliothek.de/mir/receive/DEHeft_mods_00097098 [Accessed 27 November 2020].

Federal Statistical Office (2017b) 'Statistiken der Kinder- und Jugendhilfe. Erzieherische Hilfe, Eingliederungshilfe für seelisch behinderte junge Menschen, Hilfe für junge Volljährige Heimerziehung, sonstige betreute Wohnform' ['Statistics on children and youth welfare. Residential care 2015'], Wiesbaden. Available at: www.statistischebibliothek.de/mir/receive/DEHeft_mods_00097077 [Accessed 27 November 2020].

Federal Statistical Office (2018a) 'Statistiken der Kinder- und Jugendhilfe. Erzieherische Hilfe, Eingliederungshilfe für seelisch behinderte junge Menschen, Hilfe für junge Volljährige Vollzeitpflege' ['Statistics on children and youth welfare. Foster care 2016'], Wiesbaden. Available at: www.destatis.de/DE/Themen/Gesellschaft-Umwelt/Soziales/Kinderhilfe-Jugendhilfe/Publikationen/Downloads-Kinder-und-Jugendhilfe/erzieherische-hilfe-vollzeitpflege-5225115167004.pdf [Accessed 27 November 2020].

Federal Statistical Office (2018b) 'Statistiken der Kinder- und Jugendhilfe. Erzieherische Hilfe, Eingliederungshilfe für seelisch behinderte junge Menschen, Hilfe für junge Volljährige Heimerziehung, sonstige betreute Wohnform' ['Statistics on children and youth welfare. Residential care 2016'], Wiesbaden. Available at: www.destatis. de/DE/Themen/Gesellschaft-Umwelt/Soziales/Kinderhilfe-Jugendhilfe/Publikationen/Downloads-Kinder-und-Jugendhilfe/heimerziehung-betreute-wohnform-5225113167004.pdf [Accessed 27 November 2020].

Federal Statistical Office (2019) 'Statistiken der Kinder- und Jugendhilfe. Adoptionen 2018' ['Statistics on children and youth welfare. Adoptions 2018'], Wiesbaden. Available at: www.destatis. de/DE/Themen/Gesellschaft-Umwelt/Soziales/Kinderhilfe-Jugendhilfe/Publikationen/Downloads-Kinder-und-Jugendhilfe/adoptionen-5225201187004.pdf [Accessed 27 November 2020].

Federal Supreme Court (1996) 'Judgement of the 12th Senate for Civil Matters of 15 October 1996 – XII ZB 72/96', Karlsruhe.

Helming, E. (2011) 'Organisationsstrukturen und Schlüsselzahlen' ['Organisational structures and key figures'], in H. Kindler, E. Helming, T. Meysen and K. Jurczyk (eds) *Handbuch Pflegekinderhilfe* [*Handbook Foster Care*], Munich and Heidelberg: German Youth Institute and German Institute for Youth Human Services and Family Law, pp 108–22.

Helms, T. and Botthof, A. (2017) *Besuchskontakte nach Adoption und Formen schwacher Adoption. Rechtsvergleichende Studie unter Einbeziehung des schweizerischen, französischen, italienischen, spanischen, griechischen, englischen und US-amerikanischen Rechts. Eine Expertise für das Expertise- und Forschungszentrum Adoption* [*Contact after Adoption and Forms of 'Weak' Adoptions. A Comparative Study on the Swiss, French, Italian Spanish, Greek, British and US-American Adoption Legislation. A Review for the German Research Centre on Adoption*], Munich: German Youth Institute.

Hoffmann, B. (2011) 'Adoptionsoption in der Hilfeplanung – Perspektive der Fachkräfte in der Hilfeplanung' ['Adoption in the care planning process – case workers' view'], *JAmt*, 84: 10–16.

Kindler, H. (2011a) 'Perspektivklärung und Vermeidung von Abbrüchen von Pflegeverhältnissen' ['Permanency planning and avoiding foster placement break-ups'], in H. Kindler, E. Helming, T. Meysen and K. Jurczyk (eds) *Handbuch Pflegekinderhilfe* [*Handbook Foster Care*], Munich and Heidelberg: German Youth Institute and German Institute for Youth Human Services and Family Law, pp 344–66.

Küfner, M., Kindler, H., Meysen, T. and Helming, E. (2011) 'Weiterführende Fragen' ['Pending issues'], in H. Kindler, E. Helming, T. Meysen and K. Jurczyk (eds) *Handbuch Pflegekinderhilfe* [*Handbook Foster Care*], Munich and Heidelberg: German Youth Institute and German Institute for Youth Human Services and Family Law, pp 852–71.

Reinhardt, J., Kemper, R. and Weitzel, W. (2019) *Adoptionsrecht. AdVermiG, AdÜbAG, AdWirkG, BGB, EGBGB, FamFG* [*Adoption Legislation*] (3rd edn), Munich: C.H. Beck.

Ristau-Grzebelko, B. (2011) 'Entwicklungslinien in der DDR: Sorge für elternlose bzw. "familiengelöste" Kinder und Jugendliche, einschließlich Pflegekinder' ['Historical development in the GDR: care for parentless or "family disengaged" children and youth, including foster children], in H. Kindler, E. Helming, T. Meysen and K. Jurczyk (eds) *Handbuch Pflegekinderhilfe* [*Handbook Foster Care*], Munich and Heidelberg: German Youth Institute and German Institute for Youth Human Services and Family Law, pp 37–45.

Sommer, J., Ornig, N. and Karato, Y. (2017) *Evaluation zu den Auswirkungen aller Maßnahmen und Hilfsangebote, die auf Grund des Gesetzes zum Ausbau der Hilfen für Schwangere und zur Regelung der vertraulichen Geburt ergriffen wurden* [*Evaluation of the Effects of Measures and Support Services Taken and Provided in the Course of the Act on the Extension of Services for Pregnant and on the Regulation of the Confidential Birth*], Berlin: Federal Ministry for Family Affairs, Senior Citizens, Women and Youth.

Thoburn, J. (2008) *Globalisation and Child Welfare: Some Lessons from a Cross-National Study of Children in Out-Of-Home Care*, Norwich: School of Social Work and Psychosocial Sciences, University of East Anglia.

Wapler, F. and Frey, W. (2017) *Die Ersetzung der Einwilligung in die Adoption. Rechtslage und Reformbedarf. Eine Expertise für das Expertise- und Forschungszentrum Adoption* [*Substitution of Parental Consent to Adoption. Legal Status and Need for Reforms. a Review for the German Research centre on Adoption*], Munich: German Youth Institute.

Witte, S., Miehlbradt, L.S., van Santen, E. and Kindler, H. (2019) 'Preventing child endangerment: child protection in Germany', in L. Merkel-Holguin, J.D. Fluke and R.D. Krugman (eds) *National Systems of Child Protection: Understanding the International Variability and Context for Developing Policy and Practice*, Cham: Springer International Publishing, pp 93–114.

9

Adoption from care in Norway

Hege Stein Helland and Marit Skivenes

Introduction

In Norway – a social-democratic welfare state in the north of Europe with 5.4 million citizens, of whom 1,118,608 are children (aged 0–17) – adoption as a child protection measure is hardly used. Norway is consistently ranked high on indexes of child well-being (UNICEF, 2019), due process for children (CRIN, 2020) and respecting children's rights (Falch-Eriksen and Skivenes, 2019; KidsRights Foundation, 2019; Clark et al, 2020); however, it remains of concern that a majority of the around 8,800 children that, on any given day, are under a formal care order of the state will spend much of their childhood in public care (Helland and Skivenes, 2019). Children that cannot be reunified with birth parents may be considered for adoption, but adoptions against parents' wishes are decisions that are difficult, complex and crucially important for all parties. Adoption results in a child's legal bonds with their parents, which are established at birth, being transferred to new parents. This type of intervention, as all execution of state force against individual citizens, requires statuary basis and sound justifications. In Section 4-20 ('Deprival of parental responsibility. Adoption') of the Norwegian Child Welfare Act 1992 (CWA), the terms for removal of parental responsibility and adoption as a child protection measure are regulated. It is the county social welfare boards that are given the authority to make decisions about adoption from care and all other intrusive, non-voluntary child protection interventions (see Skivenes and Søvig, 2017). Although Norway is a country that is considered to have child-centric systems (Skivenes, 2011; Hestbæk et al, 2020), only around 50–60 children are adopted from care per year, despite it being widely held and documented that adopted children grow up having better prospects for their adult life than children in continuous foster care (see NOU, 2009:21, 2012:5; for research overviews, see also Skivenes, 2010; Vinnjerlung and Hjern, 2011; Christoffersen, 2012; Skivenes and Tefre, 2012; Palacios et al, 2019). In this chapter, we first summarise the legal provisions, policy framework and child protection system, and present results from the largest study in Norway on adoption as a child protection measure. We then consider why adoption is so rarely used in Norway and explore the position and voice of the child in policy and decision-making processes in the Norwegian context.

Guiding principles in the Norwegian child welfare system

Norway has a child protection system that is family service-oriented and child-centric (Gilbert et al, 2011; Skivenes, 2011, 2015; Falch-Eriksen and Skivenes, 2019). A basic principle is that the child protection system should be part of a broader child welfare system that provides services and therapeutic assistance to prevent more serious harm and, as a result, avoid out-of-home placements.

The Norwegian system is based on three main governing principles: (1) the best interest of the child; (2) the principle of least intrusive form of intervention; and (3) the biological principle (Skivenes, 2011; Skivenes and Thoburn, 2016). In addition to serving as a general guiding principle for the implementation of the CWA, the child's best interest is defined as a condition for consenting to an adoption by Section 4-20 of the CWA. This requires that the principle must have a decisive impact on the assessments on whether a decision to permit adoption is or is not given. The principle of 'least intrusive form of intervention' provides the procedural (and ethical) norm that any decision to intervene should seek to limit the level of intrusion in the family. This principle can be seen as a protection of parental rights against excessive state intervention. Thus, a decision to deprive birth parents of their parental responsibility, which is a prerequisite for an adoption to be considered, can only be taken if it is considered necessary in the child's current situation. As the strongest measure available in the CWA, adoption clearly evokes some controversy and confronts the fundamentals of the least intrusive principle as it contradicts the assumption that placement in care is temporary (NOU, 2016:16; Tefre, 2020). Adoption is, however, not necessarily in conflict with the idea of the least intrusive intervention because the child is already in public care and living in a foster family, and an adoption can only be undertaken if it is considered to be in the best interest of the child. The biological principle is a strong tenet in Norwegian child law, to the degree that 'serious neglect' has to be determined before changes can be made to this 'natural' constellation (Stortinget, 1991/92; see also Skivenes, 2002, 2010). The biological principle in Norwegian child welfare builds on the normative idea that it is a fundamental social value in Norwegian society that children grow up with their parents. The state's responsibility is considered secondary to the parents', and even if children cannot stay with their parents, their shared biological ties mean that the state should facilitate continued contact. The possibility of adoption would typically place the biological principle and the principle of the least intrusive intervention in direct conflict with the child's interests to have stable care. This tension is formulated by the Norwegian Supreme Court (1997: 534) in a 1997 decision on adoption, which stated that 'weighting these interests against one another is the greatest challenge in making judgments about adoption'. Research has also shown that arguments related to maintaining biological ties through contact, and of biological parents' negative reactions to an adoption, are given weight in the Supreme Court's assessments, though less space is given to discussing and reflecting on the arguments assumed to be present within the 'biological presumption' (Skivenes, 2010; NOU, 2012:5; Helland and Skivenes, 2019).

Legislation, policy and processes

Decisions to present a case about adoptions from care to the county social welfare boards lie within the responsibility of the municipal child protection agencies.[1] There are ten boards in Norway, covering one or two counties each. A decision from the boards can be appealed without further reasons or costs before the Norwegian courts of justice.[2] The regional state agency responsible for state-funded child welfare and family counselling services (Bufetat) issues an adoption permit. For an adoption to be decided by the boards, the child has to be under official state care by a care order (pursuant to ss 4-12 or 4-8 (2)(3) CWA), according to Section 4-20 (2)(3) of the CWA and Section 12 (2) of the Adoption Act.[3] A care order can be made simultaneously with the deprival of parental responsibility and adoption, though this rarely happens in practice (Helland and Skivenes, 2019). Only the child's foster parents are allowed to adopt the child following an assessment of their fitness to continue to care for the child.

In 2010, legislation providing for post-adoption contact was introduced (s 4-20a, of the CWA). The provision gives the boards, and subsequently the courts, the opportunity to authorise adoption and, at the same time, to grant contact rights to the biological parents (and *only* biological parents). Prior to this, on several occasions, the Norwegian Supreme Court (1990, 1997) had encouraged Norwegian legislators to make post-adoption contact available in the legislation (see also Skivenes, 2010).

The basic conditions for such post-adoption contact to be granted are that the prospective adopters' consent to contact and, importantly, that limited contact is considered *in the best interest of the child*. Section 4-20a is naturally closely connected to Section 4-20 on deprivation of parental responsibility and adoption, and should be included in the best interest assessments when a decision by Section 4-20 is made, though if, and only if, limited contact is considered to be in the child's best interest. A lack of consent to contact of the prospective adopters cannot be taken into consideration by the judicial decision-makers as an argument against adoption. In short, the *right* to contact is limited in the sense that arranging contact cannot be forced and the child protection system has no ability to sanction the parties for not upholding the visitation rights (Barne- og likestillingsdepartement, 2009/10). While the amendments to the legislation allowing for post-adoption contact have been interpreted as a measure to encourage more adoptions from care, both the Norwegian government and the Supreme Court have emphasised that consent to post-adoption contact does not cause a lowering of the threshold for adoption (NOU, 2009:21; Skivenes, 2009; Barne- og likestillingsdepartement, 2009/10; Tefre, 2020). However, in our survey of decision-makers' attitudes and knowledge about adoption, we found that well over half of the child protection workers (60 per cent) and board decision-makers (55 per cent) responded that they felt that having the option of post-adoption contact makes adoption more accessible as a measure. This implies that experience within the practice field is nonetheless that the threshold has been lowered (Helland and Skivenes, 2019). However, there is no demonstrable causal effect of the implementation of post-adoption contact on adoption rates.

There has been increased political attention to adoption as a measure in the child protection system since 2000 (Tefre, 2020). In an analysis of policy documents and legislation, Tefre (2020: 1) shows that:

> First, research and expert discourse gained influence in the framing of adoption policy over time. Second, the ethical response to this knowledge base has been to shift attention from shared family needs to the child's individual and developmental needs. There are signs that legislators view adoption in relation to children as independent legal subjects with rights.

In 2012, the Raundalen Committee composed of prominent child protection experts in Norway, delivered an expert report, mandated by the government (NOU, 2012:5). Chapter 10 of the report discusses adoption as a child protection measure and concludes: 'Based on developmental psychological perspectives and the research-based knowledge of vulnerable children, as we have explained several places in this report, there is a basis to claim that adoption should be a measure that the child protection system considers in cases involving long-term placements' (NOU, 2012:5: 130). A sober estimate is that between one third and one fifth of the children in care in Norway are in long-term placement, which amounts to 3,000–4,500 children.

Data on adopted children and children in care in Norway

There is a scarcity of research focusing on all aspects of adoptions in Norway and this is particularly evident when it comes to the recent phenomenon of adoptions from care (NOU, 2009:21: 40). In the Act on Child Welfare 1953, there was no legal basis for adoptions from care without parental consent (NOU, 2000:21: 203), and nor was it an option through the Guardianship Act 1986. Both provided legal provisions to deprive parents of their parental responsibility but this was not as a step in an adoption process (Bendiksen, 2008). However, in a study of all appeal cases pertaining to deprival of parental responsibility decided by the Ministry of Social Affairs between 1954 and 1965, Benneche (1967) found that in six out of 64 cases, adoption was the result. In other words, case law had allowed for adoptions, a custom that was further supported by a circular from the Department of Social Affairs in 1954. In a decision on the principle from 1982, the Norwegian Supreme Court confirmed that deprivation of parental responsibility with the prospect of adoption against the parents' will was legal.

Until around 1960, the majority of adoptions in Norway were of Norwegian nationals. In the years following, international adoptions grew while the number of national adoptions declined. This was a result of, on the one hand, a more liberal policy on abortion and a better and more progressive welfare schema nationally, and, on the other hand, an increasingly distressed global scene due to war and crisis (Gärtner and Heggland, 2013). From 1975, the number of international adoptions grew steadily but the years 2000–10 saw a steep decline (see Table 9.1).[4] As seen in Table 9.1, most Norwegian adoptions are now adoptions of stepchildren, with a much smaller number being voluntary and non-voluntary adoptions from care. Only a handful of children are freed for adoption by their biological parents each year. Statistics on adoptions from care are uncertain up until 2011, and there are no official statistics on these adoptions from before 2006 (collated into the category of 'other adoptions'). After 2006, statistics may include voluntary adoptions from care and persons above the legal age. Relying on data from the boards, the number of adoptions in 1993 and 1994 were 25 per year (NOU, 2000:12: 205). The number of non-voluntary adoptions from care were at the same level in 2011, with 27 granted adoptions by the boards (see Table 9.1), while in 2015 and 2018, the number of granted adoptions increased to 62 and 50, respectively.

Who are the children being adopted in Norway?

In a study from 2019 (Helland and Skivenes, 2019), all decisions made by the boards in the years 2011 to 2016 on adoption applications from care were studied, constituting a total of 283 cases concerning 302 children. During this period, 285 children (94 per cent of all children in the cases) aged three months to 17 years were adopted from care. Half were aged between two and four years old. The median age of those adopted was four years, and for the 17 who were not adopted, the median age was three years. A total of 72 per cent of the adopted children had been placed with the prospective adopters (their foster parents) before turning one year old. Most of the children (82 per cent) were removed from their birth parents before the age of one and the median age at placement with the foster parents who adopted them was three years. They had lived with the adoption-seeking foster parents for a median of three years. Two thirds had one or more full or half-siblings, and of these, 70 per cent of their siblings were in care or adopted. Among the 283 cases that were decided by the boards, only 19 concerned a sibling pair (all resulting in adoption).

The majority of the children (52 per cent) were born of two Norwegian-born parents and 16 per cent of the children had two parents born outside Norway. A total of 14 per cent had one Norwegian-born parent and one parent born outside of Norway, while 13 per cent had one Norwegian-born parent and one parent whose origin was unknown. Country background was not available in all cases, but from available data, most non-Norwegian parents were from African or Asian countries (at least 65 per cent). A smaller proportion of parents had a European background (at least 32 per

Table 9.1: Child population, number of children in care at year end, number of adoptions per year and type of adoption (children 0–17 years) (rates per 100,000 children)

	2000	2005	2006	2010	2011	2015	2018
Child population	1,060,857	1,092,728	1,096,003	1,114,374	1,118,225	1,127,402	1,122,508
Children in care	5,124 (483)	6,002 (549)	6,116 (558)	6,975 (626)	7,270 (650)	9,008 (799)	8,868 (790)
Adoptions from care							
Voluntary			23[a] (2)	16 (1)	6 (< 1)	6 (< 1)	5 (< 1)
Non-voluntary					27 (2)	62 (5)	50 (4)
Other adoptions							
International adoptions	657[b] (62)	704[b] (64)	438 (40)	343 (31)	297 (27)	132 (12)	77 (7)
Stepchild adoptions	105[b] (10)	138[b] (13)	79 (7)	88 (8)	85 (8)	90 (8)	72 (6)
Other national adoptions	30[c] (3)	48[c] (4)	8 (< 1)	3 (< 1)	4 (< 1)	8 (< 1)	0 (0)

Note: Statistics on reunifications and average stay in care (years) are not available. [a] Not differentiated between voluntary and non-voluntary adoptions from care. [b] Not differentiated by age, the data could possibly include persons aged over 18 years. [c] Including adoptions from care, both voluntary and non-voluntary. Not differentiated by age, the data could include persons aged over 18 years.

Source: Statistics Norway (2020a, 2020b, 2020c, 2020d), Helland and Skivenes (2019) and Bufdir (2019, 2020)

cent), weighted towards parents from Eastern European countries. A total of 23 per cent of the cases were with consent from one or both parents (mother = 10 per cent; father = 9 per cent; both of the parents = 4 per cent). Among these were cases in which parents gave consent under the condition of visitation rights (Helland and Skivenes, 2019).

Research in a national and international context

A considerable body of research is available from other countries, especially the US and England, where there is a longer tradition of adoptions from care (see Chapters 5 and 2, respectively). In the Norwegian context, there are very few studies on adoptions from care (for an overview of relevant Norwegian research, see Helland and Skivenes, 2019). One of the few studies is that of Skivenes and Tefre (2012). They reported that when presented with a vignette depicting a situation of a child in long-term care, a much higher proportion of the English (97.8 per cent) and American (95.5 per cent) social workers suggest adoption than Norwegian (61.7 per cent) social workers. The authors explain these findings as related to the lack of guidelines and clear instructions for the use of adoption as a child welfare measure in Norway when compared to the US and England, where the social workers appeared to have a clearer conception of their role in working with children in long-term care. The most comprehensive study to date is the previously mentioned research of Helland and Skivenes (2019) on adoption decision-making based on surveys of and interviews with both the front-line workers and the decision-makers in the boards. However, few clear-cut and specific explanations emerged as to why decision-makers did or did not prefer adoption compared to continued foster care. While most decision-makers exhibited positive attitudes towards adoption and adequate levels of knowledge about adoption as a measure, the main explanatory factor appeared to be that adoption was not 'on the agenda' and there was a lack of formal guidance for practice. For the front-line workers, the lack of managerial and local political focus on adoption was seen to point to reluctance to change placement policy towards increasing adoption. The researchers concluded from the cases studied that local agencies appeared to use a high threshold when deciding whether a case should be forwarded to the boards, while the surveys also revealed that the social workers were under the impression that the boards were very strict in cases concerning adoption.

However, presented with a vignette case about a possible adoption or continued foster care, a large majority of child protection workers ($n = 461$), experts ($n = 158$) and county board leaders ($n = 32$) chose adoption (see Helland and Skivenes, 2019; Helland, 2020). Among child protection professionals, 86 per cent opted for adoption rather than foster care. The main arguments for adoption were: the child's needs and attachment to the foster home; parents lack of change or lack of care capacity; the age of the child; and the duration of the placement. The 14 per cent who chose foster care explained that: it would be a 'closed adoption'; 'biological bonds would be broken'; there would be the need for coercion; and they would be taking into account the views of the biological parents. Among the decision-makers from the boards, the experts and the judges, 87.5 per cent of the judges and 93.7% of the experts chose adoption as the appropriate measure, giving similar arguments to the practitioners. Only a handful of board decision-makers ($n = 14$) chose foster care, giving as reasons: that the adoption was too early because it would break bonds too soon; and that maintaining contact with the biological parents could be valuable and important at later stages in the child's life.

With respect to outcomes from adoption and alternative placement options for children who cannot return safely to parents, there is as yet no body of specifically Norwegian research to inform the debates currently taking place. There is a widely held view (supported by practitioner opinions and small-scale studies) that children too often move between foster families, whether because of managerial policies or placement breakdown.

From a wide range of studies in other countries, it is generally agreed that adoption is better for children than foster care (see, for example, Christoffersen, 2012; Christoffersen et al, 2008; Skivenes and Tefre, 2012; Hjern et al, 2019; Palacios et al, 2019). Breakdown rates for children placed for adoption from care are low, less than 4 per cent, as displayed in two recent longitudinal studies of large sample in the UK by Wijedasa and Selwyn (2017) and Neil et al (2015). Of specific relevance for Norway is the Vinnerljung and Hjern (2011) administrative data-based study of the outcomes for three groups of Swedish children: 900 adopted previous foster children; 3,062 children in long-term foster care; and 900,000 children from the majority population. They concluded:

> Crude outcomes for both groups were substantially weaker than for majority population peers. The foster children fell clearly short of adoptees on all outcomes; school

performance at 15 years, cognitive competence at 18 years, educational achievement and self-support capability in young adult years, also after adjustments for birth parent related confounders and age at placement in substitute care. (Vinnjerlung and Hjern, 2011: 1902)

Among the small number of Norwegian studies is that of Berg (2010). Based on case files and in-depth interviews with Norwegian adoptive parents of 13 children adopted without parental agreement from the child protection system, as well as six of the adopted children aged 17 plus, the study reports that children had varied challenges during their upbringing, in which two had big problems, four had some problems and seven had no problems. Children and adoptive parents report that despite the difficulties they experience, the young people are generally positive about having been adopted.

Research on citizens' views on adoption from care

Skivenes and Thoburn (2017) used a survey vignette methodology to report on attitudes towards adoption from care in the general population in England, Finland, Norway and California, USA. A total of 68 per cent of Norwegian citizens chose adoption over continued foster care for a two year old well settled in his foster family. Similar positive attitudes to adoption as a child protection measure are found in a recent study, also of a representative sample of the Norwegian population (Helland et al, 2020). There is also overwhelming support from all the main actors (organisations, unions and decision-making bodies) in the field of child protection. In 2009, the Government issued a white paper arguing a need for increased use of adoption as a child protection measure: 'A total of 107 consultation bodies have agreed to the proposal (white paper). 104 of the consultation bodies support the main ministry proposal to facilitate increased use of adoption as a child protection measure' (NOU, 2012:5:123).

Views on adoption from children and parents

To a large degree, available research has left unanswered questions about: if and how Norwegian children are involved; whether children give their consent; whether children have views on foster care versus adoption as a placement alternative; and whether children have a view on their contact with the birth family. A study of *all* judgements on adoptions from care made in Norway in a six-year period (2011–16) involving children aged 4–17 years old, a total of 169 judgements (McEwan-Strand and Skivenes, 2020), concluded that, overall, children are absent in the decision-makers' justifications and conclusions about adoption. However, those that were heard wished to be adopted. The children interviewed for the small-scale in-depth study of Berg (2010) (referred to earlier) were also generally positive about having been adopted.

The statements on adoption as a child protection measure made by the national Association for Foster Children, the Organisation for Foster Parents and *BarnevernsProffene* (young persons with experience from foster care) are important. They were generally positive towards adoption as a child protection measure as long as the requirements as stated in relevant laws are met. The statements, however, emphasise that the child's right to express their opinion and to be involved in the decision must be respected. The associations further noted several times that the narrow interpretation of 'family' is problematic and that siblings and other family members besides the biological parents can be important for the child:

> Furthermore, one should have in mind the child's attachment to other relatives but the biological parents, such as siblings, grandparents, aunts/uncles and others. Those relations can be utterly important for the future development and safety of the child. The Association for Foster Children thus would like to see a bigger emphasis on those factors in care order and/or adoption proceedings. (Association for Foster Children, 2012)

With respect to the views of biological parents, the Organisation for Parents in the Child Protection System has commented negatively on adoption without parental consent as a child protection measure: 'Forced adoption/adoption should not be subject of the child protection services' (see: https://barnevernsforeldrene.no/om-organisasjonen/utviklingsplan/). It is not explicitly stated, but we interpret the statement as meaning that they wish for other instances to prepare adoption cases, that is, adoption should not be a measure initiated under the CWA. The Organisation for Foster Parents (2012) have expressed that they are positive about adoption.

A study of foster parents ($n = 864$) showed that about 20 per cent have considered adoption, and half of them have seriously considered it (Havik, 2007). The aforementioned small-scale study of adoptive parents (Berg, 2010) showed that they are very satisfied with the adoption.

Conclusion

Adoption is a measure that, like all child protection interventions, should be undertaken with the highest regard to the specific child's best interests, and in accordance with due process and decision-making processes that fulfil criteria for rational reasoning and critical reflection. Adoption as a child protection measure should only be considered for children that cannot be reunified with birth parents or wider family, and thus will grow up in public care. However, from a child's perspective, adoption provides a new chance for permanence in a family for life. An international, interdisciplinary group of recognised researchers in the field published an article about adoptions in child protection in 2019 (Palacios et al, 2019), and they conclude that adoption must be considered as a measure to secure the child's interests because it provides permanence and belonging for the child on a lifetime basis. They argue that adoption is a legitimate model for the alternative care of children given that adoption decisions follow conventions and laws and keep the focus on the children's best interests:

> The one thing that is agreed is that the child's safety, needs, welfare and development are the core issues to consider not only in the short term, but also for the rest of their lives. Embedded within this is a fundamental recognition that family life is the basic structure that enables this, and if that cannot be with the family of origin, an alternative permanent family solution must be found. (Palacios et al, 2019: 68)

In 2009, the Norwegian government issued a white paper arguing for increased use of adoption as a child protection measure, with overwhelming support from all relevant consultation bodies. The question that remains unanswered is why, in the light of these official reports going back for some years, supportive opinions from professionals and the public, and an increasing children's rights focus, there are still so few adoptions from care in Norway. To complement the research already available on the decision-making process, more research that has a child perspective in its approach may point to a way forward that builds on the strengths of Norway's existing position as a child-centric society that ensures high performance on the rule of law.

Acknowledgements

This project has received funding from the Research Council of Norway under the Independent Projects – Humanities and Social Science program (grant no. 262773) and European Research Council under the European Union's Horizon 2020 research and innovation programme (grant agreement No 724460). Disclaimer: This chapter reflects only the authors' views and the funding agencies are not responsible for any use that may be made of the information contained therein.

Notes

[1] Decisions made by the boards are pursuant to the CWA, the Act Relating to Municipal Health and Care Services, and the Act Relating to the Control of Communicable Diseases. For details on the functioning of the boards, see Skivenes and Søvig (2017).

[2] Access to judicial review of cases decided in the boards are regulated in Chapter 36 of the Dispute Act 2005 (see also s 7-24 CWA).

[3] Section 4-20 of the CWA ('Deprival of parental responsibility. Adoption') has the following wording:

> If the county social welfare board has made a care order for a child, the county social welfare board may also decide that the parents shall be deprived of all parental responsibility. If, as a result of the parents being deprived of parental responsibility, the child is left without a guardian, the county social welfare board shall as soon as possible take steps to have a new guardian appointed for the child.
>
> When an order has been made depriving the parents of parental responsibility, the county social welfare board may give its consent for a child to be adopted by persons other than the parents.
>
> Consent may be given if
>
> a) it must be regarded as probable that the parents will be permanently unable to provide the child with proper care or the child has become so attached to persons and the environment where he or she is living that, on the basis of an overall assessment, removing the child may lead to serious problems for him or her and
>
> b) adoption would be in the child's best interests and
>
> c) the adoption applicants have been the child's foster parents and have shown themselves fit to bring up the child as their own and
>
> d) the conditions for granting an adoption pursuant to the Adoption Act are fulfilled.
>
> When the county social welfare board consents to adoption, the Ministry shall issue the adoption order. The Social County Board may decide for a child to be adopted when the parents' consent, as far as the conditions in sub-section three are fulfilled.

[4] For a broader historical perspective on the development, see NOU (2009: 33–7).

References

Association for Foster Children (2012) 'Høringsuttalelse til NOU 2012:5 Bedre beskyttelse av barns utvikling' ['Submission to the hearing regarding NOU 2012:5 – Better protection of the development of children'] Oslo. Available at: www.regjeringen.no/contentassets/ f9942dde910645d1854b4c4edc3820a9/landsforeningen_for_ barnevernsbarn.pdf?uid=Landsforeningen_for_barnevernsbarn.pdf (accessed 9 December 2020).

Barne- og likestillingsdepartement (2009/10) 'Endringer i adopsjonsloven og barnevernloven' ['Proposition on changes in the adoption law and child welfare law'], Prop. 7 L. Available at: www. regjeringen.no/no/dokumenter/ prop-7-l-2009-2010/id579198/ (accessed 4 March 2020).

Bendiksen, L. (2008) *Barn i langvarige fosterhjemsplasseringer – foreldreansvar og adopsjon* [*Children in Long-Term Foster Care – Parental Responsibility and Adoption*], Bergen: Fagbokforlaget.

Benneche, G. (1967) *Rettssikkerheten i Norge* [*The Rule of Law in Norway*], Oslo: Universitetsforlaget.

Berg, T. (2010) 'Adopsjon som barneverntiltak – Hvordan gikk det med barna? Rapport fra praksis' ['Adoption as a child welfare measure – how did it turn out for the children? A report from practice'], *Tidsskriftet Norges barnevern*, 87(1): 48–59.

Bufdir (2019) *Yearly Report 2018* [*Årsrapport 2018*], Oslo: Directorate for Children, Youth and Family Affairs.

Bufdir (2020) Data on granted voluntary adoptions years 2011, 2015 and 2018 received directly by email (received 4 March 2020) from the Directorate for Children, Youth and Family Affairs.

Christoffersen, M.N. (2012) 'A study of adopted children, their environment, and development: a systematic review', *Adoption Quarterly*, 15(3): 220–37.

Christoffersen, M.N., Hammen, I., Raft Andersen, K. and Jeldtoft, N. (2008). 'Adoption som indsats: En systematisk gennemgang af udenlandske erfaringer.' ['Adoption as an effort: A systematic review of foreign experiences.'], SFI - Det Nationale Forskningscenter for Velfærd. SFI-Rapport Nr. 07:32.

Clark, H., Coll-Seck, A., Banerjee, A., Peterson, S., Dalglish, S., Ameratunga, S., Balabanova, D., Bhan, M., Bhutta, Z., Borrazzo, J., Claeson, T., Doherty, T., El-Jardali, F., Geroge, A., Gichaga, A., Gram, L., Hipgrave, D., Kwamie, A., Meng, Q., Mercer, R., Narain, S., Nsungwa-Sabiiti, J., Olumide, A., Osrin, D., Powell-Jackson, T., Rasanathan, K., Rasul, I., Reid, P., Requejo, J., Rohde, S., Rollins, N., Romedenne, M., Sachdev, H., Saleh, R., Shawar, Y., Shiffman, J., Simon, J., Sly, P., Stenberg, K., Tomlinson, M., Ved, R. and Costello, A. (2020) 'A future for the world's children? A WHO–UNICEF–Lancet Commission', *The Lancet*, 395(10224): 605–58.

CRIN (Child Rights International Network) (2020) 'Access to justice for children: Global ranking'. *Child Rights International Network*. Available at: https://archive.crin.org/en/access-justice-children-global-ranking (Accessed 9 December 2020).

Falch-Eriksen, A. and Skivenes, M. (2019) 'Right to protection', in M. Langford, M. Skivenes and K. Søvig (eds) *Children's Rights in Norway: An Implementation Paradox*, Oslo: Universitetsforlaget, pp 107–34.

Gärtner, K. and Heggland, J. (2013) 'Adopterte barn, ungdom og voksne: en kunnskapsoppsummering om kognitiv kompetanse, psykisk helse og bruk av hjelpetjenester' ['Adopted children, youth, and adults: a knowledge summary on cognitive skill, mental health, and use of help services'], Rapport 2013/8, Folkehelseinstituttet. Available at: www.fhi.no/publ/2013/adopterte-barn-ungdom-og-voksne-en-/ (accessed 4 March 2020).

Gilbert, N., Parton, N. and Skivenes, M. (eds) (2011) *Child Protection Systems. International Trends and Emerging Orientations*, New York: Oxford University Press.

Havik, T. (2007) *Slik fosterforeldre ser det – II. Resultat fra en kartleggingsstudie i 2005* [*How Foster Parents See It – II. Results from a Mapping Study in 2005*], Bergen: BVUS-V. Available at: https://hdl.handle.net/1956/3142 (accessed 9 December 2020).

Helland, H. (2020). 'Tipping the scales: The power of parental commitment in decisions on adoption from care'. *Children and Youth Services Review*, 119: 105693.

Helland, H. and Skivenes, M. (2019) *Adopsjon som barneverntiltak* [*Adoption from Care as a Child Welfare Measure*], Bergen: University of Bergen.

Helland, H., Pedersen, S. and Skivenes, M. (2020) 'Befolkningens syn på adopsjon' ['Population's view on adoption from care'], Tidsskrift for Samfunnsforskning.

Hestbæk, A.-D., Höjer, I., Pösö, T. and Skivenes, M. (2020). 'Child welfare removal of infants: Exploring policies and principles for decision-making in Nordic countries'. *Children and Youth Services Review*, 108: 104572.

Hjern, A., Vinnerljung, B. and Brännström, L. (2019) 'Outcomes in adulthood of adoption after long-term foster care: a sibling study', *Developmental Child Welfare*, 1(1): 61–75.

KidsRights Foundation (2019) 'The KidsRights Index'. Available at: www.kidsrightsindex.org (accessed 19 November 2019).

McEwan-Strand, A. and Skivenes, M. (2020) 'Deciding on adoptions from care or continued public care – does the judiciary involve children? An analysis of the Norwegian County Social and Child Welfare Boards decision making', *International Journal of Children's Rights*, 28(2020): 632–65.

Neil, E., Beek, M., Ward, E. (2015) *Contact after Adoption: A Longitudinal Study of Post Adoption Contact Arrangements*, London: Coram-BAAF.

Norwegian Supreme Court (1990) 'Judgment from the Norwegian Supreme Court', Rt-1990-1274. Available at: www.lovdata.no

Norwegian Supreme Court (1997) 'Judgment from the Norwegian Supreme Court', Rt-1997-534. Available at: www.lovdata.no

NOU 2000:12 (2000) *Barnevernet i Norge – Tilstandsvurderinger, nye perspektiver og forslag til reformer [Child Welfare in Norway. Status Evaluation, New Perspective and Reform Proposals]*, Oslo: Barne- og likestillingsdepartementet.

NOU 2009:21 (Noregs offentlege utgreiingar) (2009) *Adopsjon - til barnets beste; En utredning om de mange ulike sidene ved adopsjon [Adoption – For the Child's Best. A Commentary on the Many Different Perspectives on Adoption]*, Oslo: Barne- og likestillingsdepartementet.

NOU 2012:5 (2012) *Bedre beskyttelse av barns utvikling; Ekspertutvalgets utredning om det biologiske prinsipp i barnevernet [Better Protection of Children's Development: An Expert Committee's Commentary on the Biological Principle in Child Welfare]*, Oslo: Barne- og likestillingsdepartementet.

NOU 2016:16 (2016) *Ny barnevernslov- Sikring av barnets rett til omsorg beskyttelse [New Child Welfare Law – Securing the Child's Right to Care Protection]*, Oslo: Barne- og likestillings- og inkluderingsdepartementet.

Organisation for Foster Parents (2012) 'Høring – NOU 2012:5 Bedre Beskyttelse av barns utvikling' ['Hearings on NOU 2012:5: better protection of the child's development']. Available at: www.regjeringen. no/contentassets/f9942dde910645d1854b4c4edc3820a9/norsk_ fosterhjemsforening.pdf?uid=Norsk_fosterhjemsforening.pdf

Palacios, J., Adroher, S., Brodzinsky, D.M., Grotevant, H.D., Johnson, D.E., Juffer, F., Martínez- Mora, L., Muhamedrahimov, R.J., Selwyn, J., Simmonds, J. and Tarren-Sweeney, M. (2019) 'Adoption in the service of child protection: an international interdisciplinary perspective', *Psychology, Public Policy, and Law*, 25(2): 57–72.

Skivenes, M. (2002) *Lovgivning og legitimitet – En evaluering av lov om barneverntjenester av 1992 i et deliberativt perspektiv* [*Legislation and Legitimacy – An Evaluation of the Law-Making Process of the Child Welfare Act of 1992*], Rapport nr 79, PhD thesis, Bergen: UiB, Institutt for administrasjon og organisasjonsvitenskap.

Skivenes, M. (2009) 'Kontakt med biologisk familie etter adopsjon i barnevernet – til barnets beste?' ['Post-adoption contact in child welfare cases – in the child's best interests?]', *Tidsskrift for arverett, familierett og barnevernrettslige spørsmål*, 7(3): 134–55.

Skivenes, M. (2010) 'Judging the child's best interests: rational reasoning or subjective presumptions?', *Acta Sociologica*, 53(4): 339–53.

Skivenes, M. (2011) 'Norway – toward a child centric perspective', in N. Gilbert, N. Parton and M. Skivenes (eds) *Child Protection Systems: International Trends and Emerging Orientations*, New York: Oxford University Press, pp 153–82.

Skivenes, M. (2015) 'Handlingsrommet for barns deltagelse i barnevernssaker' ['The margin for children's participation in child welfare cases'], *Tidsskrift for Velferdsforskning*, 18(1): 48–60.

Skivenes, M. and Søvig, K.H. (2017) 'Norway – child welfare decision-making in cases of removals of children', in K. Burns, T. Pösö and M. Skivenes (eds) *Child Welfare Removals by the State: A Cross-Country Analysis of Decision-Making Systems*, New York: Oxford University Press, pp 40–64.

Skivenes, M. and Tefre, Ø. (2012) 'Adoption in the child welfare system – a cross-country analysis of child welfare workers' recommendations for or against adoption', *Children and Youth Services Review*, 34(11): 2220–8.

Skivenes, M. and Thoburn, J. (2016) 'Pathways to permanence in England and Norway. A critical analysis of documents and data', *Children and Youth Service Review*, 67: 152–60.

Skivenes, M. and Thoburn, J. (2017) 'Citizens' views in four jurisdictions on placement policies for maltreated children', *Child and Family Social Work*, 22(4): 1472–79.

Statistics Norway (2020a) 'Population. Table 07459: population, by sex and one-year age groups (M) 1986–2020 (measured January 1st)'.

Statistics Norway (2020b) 'Child welfare. Table 04443: children with measures from the Child Welfare Services per 31 December, by assistance or care measure (M) 1994–2018'.

Statistics Norway (2020c) 'Adoptions. Table 06685: adopted, by type of adoption, sex and age 2006–2018'.

Statistics Norway (2020d) 'Adoptions. Table 06683: adoptions, by type of adoption 1986–2018'.

Stortinget (1991/92) 'Om lov om barneverntjenester (barnevernloven)' ['On the Child Welfare Act'], Ot. Prp. No. 44. Available at: www.stortinget.no/no/Saker-og-publikasjoner/Stortingsforhandlinger/Lesevisning/?p=1991-92&paid=4&wid=c&psid=DIVL312 (accessed 4 March 2020).

Tefre, Ø. (2020) 'The child's best interests and the politics of adoptions from care', *International Journal of Children's Rights*, 28(2): 288–321.

UNICEF (United Nations Children's Fund) (2019) *For Every Child, Every Right: The Convention on the Rights of the Child at a Crossroads*, New York: UNICEF.

Vinnerljung, B. and Hjern, A. (2011) 'Cognitive, educational and self-support outcomes of long-term foster care versus adoption. A Swedish national cohort study', *Children and Youth Services Review*, 33: 1902–10.

Wijedasa, D. and Selwyn, J. (2017) 'Examining rates and risk factors for post-order adoption disruption in England and Wales through survival analyses', *Children and Youth Services Review*, 83: 179–89.

10

Adoption from care in Spain

Sagrario Segado, Ana Cristina Gomez Aparicio and
Esther Abad Guerra

Introduction

In the late 1980s, newly democratic Spain needed to radically transform mechanisms and institutions inherited from Franco's dictatorship, which were imbued with a paternalistic philosophy (Ferrandis Torres, 2018). A series of bold legal reforms saw the definitive take-off of children as a group with their own characteristics and needs, and requiring special protection. Following on from the Spanish Constitution of 1978 and the Law 1/1987 (11 November), which modified the Civil Code and the Law of Civil Procedure in matters of adoption, the Law 1/1996 (15 January) as amended by Law 26/2015 and Organic Law 8/2015 (22 July) legislated for the protection of children and adolescents, including those who might be adopted (Figure 10.1). In summary, within the framework established by the Constitution of 1978, the 17 autonomous communities and two autonomous cities (Ceuta and Melilla) have delegated responsibility for the protection of minors, including in matters of adoption.

All adoptions in Spain require a judicial decision, which gives full and irrevocable status to the adopters and adoptees, and ends all existing ties with the biological family. This chapter examines social policy, legislation, assessment and decision-making processes for the adoption of children from state care. It considers system reforms over the last decade, and notes that legislative reform in 2015 opens the way for a greater number of children to be eligible for adoption from the care system. This reform requires that children be heard and introduces the possibility that adopted children may continue to be in contact with their family of origin, provided that this is in the child's best interest. Due to the high level of delegation of responsibility for care and adoption services, some detailed references are to the Madrid autonomous community (with 6,778,000 inhabitants, of which 1,256,000 are minors under 18 years old). Provisions in other parts

Figure 10.1: A simplified sequence of the most significant processes that have shaped the child protection system according to Law 1/1996, Law 26/2015 and Organic Law 8/2015

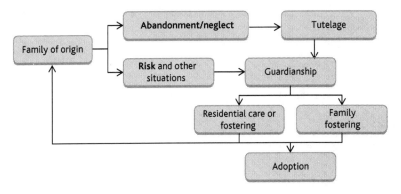

Source: Observatory for Childhood (2017) and Ministry of Health, Social Services and Equality (2017)

of the country are similar, and where available, data are provided for the whole of Spain.

Adoption from care in legislation and guidelines

The framework for adoption in Spain follows the United Nations Convention on the Rights of the Child (CRC) (ratified by Spain in 1990), the European Charter of the Rights of the Child (adopted by the European Parliament in 1990) and the 1993 Hague Convention on International Adoption. Spain was the first country to ratify this convention in 1995, followed by the majority of Western countries in 1995. The Strasbourg European Adoption Agreement of 27 November 2008 completes the international legal framework for adoptions in Spain.

Article 39 of the 1978 Constitution requires the regional governments to ensure the social, economic and legal protection of the family, and, together with the 1987 reform of the Spanish Civil Code, can be said to have 'de-judicialised' the child protection system. It delegated the protection of minors, including responsibility for providing an adoption service (previously carried out by notaries or through charity organisations), to the autonomous communities:

> After presumable abuses committed in the previous decades, the constitutional Spain turned the adoption into a public monopoly and armored against the hateful traffic of

children. This reform ended the negotiation of adoption as a business act between individuals that allowed the delivery of children by agreement between biological parents and adopters. (Ferrandis Torres, 2017: 2)

This legislation introduced two fundamental principles on which adoption is based. On the one hand, adoption results in the adopted child being fully integrated within the adoptive family. On the other hand, the role of public bodies with responsibility for child protection was enhanced and adoption from care was recognised as a child protection measure that provides a legal family to children who cannot remain with their family of origin.

Following on from the 1987 reform, a review of child and adolescent protection services was carried out, resulting in an amendment to Law 1/1996, known as Legal Protection of the Minor, which resulted in a partial modification of the Civil Code and Civil Procedure Law. It introduced the requirement for the suitability of adopters to be approved by the public bodies, and it also regulated international adoption (Callejo, 2017).

Law 26/2015 made further detailed requirements for the assessment of the suitability of adopters. It also created the legal status of 'guardian' specifically for the purposes of adoption in order to avoid the child having to be in public care prior to the public bodies applying to the judge for an adoption to be formalised. During this period, the parents retain their parental rights and the 'guardian' decides with the child protection system where the child will be placed.

This law also introduced the new concept of 'open adoptions'. Although the adoption order extinguishes the legal links between the adoptee and the family of origin, through open adoption provisions, the adoptee may maintain a relationship with members of the original family through visits or other means of communication. An open adoption may be agreed by the judge when this is proposed by the public bodies following a professional assessment that this is in the interest of the child, and with the consent of the adoptive parents and the child who has sufficient maturity and is at least 12 years old. While 'under guardianship', the professionals employed by the public bodies must provide support to the parties, monitor relationships within the adoptive family and report on the stability of the placement, prioritising the well-being of the child ahead of the interests of the adopters and family of origin.

By issuing Organic Law 8/2015, Spain satisfied the CRC request to ensure that children's rights to protection were standardised across the different autonomous communities. This legislation also reinforced the 'best interests of the child' as a guiding principle of child protection procedures. The legislators in 2015 also emphasised the importance of evaluation for purposes of public accountability, further opening up access for researchers (see later).

Each autonomous community has the discretion to enact its own laws, based on but adapting the national regulations. For example, the Community of Madrid enacted Law 6/1995 of Guarantee of the Right of Infants and Adolescents.[1] In the Community of Madrid, the body responsible for adoption is the General Directorate of the Family and the Minor of the Ministry of Social and Family Policies. However, the possibility of variability between autonomous communities does not substantially change child protection services in Spain as a whole, and since 2015, efforts have been directed at the convergence of autonomous laws and interventions. In this chapter, we will focus in detail on the Autonomous Community of Madrid as an example of how adoption works in the rest of the country.

The rights of children and parents in adoption from care

As noted earlier, children's rights are guaranteed in law but interventions are also governed by guarantees on the rights of parents, who can appeal decisions of the removal of parental rights at very little cost and within an extended time frame. The Supreme Court has regard to these guarantees for parental rights, as demonstrated in several judgments stating that the removal of parental rights should be used restrictively, not as a punishment to the parent who fails to fulfil their duties, but for the benefit and interest of the child. If deprivation of parental rights does not result in benefit to the child, it should not be agreed (on the removal of parental rights, see, for example, Supreme Court Judgments of 16 February 2012, EDJ 2012/19020[2]).

However, recent decisions of the executive branch have challenged this legal position. Specifically, the government approved decree-law 9/2018[3] to introduce 'urgent measures' against gender violence. This decree-law modifies Article 156 of the Civil Code with a new article:

> when there is a conviction or simply when a criminal proceeding has been initiated against one of the parents for attempting against the life, physical integrity, liberty, moral integrity or sexual freedom and indemnity of the minor sons and daughters, or for attempting against the other parent,

the latter's consent will be sufficient for the psychological care and assistance of minor children.

The convicted or suspected parent is deprived of their decision-making capacity with respect to children and will only have the right to be informed; their consent is considered not to be required, though they have the right to appeal to the judge. According to this, a social services report is sufficient to confer the condition of 'victim of gender violence'.

Decision-making on adoptions

Children who are considered for adoption in the Community of Madrid will be in one of the following groupings (General Directorate of the Family and the Minor[4]):

- young children whose biological mother, because of adverse circumstances that prevent her from taking care of her child, freely and voluntarily decides that her child be placed under the guardianship of the Community of Madrid prior to being adopted;
- children who are abandoned shortly after birth in the hospital, without the mother having formally requested adoption;
- any other children abandoned without identifying information;
- children removed from their family because of abuse or neglect whose guardianship is then taken over by the Community of Madrid and for whom there is no plan for return to their original family; and
- children living in childcare centres, with a legal decision taken that there is no possibility for them to return to their family.

The decision-making process

The Child Protection Service (CPS) is responsible for the adoption process and services, and makes the adoption application to court through the Commission of Tutelage for Minors (CTM) – a seven-member collegiate body and the highest child protection decision-making body in the autonomous region of Madrid. Two members of the CTM are the heads of the Division for Adoption and Fostering and the General Deputy of the Sub-Directorate for Protection of the Minor (these two are civil servants and co-authors of this chapter). Both the Division for Adoption and Fostering and the General Sub-Directorate are units of the General Directorate of the Family and

Figure 10.2: General Directorate of the Family and the Minor in the Community of Madrid

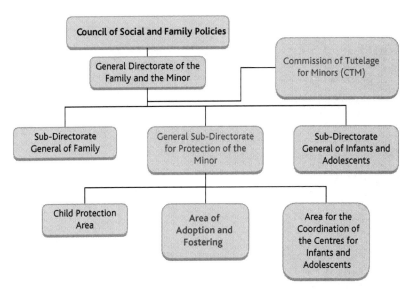

the Minor (whose chief is a political appointment of the autonomous community government) (see Figure 10.2).

Prospective adopters have to obtain a prior declaration of suitability by applying to the relevant CPS. Although adoptions generally require the consent of the birth parents, the law provides for cases where parents are unable to consent or whose consent is dispensed with. Before the adoption process can start, the CPS must remove parental rights through an *abandonment* declaration. This may occur for different reasons: (1) when parents fail to recognise the problem; (2) when they deny the negative influence of current circumstances on the child; (3) when they reject support measures; (4) when they fail to meet the child's needs; or (5) when there is an endangerment situation for the child. The CPS workers meet individually with each party before presenting reports and recommendations for the CTM to decide on the removal of parental rights for the purpose of adoption. Parents, as well as the public prosecutor for minors, are notified of the decision. Parents have the right to appeal against the removal of their parental rights to the family court for up to two years, after which the child will either be adopted or will be in the guardianship of the state.

Following the 'declaration of abandonment', the process from child removal to legal adoption can be lengthy, especially in cases of involuntary placement. During this period, the CPS delegates custody 'for the purpose of adoption' to a childcare centre or foster family until the judicial decision of adoption is issued. The guardian may agree to the child being placed as a foster child with the prospective adopters. Within three months of the CTM decision, the CPS sends the complete file along with a proposal to the family court to initiate adoption proceedings, which proceed even though the parents have a two-year appeal period.

Final adoption decisions are court orders issued by a judge following separate hearings with the adopting parents and the child over 12 years old, or younger if sufficiently mature. Children are heard in safe and private conditions. Although it is not mandatory to hear biological parents who have lost their parental rights, in practice, the judge usually gives them a hearing. The judge can commission any additional expert evidence required before issuing a court order ratifying or dismissing the CPS proposal for adoption. If the proposal is dismissed, the child will remain in foster care or in a childcare centre.

Adoption appeals are made to the family court in the first instance and to the region's court in the second instance. An appeal may be made on all grounds, and the case will be heard by four or five judges at second instance. In general, observers (including researchers and the media) are not allowed during the proceedings, but an access permit may be requested from the General Council of Judges stating the importance of that observer being present. The written decision is sent to the parents, the adoptive parents, the public prosecutor and the CPS but is not publicly available.

All case files, including those from the CPS and the final adoption decision from the court, are stored by both the regional CPS and the family court. Before 2015, it was difficult to access these decisions on the grounds of children's privacy but, as noted earlier, this has been relaxed to allow for researcher access. From 2015, there is no requirement for parental agreement to adoption if two years have passed without a parent taking steps to revoke the CPS declaration of neglect. Also, with respect to newborn infants, the mother's consent may not be given until six weeks have elapsed from delivery. The length of the adoption process is greatly reduced for consensual newborn adoptions, where the process may take only six weeks. This could be seen from various angles as a measure of protection more for women than for babies, since at the point when parental rights are given up, the 'abandonment' has not been legally certified, something that is necessary to start the adoption process. On the other hand, it could also constitute an act of protection of the minor, since being a mother who does not initially wish to be a mother increases the possibility of parental failure.

The roles of different parties and service providers

The adoptive parents

Prospective adoptive parents must follow a complex path before achieving adoption. This path has the following steps:[5]

1. *Submit the application and attend an information meeting.* When more adopters are needed in the Community of Madrid, a time-limited public call is made by order of the Council of Social and Family Policies. However, because of the difficulty of placing children with special needs due to illness and/or disability, there is no deadline for submitting applications to adopt. Any offers that imply prejudice on the part of the applicants based on sex, race, ethnicity or other circumstances of the children to be adopted are not accepted (Law 6/1995 of March 28 on Guarantees of the Rights of Children and Adolescents). The applicants are then invited to an information meeting in strict order of entry onto the register of potential adopters.
2. *Training course.* Applicants are required to attend mandatory training organised by the public body or by an approved collaborating agency (Art 176 Civil Code).
3. *Psychosocial study.* The psychosocial study builds on the information from at least three interviews with professionals from the specialist adoption team and a home visit. If necessary, additional information may be requested. The CPS then submits a report to the Child Custody Commission, which may accept or reject the application to adopt. If accepted, the proposed adoption will be entered in the Family Registry for Adoption as an 'accepted offer'.
4. *Guardian delegation for adoption purposes.* Once a child is matched with an adoptive family, the Child Custody Commission will delegate guardianship (usually to the prospective family) until the judicial hearing, when all the parties to the adoption can be heard. Parents who are deprived of parental rights will be notified of this decision. The prospective adopters have the same rights and obligations as foster family members. However, those actions that exceed the scope of everyday life (such as surgical operation) must be authorised by the Child Custody Commission.
5. *Judicial process.* For adoptions from care, the judicial process takes place while the child is already placed with the prospective adopters. The adoption proposal is submitted to the judge by the General Directorate for the Family and the Minor (see Figure 10.2) in the

shortest time possible and, in any case, within three months from the day on which the guardian delegation has been agreed.

6. *Monitoring.* During the period in which the judicial procedure is carried out and until the adoption order is made, caseworkers of the General Directorate will carry out follow-up checks in order to assess the child's adaptation to the family.

The child

Since 2015, the best interest of the child must always be evaluated by child welfare professionals and lawyers, as well as by institutions (whether public or private), courts and legislative bodies. Key requirements in the protection of minors in Spain are: first, that when making a decision about a minor, their best interest has been previously evaluated; second, as a general principle, when different interpretations of a rule arise, the one that reflects the best interests of the child will always be chosen; and, third, a procedural rule is that if the procedure stipulated for each case is not followed, the best interest of the child is likely to be prejudiced and an appeal to court will occur (see Moreno Torres, 2015). Consequently, the measures adopted must be in the child's best interest, regardless of what is requested by the parties. As part of each decision, resolution or technical report, professionals and decision-makers must specify the criteria and values that have been considered.

However, finding an agreed way of acting upon these principles is one of the most complex tasks judges face, and although they are included in legislation, a uniform process for their implementation is missing. With the enactment of the (national) 2015 laws, the understanding and application of the principle has been standardised in order to reconcile the persistent differences in practice in each autonomous community. However, even today, the criteria and elements established for this concept are broad and their formulation still leaves a gap for interpretation.

Prior to 2015, adoption ended all pre-existing links with the biological family and created new ones with the adoptive family. However, the 2015 laws raise the new possibility of 'open adoption'. According to the legislation, the best interest of the child and respect for their rights must be prioritised and must take precedence over the wishes of the prospective adoptive parents in any case of conflict. The child's participation is one way to ensure this. Children aged 12 or over (and younger if considered sufficiently mature) must consent to adoption, and to obtain that consent, the child must be heard. However, the processes for ensuring that children are fully informed have sometimes proved to be weak (Balsell et al, 2017), and while children must be heard, their opinion is not binding. Although open adoption is now possible, there are few cases to date where this has been agreed by the courts. In part, this is because, in most cases, by the time an adoption order is applied for, there are no longer links of any significance between the parent(s) and the child.

Children in care in Spain and adoption from care: numbers and profiles

The Observatory of Infancy, associated with the Ministry of Health, Social Services and Equality, provides data and has published 21 'Bulletins of statistics of child protection' to date, in which data about the number of adoptions in Spain from 2010 onwards can be found (Bulletin no. 13[6]). Table 10.1 shows that rates in public out-of-home care (377 per 100,000 in 2015 and 426 per 100,000 in 2017) are going up but still low compared to most European countries. Also of note is that a considerably higher proportion is in kinship foster care than in most 'high-income' countries. Figures for 2017 show that around 40 per cent were in residential care provision and around 30 per cent were in foster family care. What is strikingly different from most of the countries described in this volume is the high proportion of foster care placements that are kinship foster placements (around 70 per cent of foster care placements and 35 per cent of all placements in care), with only around 20 per cent of all in-care placements with non-related foster carers. This comes as no surprise since Spain is a 'familist' country where the 'blood tie' is given importance. Relatives tend to stay closely connected and feel that they are bound to take care of a child that 'belongs' to the family. Therefore, for the CPS, it is a priority to place the child with relatives. This is relevant to the understanding of adoptions from care in Spain since, as with most countries in Europe but unlike the US, adoption by kin (other than by step-parents) is unusual.

Foster care in Spain has not had as high a profile in political and professional thinking as in some other countries, and awareness and knowledge about the need for family placement is still not widespread in the general population. For example, in contrast to the position in most Western countries, there is no funding to support foster families, which greatly discourages this alternative to residential care, and it is not an important part of the culture and training of children's services professionals.

Table 10.1: Numbers and rates per 100,000 children (from 0 to 17 years old) in public out-of-home care and placements in care in Spain

		2010	2015	2016	2017	2018
Children adopted from care	Numbers	793	553	588	680	639
	Rate	10.2	6.8	7.1	8.2	7.7
Children in care at year end (number and rate per 100,000 children)			30,677 (377)	31,913	34,744 (426)	
In residential care/care centre[a] (number and % of all in care)			13,596 (40%)		17,527 (44%)	
In kinship foster care (number and % of all in care)			12,851 (38%)		12,748 (35%)	
In non-relative foster care (number and % of all in care)			7,321 (22%)		6,256 (17%)	

Note: [a] The totals for placements are slightly higher than for those in care as a small number under assessment are included.

Source: Boletín de datos estadísticos de medidas de protección a la infancia. Bulletin number 20. Report, Studies and Research 2018. Ministerio de Derechos Sociales y Agenda 2030 (last updated June 2020). Available at: https://observatoriodelainfancia.vpsocial.gob.es/productos/pdf/Boletin_Proteccion_21_Accesible.pdf (accessed 16 December 2020)

Research teams in Spain are internationally recognised in the field of adoption. (on the dynamics of the adoptive family, see, for example, Palacios and Sanchez-Sandova, 2006). Studies on the effects that the adoption process has had on children from the physical point of view are those of Oliván (2007), Truchis and Focaud (2010) and Callejón-Poo et al (2012), while León et al (2018) study adoptive parents' health. However, Castón Boyer and Ocón Domingo (2002) comments that there is a shortage of research that explores the 'phenomenon' of adoption and its relationship and location in past and present Spanish society (what some authors refer to as the sociology of Spanish adoption). With respect to residential care, del Valle et al (2008) have reported on long-term outcomes and del Valle and Bravo (2013) report on a comparative study of child placement alternatives. Until fairly recently, there has been little outcome research on foster care, but an important exception is the study of transitions to adulthood from kinship foster care of del Valle et al (2011). Through the 2015 legislation, the Autonomous Community of Madrid leads the way in allowing researcher access to adoption files, and this increased openness is an important step in facilitating research on child welfare decision-making and practice.

Table 10.1 shows that numbers adopted from care in Spain went down between 2010 and 2011 but then remained broadly constant at a rate of less than 1 per 100,000 children. The data show no differences with respect to sex and that, usually, 50 per cent of the total adoptions in a year are of children aged under three years, 35 per cent are aged between four and ten years, and the others are aged from 11 to 17 years. Finally, we should note that the CPS reports substantial difficulties in placing for adoption children with disabilities or sibling groups (Ferrandis Torres, 2018). In the Community of Madrid, with an approximate population of 6.5 million inhabitants and about 60,000 births per year, during the last decade, the number of babies placed for adoption was around 40 and went down from 46 in 2013 to 39 in 2017 (Ferrandis Torres, 2017).

The position and perceptions of adoption from care in Spain

From Law 21/1987 onwards, the legalisation of adoption was entrusted solely to public bodies, with the overarching proviso that adoption should be a measure not to be used frequently due to its drastic nature in definitively extinguishing ties with the family of origin. As far as possible, the CPS should provide support for families so that they can assume their responsibilities, and intervention from public services should end when family members resume full care and protection responsibilities (Ferrandis Torres, 2017).

In Spain, numbers available for inter-country adoptions have progressively reduced, as occurred in all Western countries (Selman, 2018). The abandonment of babies solely as a result of poverty or the social stigma of extramarital childbirth no longer occurs, and the focus of the protection system has moved towards finding families for children with special needs who do not meet the traditional expectation of 'a healthy baby as young as possible'. These children may have physical or cognitive disabilities, have psychological or behavioural problems, be part of a sibling group, be aged over eight years, or be from a minority ethnic group or immigrant family. Another point to note is that numbers in care who are available for adoption in Spain are likely to be lower than in some other countries, in part, because of fairly low numbers in care and also because of the lower frequency of non-relative foster carers who might apply to adopt the children placed with them.

In contrast to foster care, adoption began to have visibility among the general population because of the increase in international adoptions over the last decade of the century, which had risen to 5,423 in 2005 (see Table 10.2). This is relevant to adoptions from care in Spain since the difficult process of adopting young Spanish children (Rodriguez Jaume, 2015) influenced the start of international adoption. International adoption in Spain started late in comparison to neighbouring European countries, though it had greater intensity once it started. The number of international adoptions dropped by 85 per cent between 2005 and 2015, and international adoption agencies predict that such adoptions will tend to disappear (*El Mundo*, 2018). In part, this is because social development in origin countries includes greater protection for homeless minors. Most of the children now available from overseas for adoption in Spain are in sibling groups or have special medical or psychological needs (*Adoptantis*, 2011).

With respect to the perception of citizens, little by little, adoption has moved from its status as a private and stigmatised event – to which little importance was attached from the perspective of society and where adoptive families considered themselves as an 'inferior category' for not having their own children (Castón Boyer and Ocón Domingo, 2002) – to become a phenomenon with high social acceptance. Adopters have become respected and perceived as 'generous' people, in large part, because of the rise in international adoption. Data about numbers of international adoptions are rudimentary but we can find reference to 2005 in Bulletin no. 13 (see Table 10.2).

Conclusion

We anticipate that adoptions from care in Spain will follow a similar pattern as in the past, where most adoptions are of children under three years old and numbers will remain fairly low. Furthermore, most of them were requests for adoption from the mother at the time of her delivery at the hospital. Among these cases of newborns, there are very few in which the initial protection measure is adoption, and these are

Table 10.2: Number of international adoptions and rate per 100,000 children aged 0–17

		2005	2010	2015	2018
International adoptions	Numbers	5,423	2,891	799	444
	Rate per 100,000	71.02	35.53	9.6	5.4

Source: Boletín de datos estadísticos de medidas de protección a la infancia. Bulletin number 20. Ministerio de Derechos Sociales y Agenda 2030 (last updated January 2019). Available at: https://observatoriodelainfancia.vpsocial.gob.es/productos/pdf/Boletin_20_DEFINITIVO.pdf (accessed 16 December 2020)

mainly related to parental drug abuse or neglect of the child. For older children, the usual path is to have another child protection measure, including foster care or in a childcare centre.

Those children considered to be 'hard to place' (as listed earlier) will continue to have special difficulty in finding a family, either for adoption or foster care. According to the Division for Adoption and Fostering, the urgent task is to more fully develop the potential of foster family care alongside adoption as an alternative to residential care. To do so, it is necessary to explain to the population the nature and purpose of foster family care and, if not incentivising economically, at least covering the expenses generated by the foster child as a member of the family.

Progress in child protection has been very considerable in just 19 years (from 1996 to 2015). In fact, the last two laws of 2015 have undoubtedly pushed the child protection system in the right direction. The number of adoptions from care has remained relatively low since public bodies have not considered that it is an appropriate measure for 'most' of the children because it results in breaking all ties with the biological parents.

The adoption process is inextricably linked to the child's best interests, according to laws, and procedural and training manuals. However, there is still a way for finding methods to standardise the application of this principle and how it is applied in practice. Importantly, although the adoption process begins as soon as possible once the 'abandonment' is declared, and the child will often be placed in their prospective family at the beginning of the process, it takes at least two years to complete the adoption in order to allow time for parents to appeal.

The adoption process has evolved over the years, with different reviews of the 1996 law that strengthen the guarantees for all the parties. In this evolution, since 2015, an entirely new chapter is opened up by the possibility of open adoptions. It has been shown that foster children show higher levels of mental health when compared to those who are adopted (Ferrandis Torres, 2017). Knowing where you come from, and what has influenced your eye colour, height, hair colour, preferences and phobias, definitely contributes to a healthy construction of identity. Open adoptions are so recent that we still need a few years to corroborate if this measure contributes to the best interest of the child or not. Undoubtedly, the way travelled has been long and policymakers and practitioners continue to aim to improve the understanding and implementation of the best interest of children in all the cases that affect them, including, of course, in matters of adoption.

Notes

[1] See: http://gestiona.madrid.org/wleg_pub/secure/normativas/contenidoNormativa.jsf?opcion=VerHtml&idnorma=484&word=S&wordperfect=N&pdf=S#no-back-button
[2] See: https://elderecho.com/privacion-de-la-patria-potestad-procedimiento-y-competencia
[3] This is a norm with the rank of law, emanating from the executive branch (government or administration), without having prior authorisation from a Congress or Parliament. It is dictated for reasons of urgency that prevent, for example, obtaining authorisation by the legislative branch or the enactment of a law itself.
[4] See: www.comunidad.madrid/servicios/asuntos-sociales/adopcion
[5] See: www.comunidad.madrid/servicios/asuntos-sociales/adopcion
[6] See: www.bienestaryproteccioninfantil.es/imagenes/tablaContenidos03SubSec/Medidas%20Proteccion%20Infancia%20%20Bolet%C3%ADn%2013.pdf

References

Adoptantis (2011) 'El periódico de la adopción' ['The adoption newspaper'], Madrid, *Adoptantis*, no. 90.

Balsell, M.A., Fuentes, N. and Pastor, C. (2017) 'Listening the voices of children in decision-making: a challenge for the child protection system in Spain', *Children and Youth Services Review*, 79: 418–25.

Callejo, C. (2017) 'Análisis de la reforma de la adopción tras la Ley 26/2015, de 28 de julio, de modificación del sistema de protección a la infancia y a la adolescencia' ['Analysis of the adoption reform after Law 26/2015, of July 28, on the modification of the protection system for children and adolescents'], in A. Berrocal and C. Callejo (eds) *La protección jurídica de la infancia y la adolescencia tras la Ley Orgánica 8/2015, de 22 de julio y la Ley 26/2015 de 28 de juli* [*The Legal Protection of Childhood and Adolescence after Organic Law 8/2015, of July 22 and Law 26/2015 of July 28*], Spain: Ministry of Health, Consumption and Social Welfare, pp 323–418. Available at: www.mscbs.gob.es/ssi/familiasInfancia/Infancia/pdf/Ley_26_2015_INGLES.pdf (accessed 16 December 2020).

Callejón-Poo, L., Boix, C. and Lopez-Sala, R. (2012) 'Perfil neuropsicológico de niños adoptados en internacionalmente en Cataluña' ['Neuropsychological profile of internationally adopted children in Catalonia'], *Anales de Pediatría*, 76(1): 23–9.

Castón Boyer, P. and Ocón Domingo, J.O. (2002)). 'Historia y Sociología de la adopción en España' ['History and sociology of adoption in Spain'], *Revista Internacional de Sociología*, 60(33): 173–89.

Del Valle, J. and Bravo, A. (2013) 'Current trends, figures and challenges in out of home care: an international comparative analysis', *Psychosocial Intervention*, 22: 251–7.

Del Valle, J., Bravo, A., Alvarez, E. and Fernanz A. (2008) 'Adult self-sufficiency and social adjustment in care leavers from children's homes: a long-term assessment', *Child and Family Social Work*, 13(1): 12–22.

Del Valle, J., Lazaro-Visa, S. and Lopez, M. (2011) 'Leaving family care: transitions to adulthood from kinship care', *Children and Youth Service Review*, 33(12): 2475–81.

El Mundo (2018) 'Las adopciones internacionales caen un 85%' ['International adoptions drop 85%']. Available at: www.elmundo. es/sociedad/2017/02/19/58a7518fca47416c048b45e0.html (accessed 26 June 2020).

Ferrandis Torres, A. (2017) 'Thirty years since the adoption reform', *Revista Clínica Contemporánea*, 8: 1–12.

Ferrandis Torres, A. (2018) 'Una introducción a la situación actual y perspectivas de la adopción en la Comunidad de Madrid' ['An introduction to the current situation and prospects for adoption in the Community of Madrid'], in J.L. Pedreira (ed) Adopción y Psicopatología [Adoption and Psychopathology], *Monografías de Psiquiatría*, 20(2): 14–20.

León, E., Steele, M., Palacios, J., Román, M. and Moreno, C. (2018) 'Parenting adoptive children: reflective functioning and parent–child interactions. A comparative, relational and predictive study', *Children and Youth Services Review*, 95: 352–60.

Ministry of Health, Social Services and Equality (2017) 'Statistical data bulletin of protection measures to childhood, number 18. Data 2015'. Available at: https://observatoriodelainfancia.vpsocial.gob. es/productos/pdf/Boletin_18_Medidas_impuestas_a_menores_ infractores_accesible.pdf

Moreno Torres, J. (2015) *Modificación del Sistema de Protección a la infancia y a la adolescencia. Guia para profesionales y agentes sociales* [*Modification of the Child and Adolescent Protection System. Guide for Professionals and Social Agents*], Málaga: Save the Children.

Observatory for Childhood (2017) 'Statistical data bulletin on child protection measures. Bulletin number 19' ['Boletín de datos estadísticos de medidas de protección a la infancia. Boletín número 19'], Data 2016. Reports, Studies and Research 2017 [Informes, Estudios e Investigación 2017], Madrid: Ministry of Health, Social Services and Equality [Ministerio de Sanidad, Servicios Sociales e Igualdad]. Retrieved from: www.mscbs.gob.es/ssi/familiasInfancia/ Infancia/pdf/Boletinproteccion19accesible2016.pdf

Oliván, G. (2007) 'Adopción en China de niños con necesidades especiales: el "pasaje verde"' ['Adoption in China of children with special needs: the "green passage"'], *Anales de Pediatría*, 67(4): 374–7.

Palacios, J. and Sanchez-Sandova, Y. (2006) 'Stress in parents of adopted children', *International Journal of Behavioural Development*, 30(6): 481–7.

Rodriguez Jaume, M.J. (2015) 'La construcción ideológica y social del fenómeno de las adopciones: avances y retos para una sociología de las adopciones' ['The ideological and social construction of the phenomenon of adoptions: advances and challenges for a sociology of adoptions'], *Política y Sociedad*, 52(2): 509–37.

Selman, P. (2018) 'Global statistics for intercountry adoption: receiving states and states of origin 2004–2017'. Available at: https://assets.hcch. net/docs/a8fe9f19-23e6-40c2-855e-388e112bf1f5.pdf

Truchis, A. and Focaud, P. (2010) 'Atención pediátrica de un niño adoptado' ['Paediatric care of an adopted child'], *EMC-Pediatría*, 45(3): 1–12.

PART III

Human rights platform and ways of belonging

11

International human rights law governing national adoption from care

Katre Luhamaa and Conor O'Mahony

Introduction

Although adoption is primarily regulated at the level of national law, it has become the subject of an increasing volume of international law and practice with which national laws are required to comply. Articles 20 and 21 of the 1989 Convention on the Rights of the Child (CRC) set general standards that must be adhered to in national and international adoptions, and these general standards are developed in more detail in a number of other international treaties, policy and supervisory instruments. Of these, Article 8 of the European Convention of Human Rights (ECHR) has generated a substantial body of adoption-related case law, while dedicated provision for adoption is made in the 1968 European Convention on the Adoption of Children (ECAC) and the 2008 European Convention on the Adoption of Children (Revised) (ECAC (Rev)). In addition, specific provision for inter-country adoptions is made by the 1965 Hague Convention on Protection of Children and Co-operation in Respect of Intercountry Adoption (Hague Convention).

The purpose of this chapter is to examine the international law standards governing adoption that the countries examined in this book have committed to, and to extract the key principles and themes from those standards. In line with the theme of the book, the analysis will focus on the issue of adoptions from care. The international standards governing this specific issue have received limited attention in the literature to date. International, inter-country or transnational adoptions have received some attention (for example, Covell and Snow, 2006; Chou and Browne, 2008; Vité and Boéchat, 2008; Lowe, 2009; O'Halloran, 2015a, 2018), with some of the discussion focusing on the position of the child and their rights in this process (Barrozo,

2010; Bartholet, 2010). The adoption requirements of Article 8 of the ECHR and its connection to the ECAC (Rev) have also been discussed (albeit often in passing) in the general international scholarship dealing with the right to respect for family life (Kilkelly, 2015, 2017; Pascual and Pérez, 2016) or the child's right to family life, as protected by the European Court of Human Rights (ECtHR) (O'Halloran, 2015b; Skivenes and Søvig, 2016; Breen et al, 2020).

However, to date, a comprehensive analysis of the combined effect of the various international provisions in the specific context of adoptions from care has not been provided. This chapter will fill that gap by asking: what are the international law standards that bind the countries featuring in this book (see Table 11.1) when making decisions to place children for adoption without parental consent? To answer this question, the various international instruments of relevance to adoption will first be introduced. This will be followed by a thematic analysis of key issues that feature in the international law provisions.

The analysis utilises the doctrinal legal method (for example, Kilcommins, 2016) to international human rights law, where the focus is on systematisation and legal interpretation of existing legal norms, with the aim of finding out the precise obligations deriving from these norms. Thus, the research focuses on the primary norms of the relevant treaties, as well as the interpretive practice of the treaties' supervisory bodies (the CRC Committee and ECtHR). Such an approach is in its nature conservative and backward-looking, and the norms defined should be seen as minimum core obligations (Young, 2008) that limit the legislative discretion of the state, as well as guide the implementation of national legislation. The discussion encompasses both the substantive

Table 11.1: Entry into force year of the conventions for the different states

Country	CRC	Hague Convention	ECHR	ECAC
Austria	1992	1999	1958	1980
Estonia	1991	2002	1996	–
Finland	1991	1997	1990	ECAC (Rev), 2012
Germany	1992	2002	1953	ECAC (Rev), 2015
Ireland	1992	2010	1953	1968
Norway	1991	1998	1953	ECAC (Rev), 2011
Spain	1990	1995	1979	ECAC (Rev), 2011
UK	1991	2003	1953	1968
US	1995[a]	2008	–	–

Note: [a] Signature only

and procedural requirements of adoptions. Exhaustive treatment of all international human rights norms related to adoption is beyond the scope of this chapter, and other themes that have featured in the source material, such as the issue of parental eligibility to adopt, have been omitted due to space constraints.

Two key themes emerge: the manner in which the law has treated the best interests principle; and the right of the child to express their views during the decision-making process. Other issues to be considered include the requirements relating to the institutional system for adoption, adoption procedure and protection for the child's right to identity.

Key international law provisions

At the outset, it should be clarified that the international law provisions discussed in this chapter are binding on the countries that subscribe to them as a matter of international law (Rehman, 2003). The position on whether those standards have been incorporated into national law and can be directly enforced in a national court varies from one jurisdiction to another, and, indeed, different international law conventions may have a different status even within a single jurisdiction. However, regardless of the level of domestic incorporation of the international law standards in a given state, it remains the case that states are legally committed to comply with international law conventions that they have signed and ratified, and to make any necessary changes to domestic law, policy and practice (for example, Article 4 CRC; Article 1 ECHR).

Non-compliance with a state's international law obligations may result in various consequences, such as a judgment of the ECtHR (for example, Strand Lobben v Norway [2019]) or critical concluding observations by the CRC Committee (for example, CRC Committee, 2010: para 29; 2017: para 51). It should be noted that the international monitoring bodies afford significant discretion to national authorities as to how the rights set down in international instruments are to be protected in national law and practice; however, nonetheless, judgments of the ECtHR are binding on the state party to which they are addressed, and execution of the judgment is monitored by the Committee of Ministers of the Council of Europe. Similarly, the CRC Committee expects that its recommendations will be complied with in substance, even if there is a degree of flexibility regarding the means by which this is to be achieved.

In the context of the current book, all of the countries considered have signed and ratified the CRC (apart from the US, which has signed but not ratified it). The eight European countries are parties to the ECHR, while seven of the countries are parties to either the ECAC or the ECAC (Rev). The ECtHR has held that state obligations under Article 8 of the ECHR relating to adoption must be interpreted in the light of these conventions (Pini et al v Romania [2004]). This holds even for those European countries that are not parties to the ECAC (Rev) (AK and L v Croatia [2013]). Thus, with the sole exception of the US, the standards outlined in this chapter are legally binding on the countries under consideration and domestic law and practice is required to comply with them.

The Hague Convention is an inter-country adoption standard for all its states parties. The ECtHR uses the Hague Convention as an interpretive aid in inter-country adoption cases (for example, Paradiso and Campanelli v Italy [GC] [2017]; Pini et al v Romania [2004]). Similarly, the CRC Committee has pointed out the importance of ratifying the Hague Convention in relation to all of the eight states, and has stressed that states should refrain from adopting children to or from countries that have not ratified the Hague Convention (for example, CRC Committee, 2010: para 45).

Convention on the Rights of the Child

The CRC, together with the supervisory practice and general interpretations of the CRC Committee (Oette, 2018), is a general frame of reference for children's rights both for states parties and for other international human rights instruments, including the interpretation of the ECHR (Kilkelly, 2015). The CRC Committee has identified the following provisions as encapsulating the 'general principles' of the CRC: non-discrimination (Article 2); the best interests of the child (Article 3(1)); the child's right to life, survival and development (Article 6); and the child's right to express the views in matters that affect the child (Article 12) (CRC Committee, 2003a).

In addition to these general principles, the CRC has two provisions that include specific individuals' rights or state obligations in the area of adoption. Article 20 provides that the state has an obligation to provide special protection and assistance for children temporarily or permanently deprived of their family environment. Article 20(3) provides:

> Such care could include, inter alia, foster placement, kafalah of Islamic law, adoption or if necessary placement in suitable institutions for the care of children. When considering solutions, due regard shall be paid to the desirability of

continuity in a child's upbringing and to the child's ethnic, religious, cultural and linguistic background.

The list of possible alternatives in this provision is not exhaustive, and it should be seen as at least partially hierarchical, giving preference to the kinship placement and other types of family-based care before any placement in an institution (UN General Assembly, 2019; Cantwell and Holzscheiter, 2007; Hodgkin and Newell, 2007). This view has also been stressed by the CRC Committee, which has discouraged the placement of children in institutional care and prefers family-based care settings (CRC Committee, 2017: para 37).

Article 21 provides both a general standard for all adoptions (para a) and specific requirements for inter-country adoptions (paras b–e):[1]

> States Parties that recognise and/or permit the system of adoption shall ensure that the best interests of the child shall be the paramount consideration and they shall:
>
> (a) Ensure that the adoption of a child is authorized only by competent authorities who determine, in accordance with applicable law and procedures and on the basis of all pertinent and reliable information, that the adoption is permissible in view of the child's status concerning parents, relatives and legal guardians and that, if required, the persons concerned have given their informed consent to the adoption on the basis of such counselling as may be necessary.

Thus, Article 21(a) emphasises the centrality of the best interests principle in adoption cases – describing it as 'the paramount consideration', in contrast with Article 3, which states that the best interests principle is 'a primary consideration' – and further stipulates both institutional and procedural requirements. These issues will be examined further in the following.

Hague Convention

The Hague Convention aims 'to establish safeguards to ensure that intercountry adoptions take place in the best interests of the child and with respect for his or her fundamental rights as recognised in international law' (Article 1(a)). From the countries included in the current book, eight receive children adopted from third countries and Estonia is the only country that allows inter-country adoption of children in care from Estonia to a limited number of other countries. The regulation of inter-country adoptions is not the focus of the current chapter, but it is shown elsewhere in the book (for example, in the chapter on Estonia) that international adoptions from care can give rise to important dilemmas in some countries. The standard used in the Hague Convention follows the requirements of the CRC, in particular, the Hague Convention stresses that the best interests principle is the main guiding principle for inter-country adoptions, together with the protection of the fundamental rights of the child (presumably including those protected by the CRC).

European Convention on the Adoption of Children

The 1968 ECAC and the 2008 ECAC (Rev) aim to unify some common principles and standards as international benchmarks for all states and state institutions included in the process. The principles underpinning both conventions are broadly similar to those espoused in the CRC (Shannon et al, 2013); for example, the ECAC (Rev) states in Article 4 that '[t]he competent authority shall not grant an adoption unless it is satisfied that the adoption will be in the best interests of the child'. However, the ECAC (Rev) goes somewhat further than other instruments on the question of child participation (Burns et al, 2019), providing that adoption should not be granted by the competent authority without 'the consent of the child considered by law as having sufficient understanding', and that a child is considered as having sufficient understanding on attaining an age that is prescribed by law and should not be more than 14 years (Article 5). Children not deemed to have sufficient understanding should, 'as far as possible, be consulted' and their 'views and wishes' taken into account having regard to their degree of maturity (Article 6).

European Convention on Human Rights

Although the ECHR does not contain dedicated provisions on the issue of adoption, a substantial body of case law on adoption, and especially adoptions from care, has developed in relation to the right to respect for family life under Article 8:

> 1. Everyone has the right to respect for his private and family life ...
> 2. There shall be no interference by a public authority with the exercise of this right except such as is in accordance

with the law and is necessary in a democratic society in the interests of national security, public safety or the economic well-being of the country, for the prevention of disorder or crime, for the protection of health or morals, or for the protection of the rights and freedoms of others.

Analysis of Article 8 practice shows that the focus of the ECtHR to date has been not on the rights of the child, but on the rights of the biological parents (Breen et al, 2020; Kilkelly, 2017), and where the right to respect for family life has been established, the state has an obligation to protect it, including through positive measures (see, for example, Kilkelly, 2010). Nevertheless, the parents' (or other adults') right to respect for family life may be overridden by the child's best interests, which might require prioritising the child's existing or emerging bonds with their non-biological family (see, for example, Kilkelly, 2017: 159–163; see also ECtHR, 2019: paras 299–308).

The ECtHR has established that the relations between an adoptive parent and an adopted child are, as a rule, protected by Article 8 (Kurochkin v Ukraine [2010]; Ageyevy v Russia [2013]). Thus, a lawful and genuine adoption may constitute family life, even in the absence of cohabitation or any real ties between an adopted child and the adoptive parents (for example, Topčić-Rosenberg v Croatia [2013], para 38).

Key themes and principles

Systematic analysis of the key human rights norms cited earlier reveals two central themes: the manner in which the law treats the best interests principle; and the right of the child to express their views during the adoption decision-making process. International human rights law also guides the organisation and procedure of adoption, as well as protection for the child's right to identity.

Best interests of the child

All the instruments stress the importance of the best interests principle in adoption decisions. Under Article 21 of the CRC (cf Article 4(1) ECAC (Rev)), the best interests of the child must be the 'paramount consideration' in adoption cases. The legal requirements deriving from this provision are specified in General Comment no 14, where the CRC Committee (2013: para 36) stressed that the word 'shall' places a strong legal obligation on states and means that states do not have discretion as to whether children's best interests are to be assessed.

Thus, the best interests cannot be one among several considerations; rather, it should guide the whole adoption process and be the primary driver of the adoption (Strand Lobben v Norway [2019], para 204).

Article 21 of the CRC goes further than Article 3(1), and strengthens the implementation of the best interests principle in adoption as it is not simply to be 'a primary consideration' (as in Article 3(1)), but 'the paramount consideration'. The CRC Committee (2013: para 38) has gone even further and required that the best interest of the child is the determining factor when making decisions on adoption (see also Vité and Boéchat, 2008: paras 42–58). A uniform process is necessary to determine what is the best interest of the child (CRC Committee, 2010: paras 27–8). This principle is relevant for both national and inter-country adoptions, though ensuring it in relation to states that have not ratified the Hague Convention might prove problematic (CRC Committee, 2012: paras 42–3).

Likewise, the ECtHR has emphasised that the best interests of the child may override the rights of the parent in the cases of adoption (for example, Pini et al v Romania [2004]). However, the Grand Chamber of the ECtHR recently emphasised in Strand Lobben v Norway ([2019], paras 220, 225) that adoption decisions cannot solely focus on the best interests of the child; rather, adoption from care should be a 'last resort' measure and the child's interests must be combined with those of the parent(s), with a genuine balancing exercise being conducted between the two. Thus, adoption against the wishes of the biological parents should only occur in exceptional circumstances and should be justified by an overriding requirement pertaining to the child's best interests (see, for example, Ageyevy v Russia [2013], para 144; see also Kilkelly, 2017). Since adoption orders are irreversible, 'there is an even greater call than usual for protection against arbitrary interferences' and they 'must be subject to the closest scrutiny' (YC v the United Kingdom [2012], paras 136–7; see also Burns et al, 2019). The best interests of the child cannot be the only or central consideration for an adoption judgment; it is of most use when balancing different rights and interests.

The underlying presumption of the CRC is that children's best interests are served by being with their parents wherever possible (Articles 7 and 9) and that their parents have 'primary responsibility' for their upbringing. Adoptions from care are permissible only if parents are unwilling or are deemed by judicial process to be unable to discharge this responsibility; any legislation that permits adoptions under less stringent conditions would probably amount to a breach of both children's and parents' rights under the CRC (cf Council of Europe and PACE, 2018).

The best interests of the child principle includes a number of practical considerations. It requires that the decision-maker takes into account the child's relations and attachment, and the lack of relation or attachment to birth parents can support an adoption order (Breen et al, 2020). States would violate their obligations in cases where their conduct is responsible for the breakdown of the relationship between the child and the parent (for example, EP v Italy [1999]; Pedersen v Norway [2020]). However, when a considerable amount of time has passed since the child was taken into care, the interests of the child not to have their de facto family changed again may override the interests of the parents to have the family reunified (for example, K and T v Finland [2001], para 155; R and H v United Kingdom [2011], paras 82–9).

Several judgments have found adoption orders to be justified, including: where there was a loss of attachment with parents, when the child was particularly vulnerable, and the parents were unable to care for the child (for example, Aune v Norway [2010]; Mohamed Hasan v Norway [2018]); and where the parents were unable to care for children even after appropriate efforts were made by the authorities to provide support (for example, SS v Slovenia [2018]). While adoption terminates all de jure parental ties between the child and the biological parents, the ECtHR has commented positively on cases where the contact was retained after adoption (Aune v Norway [2010]; SS v Slovenia [2018]). In Pedersen v Norway ([2020], para 70), the ECtHR went further and noted that such contact should create a meaningful relationship. The ECtHR was unclear whether post-adoption contact should become a mainstream (cf Burns et al, 2019).

The ECtHR has found violations of Article 8 due to, for example: the initial care order being found unjustified (RMS v Spain [2013]); a failure to take account of changes in circumstances (Strand Lobben v Norway [GC] [2019]); and a failure to commission expert reports or to take adequate account of reports that were commissioned (SH v Italy, [2015]; Strand Lobben v Norway [GC] [2019]). However, when the ECtHR establishes a violation, this does not mean that the biological relationship has to be re-established as the child's bests interests also require stability and attention to the attachment of the child (Johansen v Norway [II] [2002]).

Child's views and consent for adoption

According to Article 12 of the CRC, the child's views, together with the best interests of the child, should be at the centre of the adoption proceedings. It is both a procedural obligation of the states and a substantive requirement – the child must be heard and must have their opinions taken into account having due regard to their degree of maturity as far as possible. The CRC Committee has linked these two concepts and stressed, for example, in General Comment no 12, that '[i]n decisions on adoption, kafalah or other placement, the "best interests" of the child cannot be defined without consideration of the child's views' (CRC Committee, 2009: para 56).

The same emphasis on child participation in involuntary adoption cases is not evident in ECHR case law. Breen et al (2020) noted that the incorporation of the child's views of what is in their best interests is lacking in much of the ECtHR adoption-related jurisprudence, as is any independent representation for the child in such ECtHR proceedings. This potential oversight reflects broader questions about the application of children's rights and their exercise by children themselves. These questions are important because in many national child protection laws, the opinion of the child is an essential component for defining the child's best interests (Skivenes and Sørsdal, 2018), a point that underpins the views of the CRC Committee (2013) as developed in its General Comment no 14 on the interpretation of the child's best interests principle.

The approach seen in the majority of the adoption cases can be contrasted with that taken in Pini et al v Romania (2004), where the ECtHR considered that the interests of two girls, who had consistently objected to their adoption by an Italian couple, should prevail over the interests of the prospective adoptive parents to create a new family with the children. The ECtHR stated that placement decisions should take into account the child's views as emotional ties cannot be created against the will of the child (para 153 et seq). This approach to incorporating the views of the child into the decision-making process is in line with the emerging approach in ECtHR judgments in other areas of child and family law (see, for example, M and M v Croatia [2015]).

Institutional and procedural requirements

Implementing the CRC requires both institutional and legal measures as Article 21 of the CRC requires that the adoption of a child is permissible only when authorised by 'competent authorities'. Neither the CRC nor the ECHR requires a specific type of institutional system, but they do stress that adoptions require inclusion of multidisciplinary services competent in child protection, which are subject to accreditation and periodic inspection by competent national authorities (Vité and Boéchat, 2008: paras 63, 110). Decisions related to adoptions must be made by bodies that have diverse and complementary professions and experiences at their disposal (Vité and Boéchat, 2008: paras 63–4). At the same time, such an institutional system should guarantee a uniform interpretation and implementation of the rights of the child in the adoption proceedings; the CRC Committee has been concerned when there have been persisting local differences and a lack of a uniform process to determine what constitutes the best interests of the child in adoption proceedings (CRC Committee, 2010: para 27).

States are free to set out their own adoption procedure, provided that it includes a formal institutional framework and guarantees the rights of all the parties (including the child, the biological parents and the adoptive parents). Thus, adoptions can only be decided by the appropriate institutions following applicable law and procedure. Failure to follow such a procedure can result in unlawfulness of the adoption for the purposes of the ECHR (Paradiso and Campanelli v Italy [GC] [2017], paras 165, 215). Where there is insufficient legislation to protect parental rights, then an adoption decision violates the parent's right to family life (Zhou v Italy [2014]).

Article 10 of the ECAC (Rev) sets forth a list of preliminary inquiries that need to be completed prior to adoption (similarly in the CRC context, see Vité and Boéchat, 2008: para 75). These procedural requirements are aimed at ensuring the suitability of the adoptive parents. A similar point has been made by the CRC Committee, which has stressed the need to: have an effective system for the screening of adoptive parents, including national standards and efficient mechanism to prevent the sale and trafficking of children; review, monitor and follow up the placement of children; and collect statistics on adoptions, including inter-country adoptions (CRC Committee, 2003b: paras 36–7).

Vité and Boéchat (2008: paras 73–4), when summarising the practice of the CRC Committee, point out that state authorities also have to gather sufficient information about the child to be adopted, including their past, present and future. Such information should be detailed and must determine, among other things, 'the child's status concerning parents, relatives and legal guardians' (Vité and Boéchat, 2008: paras 80–4). The ECtHR has similarly held that adoption decisions should be based on updated technical reports prepared by appropriate specialists, detailing the circumstances and needs of the individual child (see, most recently, Strand Lobben v Norway [GC] [2019], para 222 ff).

Involvement of the biological parents within the adoption procedures has been stressed by the ECtHR, focusing on their right to be substantively protected by informing and involving them adequately during the adoption process (see, for example, SS v Slovenia [2018]). In W v United Kingdom ([1987], paras 63–4), the ECtHR stated that:

[t]he relevant considerations to be weighed by a local authority in reaching decisions on children in its care must perforce include the views and interests of the natural parents. The decision-making process must therefore, in the Court's view, be such as to secure that their views and interests are made known to and duly taken into account … what therefore has to be determined is whether, having regard to the particular circumstances of the case and notably the serious nature of the decisions to be taken, the parents have been involved in the decision-making process, seen as a whole, to a degree sufficient to provide them with the requisite protection of their interests. If they have not, there will have been a failure to respect their family life and the interference resulting from the decision will not be capable of being regarded as 'necessary' within the meaning of Article 8.

Inclusion of biological parents in the adoption process in cases where their rights have been limited or removed is another issue that has been discussed by both the CRC Committee and the ECtHR. The CRC Committee has pointed out when national legislation has disadvantaged the situation of children born of unmarried parents, and where there was a lack of an appropriate procedure to name the father in the birth registration of the child. This had adverse impact on the implementation of other rights in relation to adoption, which could take place without the consent of the father (CRC Committee, 1998: para 17). This issue has also generated case law in the ECtHR, which found that permitting adoption of the child without the father's knowledge or consent can constitute an Article 8 violation (Keegan v Ireland [1994]). Finally, the ECtHR has stressed that child protection decision-making must not involve unnecessary delays that make family reunification more unlikely, or amount to a de facto determination of the issue; future relations between parent and child should be determined solely in the light of all relevant considerations and not by the mere passage of time (Strand Lobben v Norway [GC] [2019], para 212).

The child's right to identity

A child's right to know their origins has gained particular importance in the context of adoption. Article 8 of the CRC obliges states to respect the right of the child to preserve their identity, including nationality, name and family relations as recognised by law, without unlawful interference. The CRC Committee has made it clear that adopted children have the right to be told they are adopted and, if they so wish, to know the identity of their biological parents, which implies keeping accurate and accessible records of the adoption (Hodgkin and Newell, 2007: 115, 296).

Similarly, Article 22(3) of the ECAC (Rev) gives the adopted child the right to access information held by the authorities concerning their origins. However, the level of protection seen here is somewhat weaker than in the CRC context; Article 22 also allows states to protect the privacy of parents and give them the right not to disclose their identity as long as the child can receive some information about their origins.

The position under the ECHR follows the ECAC (Rev) and the ECtHR has recognised that 'respect for private life requires that everyone should be able to establish details of their identity as individual human beings and that an individual's entitlement to such information is of importance because of its formative implications for his or her personality' (Mikulić v Croatia [2002]). In the context of adoption, '[b]irth, and in particular the circumstances in which a child is born, forms part of a child's, and subsequently the adult's, private life guaranteed by Article 8' (Odièvre v France [GC] [2003]).

At the same time, the ECtHR accepted in the Odièvre case that the right to identity can be balanced against the right to privacy of the parent in certain circumstances, and that laws that protect the privacy of a natural mother who expressly requests that information about the birth remains confidential may fall within a state's margin of appreciation, provided that they seek to strike a balance between the competing interests. In contrast, a violation of Article 8 was found in Godelli v Italy (2012) on the basis that Italian law resulted in the applicant's request for both identifying and non-identifying information being totally and definitively refused, without any balancing of the competing interests.

In cases where a child in care is placed for adoption without the consent of their parents, the issue of identity tracing is less likely to be an issue than in other adoption cases since it is unlikely that the parent would have been afforded a legal guarantee of privacy of the sort seen in the Odièvre case. The process leading up to the placement for adoption would have been documented in the child's social work records, and in Gaskin v United Kingdom (1989), the ECtHR held that a refusal by the authorities to provide the applicant with access to his social work records violated Article 8 as 'persons in the situation of the applicant have a vital interest, protected by the Convention, in receiving the information necessary to know and to understand their childhood and early development'.

Conclusion

As shown earlier, international human rights law establishes a number of important rights and sets down minimum standards to be met by national legal systems. These standards are binding on states that commit to them, and require compliance and implementation in national laws, policies and practices. The requirements of international human rights law cover a range of institutional and procedural issues, as well as substantive rights. In the context of adoptions from care, two themes stand out, namely, the best interests principle and the obligation to allow children the opportunity to express their views. It was noted that the best interests principle could potentially be invoked on either side of these disputes: parents might argue that family reunification is in the best interests of the child (citing Articles 7 and 9 of the CRC in support); while state authorities might argue that adoption by a foster family where the child is settled is in the child's best interests (citing Articles 3 and 21 of the CRC in support).

On the obligation to ascertain the views of the child, it was seen that this is strongly protected in the CRC, and even more so in the ECAC (Rev), which goes so far as to require the consent of older children to adoption. In contrast, the ECHR case law places less emphasis on child participation in adoption decisions. This is most likely a by-product of the fact that applications challenging such decisions are invariably brought by the parents; indeed, it is notable that the ECtHR has stressed the importance of the participation of the parents in the adoption process. The case law here could become more CRC-compliant by placing a greater emphasis on the child's views and independent interests (cf Breen et al, 2020).

To date, little research has been done on the effect of the international human rights legislation in the area of adoption on national legal systems. An interesting topic for future research would be to explore the extent to which these international requirements are considered and included in national legal systems.

Acknowledgements

This project has received funding from the European Research Council under the European Union's Horizon 2020 research and innovation programme (grant agreement No 724460). Disclaimer: This chapter reflects only the authors' views and the funding agency is not responsible for any use that may be made of the information contained therein.

Note

[1] Discussions during the preparation of this provision, as well as reasons for selecting the wording that has been included in Article 21, are discussed in Vite and Boéchat (2008).

References

Barrozo, P. (2010) 'The child as a person', *Global Policy*, 1(2): 228–9.

Bartholet, E. (2010) 'International adoption: the human rights position', *Global Policy*, 1(1): 91–100.

Breen, C., Krutzinna, J., Luhamaa, K. and Skivenes, M. (2020) 'Family life for children in state care. An analysis of the European Court of Human Rights' reasoning on adoption without consent', *International Journal of Children's Rights*, 28: 715–47.

Burns, K., Križ, K., Krutzinna, J., Luhamaa, K., Meysen, T., Pösö, T., Sánchez-Cabezudo, S., Skivenes, M. and Thoburn, J. (2019) 'The hidden proceedings – an analysis of accountability of child protection adoption proceedings in eight European jurisdictions', *European Journal of Comparative Law and Governance*, 6(1): 1–35.

Cantwell, N. and Holzscheiter, A. (2007) *A Commentary on the United Nations Convention on the Rights of the Child, Article 20: Children Deprived of Their Family Environment*, Leiden: Brill.

Chou, S. and Browne, K. (2008) 'The relationship between institutional care and the international adoption of children in Europe', *Adoption and Fostering*, 32(1): 40–8.

Council of Europe and PACE (Parliamentary Assembly of the Council of Europe) (2018) 'Striking a balance between the best interest of the child and the need to keep families together', Resolution 2232 (2018).

Covell, K. and Snow, R. (2006) 'Adoption and the best interests of the child: the dilemma of cultural interpretations', *The International Journal of Children's Rights*, 14(2): 109–17.

CRC Committee (The Committee on the Rights of the Child) (1998) 'Concluding observations: Ireland', CRC/C/15/Add.85.

CRC Committee (2003a) 'General comment no 5. General measures of implementation of the Convention on the Rights of the Child (Arts. 4, 42 and 44, para 6)', CRC/GC/2003/5.

CRC Committee (2003b) 'Concluding observations: Estonia', CRC/C/15/Add.196.

CRC Committee (2009) 'General comment no. 12. The right of the child to be heard (Art. 21, para 56)', CRC/C/GC/12.

CRC Committee (2010) 'Concluding observations: Spain', CRC/C/ESP/CO/3–4.

CRC Committee (2012) 'Concluding observations: Austria', CRC/C/AUT/CO/3–4.

CRC Committee (2013) 'General comment no 14 on the right of the child to have his or her best interests taken as a primary consideration (Art. 3, para 1)', CRC/C/GC/14.

CRC Committee (2017) 'Concluding observations: Estonia', CRC/C/EST/CO/2–4.

ECtHR (European Court of Human Rights) (2019) 'Guide on Article 8 of the Convention – right to respect for private and family life', updated 31 August. Available at: www.echr.coe.int/Documents/Guide_Art_8_ENG.pdf (accessed 19 February 2020).

Hodgkin, R. and Newell, P. (2007) *Implementation Handbook for the Convention on the Rights of the Child* (3rd edn), Geneva: UNICEF.

Kilcommins, S. (2016) 'Doctrinal legal method (black-letterism): assumptions, commitments and shortcomings', in L. Cahillane and J. Schwebbe (eds) *Legal Research Methods: Principles and Practicalities*, Dublin: Clarus Press.

Kilkelly, U. (2010) 'Protecting children's rights under the ECHR: The role of positive obligations', *Northern Ireland Legal Quarterly*, 61(3): 245–61.

Kilkelly, U. (2015) 'The CRC in litigation under the ECHR', in t. Liefaard and J.E. Doek (eds) *Litigating the Rights of the Child*, Dordrecht: Springer Netherlands, pp 193–209.

Kilkelly, U. (2017) *The Child and the European Convention on Human Rights: Second Edition*, London and New York: Routledge.

Lowe (2009) 'A commentary on the United Nations Convention on the Rights of the Child – Article 21 – adoption', *The International Journal of Children's Rights*, 17(2): 344.

Oette, L. (2018) 'The UN human rights treaty bodies: impact and future', in G. Oberleitner (ed) *International Human Rights Institutions, Tribunals, and Courts*, Singapore: Springer, pp 95–115.

O'Halloran, K. (2015a) *The Politics of Adoption: International Perspectives on Law, Policy and Practice. Vol. 41. Ius Gentium: Comparative Perspectives on Law and Justice*, Dordrecht: Springer Netherlands.

O'Halloran, K. (2015b) 'Adoption, the conventions and the impact of the European Court of Human Rights', in K. O'Halloran (ed) *The Politics of Adoption: International Perspectives on Law, Policy and Practice. Ius Gentium: Comparative Perspectives on Law and Justice*, Dordrecht: Springer Netherlands, pp 107–36.

O'Halloran, K. (2018) *Adoption Law and Human Rights: International Perspectives. Human Rights and International Law*, Abingdon: Routledge.

Pascual, M.G. and Pérez, A.T. (2016) *The Right to Family Life in the European Union*, Oxford: Routledge.

Rehman, J. (2003) *International Human Rights Law*, Harlow: Pearson.

Shannon, G., Horgan, R., Keehan, G. and Daly, C. (2013) *Adoption – Law and Practice under the Revised European Convention on the Adoption of Children*, Council of Europe.

Skivenes, M. and Sørsdal, L. (2018) 'The child's best interest principle across child protection jurisdictions', in A. Falch-Eriksen and E. Backe-Hansen (eds) *Human Rights in Child Protection: Implications for Professional Practice and Policy*, Cham: Springer International Publishing, pp 59–88.

Skivenes, M. and Søvig, K.H. (2016) 'Judicial discretion and the child's best interest – the European Court of Human Rights on child protection adoptions', in E. Sutherland and L.-A.B. Macfarlane (eds) *Implementing Article 3 of the United Nations Convention on the Rights of the Child: Best Interests, Welfare and Well-Being*, Cambridge: Cambridge University Press.

UN General Assembly (2019) 'Rights of the child', Resolution 74/133. Available at: https://undocs.org/en/A/RES/74/133 (accessed 16 December 2020).

Vité, S. and Boéchat, H. (2008) *Commentary on the United Nations Convention on the Rights of the Child: Adoption*, Leiden: Brill.

Young, K.G. (2008) 'Minimum core of economic and social rights: a concept in search of content', *Yale Journal of International Law*, 33: 113.

12

Creating 'family' in adoption from care

Jenny Krutzinna

Introduction

Adoption may be defined as 'the legal process through which the state establishes a parental relationship, with all its attendant rights and duties, between a child and a (set of) parent(s) where there exists no previous procreative relationship' (De Wispelaere and Weinstock, 2018: 213). In adoptions from care, state intervention effectively converts an established, or nascent, adult–child relationship into 'family' in the legal sense. From the state's perspective, adoption thus entails the transfer of parental responsibilities for a child in public care to a private family unit, enabling the state to permanently delegate its duties towards a child to this new unit. This seemingly straightforward legal act raises deeper philosophical questions relating to such state 'family creation', particularly when the child's perspective is taken. Such a child-centric approach normatively regards children as equal moral beings, who ought to be included in actions concerning them, regardless of their capacity to form and express an opinion. Accordingly, adoption from care can be described as a *moral* decision, aimed at doing what is in the child's best interests. The purpose of this chapter is to explore a suspicion of a lack of child-centrism in adoption from care practice, and to illustrate how adopted children's rights are inferior to those of their non-adopted peers. This will shed light on a practice currently lacking transparency and accountability (see Burns et al, 2019) and will increase our understanding of how we fail to treat children as equal moral individuals in decision-making that severely impacts children's lives.

The law plays a critical role in adoption as its status-conferring power determines who falls within the state's protective sphere and who is excluded from it. 'Parent' is one example, in that the legal status of parenthood confers upon an individual certain rights and obligations concerning a child. This status may or may not align with the social reality of those involved; 'parent' or 'family' as social constructs may well differ from social life as experienced by children and parents in the non-traditional social kinship network formed by adoption, including birth and adoptive family members.

This chapter attempts to provide some child-centric insights in order to identify relevant ways to improve adoption from care for adopted children. Specifically, the basic premise of adoption, namely, the creation of a stable and permanent family for the child, will be assessed through a child lens. A critique of the current approach to adoption as adult-centric is presented, starting with a reflection on the concept of 'family' in the context of adoption. The next part introduces adoption as a moral decision from the child's perspective. The third part considers adopted children's rights, focusing on the consequences of adoption practice on children's rights. Finally, the challenges discussed in this chapter will be summarised and some moderate suggestions for reform will be proposed.

'Family'

The question of what family is has received much attention, yet no universally accepted definition exists, at least not when crossing contexts or disciplines. Some ask if a definition is even necessary, or if we can ignore the decision of *who* is part of *the* family, as long as we know *what* the characteristics of *a* family are (Ferguson and Brake, 2018: 11–12). One characteristics-based definition describes family as a multigenerational unit consisting of one or more adults, taking primary custodial responsibility for any number of dependent children (Archard, 2010: 9–10), where this unit exists over a substantial period. Temporary foster care as lacking permanence and being contract-based may thus be excluded; however, from a child perspective, placement length does not always predict relationship quality (Andersson, 2009). Many alternative 'family' definitions exist; often focusing on caring function over family form. This form–function binary, while appealing for its simplicity, fails to persuade precisely because of this simplicity: it does not capture the complexities of 'family' (Ferguson and Brake, 2018: 13), which would be necessary for any satisfactory – morally defensible and practically useful – definition of family.

The concept of family is shaped by normative assumptions about personal relationships, which is evident from the tensions between legal and moral parenthood, and the different views on what makes one a parent or a family. The law only recognises 'family' as a legal status relationship in some contexts (such as migration), while requiring a more specific familial relationship in others (such as 'parent') (Ferguson and Brake, 2018: 17). This is relevant in the present context as adoption entails a shift of status attribution, with the consequence that the adopted child receives new (legal) parents. Family is thus not simply a private entity, but a social institution supported by laws. Feminists argue that as a political institution, the family should therefore be subject to principles of justice as the state cannot avoid interference in families, especially given the state's critical interest in children as future citizens (Satz, 2017). In adoptions from care, the state interferes in families in one of the most serious ways by, first, breaking legal (and sometimes social) ties with the family of origin, and then deciding and confirming the child's alternative family. Here, the question arises as to how adopted children themselves construe family and to what extent the law's limited possibilities do justice to their experiences.

In adoption, the basic premise concerning 'family' may best be described as a compromise: birth parents unable to provide (adequate) care for their child are replaced by alternative carers to safeguard the child's welfare. Often, this is the most personally, socially and legally stable option for children (Palacios et al, 2019: 57), and in line with a children's rights emphasis on growing up in a family environment (see the United Nations Convention on the Right of the Child [CRC]). This aim to give a child a new, permanent family through adoption is persuasive, yet creating 'family' by legal deed can, at best, provide the breeding ground for emotional and social family-like bonds. In adoptions from care, this is particularly relevant as the absence of actual abandonment means the substitution of family is only unilateral and requires justification. This compares to full orphans or abandoned children, where the necessity to find alternative carers is obvious. The severity of neglect or maltreatment, and the resulting threat to the child's health (and sometimes life) seen in many child protection cases, provides a justification not only for removal, but also for finding a permanent solution outside of the birth home if the possibility of reunification has legitimately been ruled out.

Ideally, adoption will align the child's experience of de facto with de jure family, where de facto reflects actual bonds and not mere living arrangements. Again, adoption from care is a special case, where the reasons for excluding the birth family entirely from the de jure family are far less clear than in cases of abandoned or anonymously born children. From the child's perspective, social and emotional bonds, lived experience, and identity do not necessarily align with legal relationships, as shown by numerous empirical studies (for an overview, see Blake, 2017). Familial association cannot be forced, whether through the law or otherwise, and in adoption, often fails to fit neatly within the narrow legal notion of 'family'. The law itself is instructive here, in that human rights law recognises the 'right to *respect for* family life' (for example, Art 8 European Convention of Human Rights [ECHR]), rather than a 'right to family' or a 'right to family life', as the latter two are beyond the reach of the law. While the former is nonsensical in that we all have family, at least in the narrow sense of biological kin, the latter would be impossible to enforce if understood as having meaningful and loving relationships with our family members. Indeed, the human rights approach is more modest in *respecting* family life where it already exists or where it is developing, which poses challenges in cases of very young children (Breen et al, 2020). Stability, the law can provide; meaningful family life, not so much.

This is a reminder to view 'family' in adoptions from care from the child's perspective. Adoption should always be 'in the child's best interests' (Art 21 CRC), yet the child seems absent in much of the process. For instance, the beneficence of adoption is typically framed in terms of outcomes compared to children remaining in foster care (Vinnerljung and Hjern, 2011), and by reference to low adoption breakdown rates in countries such as England and Wales (Wijedasa and Selwyn, 2017) as a sign of success in providing stability.[1] This emphasis on 'hard' empirical data, however, only expresses one aspect of adoption, albeit an important one. The experience of those affected most by adoption from care – children and adult adoptees – is rarely considered adequately. Featherstone and colleagues (2018: 22) caution that while 'adoption may meet the needs of a particular calculative logic, it must be questioned from a perspective that considers ethical and human rights considerations for all concerned, including [the child] herself'. This has also been highlighted by many in the adult adoptee community, which, through the new possibilities of social media, has been given a voice that speaks from experience, for instance, via the hashtag #AdultAdoptee. The popularity of Nancy Verrier's (2009) *The Primal Wound* among adoptees demonstrates the desperation of adoptees to be seen, and for adoption to be understood from their perspective. In what has been described as 'the adoptee's bible', Verrier (2009: 10) writes:

> What the general population considers to be a concept, a social solution for the care of children who cannot or will not be taken care of by their biological parents, is really a two-part, devastating experience for the child. The first

part of the experience is the abandonment itself. ... The second part of the experience is that of being handed over to strangers.

Of course, adoption experience varies from one adoptee to another, and no voice can speak for *all* adopted children. The diversity of views emerging from these discussions is instructive in discovering themes in adoption experiences from the child's perspective, and reveals the need to give a voice to the children themselves, both during the adoption process and beyond.

The child's perspective in adoption

The child's perspective is a way of conceptualising and including the child in decision-making proceedings. At its heart is the notion of child-centrism, which puts the child at the core of one's considerations. While ideally entailing direct involvement (participation) of the child, constructing a child perspective goes further by also including the child's unvoiced situation in the context of the action to be taken. A child perspective normatively regards children as moral individuals, regardless of their capacity to form and express an opinion. In adoptions from care, this is particularly relevant as children are often too young to (fully) participate in the process.

The term 'adoption' has its roots in the Latin word '*adoptare*', meaning 'to choose for oneself' (Hoad, 2003). With a few exceptions, it is not the child who chooses to be adopted, or by whom[2]; rather, the decision is made by adults for their own reasons (see Malm and Welti, 2010), aided by the state 'in the child's best interests'. In child protection, the state makes the decision. Language is political (Orwell, 2013) and powerful (Tutu, 1999); therefore, regardless of good intentions and the empirically reported benefits of adoption, the very label we attach to a process that begins with a traumatic event for the child (and often others) implies a positivity not everyone involved may experience unequivocally. While for the adopters the completion of the process may also mark the completion of their 'family', the official term of choice for this happening appears to objectify rather than to recognise the child, and denies the fact that someone's gain is someone else's loss – and, crucially, for the child, it is both. This may or may not involve a deeper trauma or 'primal wound', but from the child's perspective, adoption is not simply an endpoint in a care history, but also the beginning of 'adopted identity' (Leighton, 2005). That many adopted children report positive feelings related to their adoption is not in conflict with the idea that this 'adopted identity' may come with significant emotional, social and practical challenges, which are unique to the individual. This highlights the need to involve the child concerned in the issue of using adoption to create a stable and loving family environment for that child.

Adoption as a moral decision requires taking the child's perspective, even where direct input from the child is limited or impossible (for instance, due to age). Treating children as moral individuals requires openness to a broad range of experiences, feelings and interpretations of facts. An example is separation trauma, which may occur even in infants. The mother–baby bond may be understood as a profound and special connection (see Winnicott, 1966), and prenatal bonding has been shown to affect child development (Glover and Capron, 2017). However, concluding that *all* children placed in care experience separation trauma, or to the same extent, would be mistaken, warranting instead a child-specific assessment.

Current deficiencies in child-centrism can be exemplified by adoption marketing. While it is not the purpose of a child to 'complete a family' or to 'be saved', this is often how adoption is portrayed by adults for adults. In extreme cases, private and public adoption agencies promote children available for adoption in the same way as animal shelters try to rehome puppies (for example, One Adoption, no date; AdoptUSKids, no date). Even if online profiles of to-be-adopted children increase the likelihood of adoption, such 'effectiveness' cannot morally justify promoting children in a way that breaches their privacy rights and objectifies them to appeal to adults. It is intrinsically wrong to promote children as if they were goods, irrespective of the outcome for the child: 'Even if buyers did not mistreat the children they purchased, a market in children would express and promote the wrong way of valuing them. Children are not properly regarded as consumer goods but as beings worthy of love and care' (Sandel, 2012). This argument has force, even where no strong or obvious commercial element exists. Practices such as 'adoption parties' and photo-listings of children available for adoption exemplify how the process of adoption is largely adopter-centric, being for adults who are enabled to 'rescue' a child in need and to 'complete' their family – the rhetoric of governments and official adoption agencies, as a simple web search for official adoption information reveals (see Table 12.1).[3]

This overview may give reason for hope: descriptions in Estonia, Finland, Norway and Spain are child-centric, and Austria is neutral, while England, Ireland, Germany and the US are adult-centric. This shows that child-centric adoption language and descriptions

Table 12.1: Adoption descriptions on states' official websites (government or official adoption agencies)

Country[a]	Description of adoption	Perspective
Austria	'Die Gründe, ein Kind adoptieren zu wollen, sind vielfältig. Eine Adoption bietet allen Beteiligten eine neue Chance' ['There are many reasons for wanting to adopt a child. Adoption offers everyone involved a new opportunity'] (Bundeskanzleramt, 2020)	Neutral
England	Government website only describes adoption process	
	Regional adoption agency (Greater Manchester): 'Adoption is life changing. You become the legal parent of a child who cannot – for whatever reason – live with their birth parents. You'll take on the same legal rights and responsibilities of a birth parent and provide a permanent home for the child you adopt. Your child will take on your surname and become a member of your family for life' (Adoption Counts, 2019)	Adult-centric
Estonia	'Adoption is a legal procedure in which the legal obligations and rights of a child are created between the adoptive parent and the child similarly to those between a biological parent and a child. The objective of adoption is to find a proper and loving family for children deprived of parental care. ... Adoption must always serve the best interest of the child' (Republic of Estonia Social Insurance Board, 2020)	Moderately child-centric
Germany	'Eine Adoption ist für viele Paare die einzige Möglichkeit, ihren Kinderwunsch zu erfüllen. Im Mittelpunkt der Adoptionsvermittlung steht immer das Wohl des Kindes' ['For many couples, adoption is the only way to fulfil their desire to have children. The welfare of the child is always at the centre of adoption placement'] (BMFSJ, 2019)	Adult-centric
Finland	'The purpose of adoption is to promote the welfare of a child by creating a child-parent relationship between the adoptee and the prospective adopter' (National Supervisory Authority for Welfare and Health, 2020)	Child-centric
Ireland	'The nature and effect of an Irish adoption order is that the child becomes the child of the adopters as if born to them in marriage with all the rights and duties of parents and children in relation to each other' (The Adoption Authority of Ireland, 2019)	Adult-centric

(continued)

Table 12.1: Adoption descriptions on states' official websites (government or official adoption agencies) (continued)

Country[a]	Description of adoption	Perspective
Norway[b]	'Formålet med adopsjon er å gi et godt og varig hjem til et barn som ikke kan bli tatt hånd om av sine biologiske foreldre' ['The purpose of adoption is to provide a good and lasting home to a child who cannot be cared for by their biological parents'] (Bufdir, 2019)	Child-centric
Spain	Government website only describes adoption process	
	Regional government: 'La adopción es una medida de protección a la infancia que proporciona una familia definitiva a niños y niñas que, por determinadas circunstancias, no pueden permanecer en su familia de origen' ['Adoption is a child protection measure that provides a definitive family to children who, due to certain circumstances, cannot remain in their family of origin'] (Comunidad de Madrid, 2019)	Child-centric
USA	'Adoption is the creation of a new, permanent relationship between an adoptive parent and child. Once this happens, there is no legal difference between a child who is adopted and a child who is born into a family' (US Government Services, 2020)	Adult-centric

Note: All translations by the author. [a] Selection based on the countries represented in this volume. [b] Refers to international adoptions. No domestic adoption description as these are rare in Norway, typically around a dozen per year.

are possible. However, the comparison also reveals 'saviour' and 'family completion' narratives, as well as those of 'normalisation' and 'opportunity', which may contribute to perpetuating the shame or stigma historically associated with adoption, or in soliciting undue gratitude from adoptees. Advocates for those affected by adoption criticise this 'positive adoption language' or 'respectful adoption language' as being respectful only to adopters (OriginsCanada, 2009). The connection between language and the perspective taken matters: how we discuss adoption reflects our attitude towards children in general, as well as towards to-be-adopted children. Table 12.1 shows that child-centrism as an approach rooted in understanding children as equal moral individuals has not been internalised to the extent that it is reflected in our language. This lack of internalised child-centrism is also apparent in the adopted children's rights. While it might be assumed that the status-conferring power of the law serves to align the protection of adopted children's rights with those of non-adopted children, this is far from the case, as will be shown in the next section.

Adopted child's rights

Children in care have been identified as a vulnerable group of children (UNCRC, 2013), and some adopted children continue to be stigmatised in society (Garber and Grotevant, 2015; Baden, 2016). Intersectionality is also often an issue as many children in care for whom adoptive families are sought are marginalised for several reasons, such as a combination of chronic illness, disability, ethnicity or gender. In addition, adoption from care may involve complex trauma, both from maltreatment leading to adoption and from separation, as described earlier. Therefore, even though adoption outcomes are typically better than available alternatives (van Ijzendoorn et al, 2005), the way adoption is handled from the child's perspective can and should be improved. A crucial point is to introduce a child-centric adoption narrative, which should consider the voices of past, present and future adoptees as a starting point. This will serve to identify shortcomings of adoption as we currently know it.

A few words on vulnerability, consent and participation are in order. Describing adopted children as vulnerable is not to victimise or disempower them, but to acknowledge that the separation of a child from their birth parents (at the time and in retrospect) is traumatic, even if we cannot quite fathom how very young children experience such separation. Crucially, the notion of vulnerability is also about responsibility, connoting special responsibilities to those whose interests are vulnerable to our actions and choices (Lindemann, 2019: 32), including an obligation to focus on and involve the child in the entire adoption process. Unfortunately, child-centrism appears to be substituted with legalistic mechanisms, such as consent. The child's consent to adoption, as required in Europe (Fenton-Glynn, 2013), constitutes no more than the bare minimum of child participation in adoption, and is far removed from actual child-centrism. Depending on age and circumstances, young children are unlikely to fully grasp the relevance of legal 'parent' status, or the wider legal and social implications of its transferral. Beyond consent, a review of cases of adoption from care before the European Court of Human Rights (ECtHR) has shown that consideration of the child's views and opinion remains the exception (Breen et al, 2020). While the child's right to be heard has been formalised in Article 12 of the CRC, and thus harmonised across the world through near-universal ratification of the CRC, the situation concerning adopted children's rights can be best described as messy. Disclosure and access to information rights are patchy, and available documentation following an adoption from care is not fit for purpose.

The role of the law here is instrumental. In adoptions from care, it defines who gets access to which information and under which circumstances. Crucial dimensions are knowledge about the adoption itself and information about birth parents and the circumstances leading to the adoption. While further relevant aspects exist, these are singled out because they relate to information that others – the state, social workers and usually adoptive parents – will have, while the adopted person may not have (full) access to the same information. This cannot be reconciled with a child-centric view of adopted children as equal moral beings. A review of relevant national legal provisions reveals that the rights of adoptees to obtain information about their histories also vary across countries (see Table 12.2). This is surprising as adopted children are unlikely to differ in a morally relevant way across borders; rather, as a group, they may 'face some unique problems in forging a sense of self' (Witt, 2005: 138).

Table 12.2 shows that information about birth parents is not easy to obtain. While non-adopted children can check their birth certificates,[4] adoptees will only see their current legal parents' names. Even where biological parents' names are recorded in the population registry, as in Austria and Germany, these are not accessible to private individuals. Some countries (England, Ireland and Norway) maintain separate Adopted Children Registries but, again, these are not publicly accessible. Names play an important role here. 'Name' is explicitly mentioned as part of the child's identity protected by law (for example, Article 8 CRC), yet emphasis is often placed on the fact that the adopted child will take on the adopter's last name, and even first names may be changed (see Table 12.1). 'Preservation', then, seems reduced to keeping a record of the child's original name for administrative purposes, and possibly for the child to access at some point (see Table 12.2). None of the countries studied issues a post-adoption certificate that includes both birth and adoptive parents, listing only current legal parents. Adoption records are kept but adoptees often face practical obstacles in gaining access to information: Ireland and California require an application; birth parent information is restricted to non-identifying information unless birth parents have consented; and files may be heavily redacted. Even in countries with a legal right to access adoption information, age limits apply: in most countries, adoptees must reach legal majority, while three countries allow adopted

Table 12.2: Information rights of adopted children in domestic[a] adoptions

	Parents listed in population/ birth registry	Birth certificate information	Duty to tell the child about the adoption	Right to access original birth record/ adoption file[b]	Access rights compared to child's consent to adoption requirement
Austria	Both birth and adoptive parents	Current legal parents	No	From age 14	No fixed age for consent to adoption (typically required from age 14)
England	Birth parents, annotated 'adopted'; separate Adopted Children Register	Original birth certificate becomes void Adoption certificate issued, names current legal parents. Short version: no information about adoption. Long version: excerpt from registry, includes date of adoption	No	Age 18	Child's consent not required for adoption, but child's wishes must be ascertained
Estonia	Current legal parents	Excerpt from registry	No	Age 18[c]	Consent age lower (age 10)
Finland	Current legal parents	Excerpt from registry	No	From age 12	Same (age 12)
Germany	Both birth and adoptive parents	Current legal parents	No	From age 16[d]	Consent age lower (age 14)

(continued)

Table 12.2: Information rights of adopted children in domestic[a] adoptions (continued)

	Parents listed in population/ birth registry	Birth certificate information	Duty to tell the child about the adoption	Right to access original birth record/ adoption file[b]	Access rights compared to child's consent to adoption requirement
Ireland	Birth parents; separate Adopted Children Register	Birth parents; sealed upon adoption Adoption certificate issued, names current legal parents	No	No legal right. Adoptee may apply to the Adoption Authority of Ireland for release of original birth certificate; usually granted where birth mother agrees or where she is deceased. Records provided are often heavily redacted, so that any information that would identify the birth parents is no longer visible	No legal right to access adoption file. Child's consent not required for adoption
Norway	Current legal parents; separate Adopted Children Register	Excerpt from registry	Yes	Age 18; actively informed	Consent age lower (age 12)

Table 12.2: Information rights of adopted children in domestic[a] adoptions (continued)

	Parents listed in population/ birth registry	Birth certificate information	Duty to tell the child about the adoption	Right to access original birth record/ adoption file[b]	Access rights compared to child's consent to adoption requirement
Spain	Birth parents, annotated 'adopted'. Adoptive parents can request to issue a new birth record omitting birth parents (original record is kept and sealed)	Current legal parents	No	Age 18	Consent age lower (age 12)
USA (California)	Current legal parents; no registry, but publicly accessible database from the California Department of Public Health. Original birth record sealed upon adoption	Birth parents; sealed upon adoption. Adoption birth certificate issued, names current legal parents	No	Limited. From age 21 where birth parent consent given. Access to file by court order only	Consent age lower (age 12)

Note: My gratitude to Salomé Adroher Biosca (Spain), Tore Lied (Norway), Katre Luhamaa (Estonia), Conor O'Mahony (Ireland) and Tarja Pösö (Finland) for their help in compiling this information. [a] International adoptees' rights are often even more limited. [b] Data are from European Union Agency for Fundamental Rights (2018). [c] Younger children may access this information with their parents' consent. Restrictions apply if biological parents or siblings did not provide consent to their identity being disclosed, or if such information is not in the child's best interests. [d] Younger children may access this information with their parents' consent.

Source: Country references, all accessed 31 March 2020: Austria – Personenstandsgesetz 2013 (see: www.ris.bka.gv.at/GeltendeFassung.wxe?Abfrage=Bundesnormen&Gesetzesnummer=20008228) and Personenstandsgesetz-Durchführungsverordnung 2013 (see: www.ris.bka.gv.at/GeltendeFassung.wxe?Abfrage=Bundesnormen&Gesetzesnummer=20008627); England – Adoption and Children Act 2002 (see: www.legislation.gov.uk/ukpga/2002/38/contents); Finland – Adoption Act 2012. 2012/22 Oikeusministeriö (see: www.finlex.fi/en/laki/kaannokset/2012/en20120022?search%5Btype%5D=pika&search%5Bkieli%5D%5B0%5D=en&search%5Bpika%5D=adoption%20act); Germany – Personenstandsgesetz 2007 (see: www.gesetze-im-internet.de/pstg/BJNR012210007.html); Norway – Lov Om Adopsjon (Adopsjonsloven) 2017 (see: https://lovdata.no/dokument/NL/lov/2017-06-16-48); Spain – Código Civil 1889 (see: www.boe.es/eli/es/rd/1889/07/24/(1)/con) and Reglamento de La Ley Del Registro Civil 1958 (see: www.boe.es/buscar/doc.php?id=BOE-A-1958-18486); and US (California) – Family Code (see: http://leginfo.legislature.ca.gov/faces/codesTOCSelected.xhtml?tocCode=fam).

children access (Austria at 14, Finland at 12 and Germany at 16). This is in contrast with child consent to adoption requirements, which – where applicable – are consistently lower (the same in Finland).

While non-adopted children typically have access to their family histories:

> [f]or an adopted child, the process of creating a narrative of the self may well require knowledge of biological or genetic origins (as far as these are available) and not because these are thought to determine any particular characteristic of the adopted child, but in order to complete the narrative of the self. (Witt, 2005: 140)

This differential in available knowledge about one's past cannot be fully remedied; however, a child-centric approach would ensure that whatever is available would be made more readily accessible. Adoptees should not have to justify their wanting to know; they should have a right to know. Only Norway imposes an obligation on adopters to inform children about their adoption *as soon as advisable* and notifies adoptees of their access rights upon reaching legal majority. All other countries rely on adopters' goodwill to inform children of their adoption.

The findings in Table 12.2 demonstrate the lack of equal moral standing adoptees have as they continue to struggle to obtain information that others hold about them. Deliberately depriving any child of this knowledge seems irreconcilable with a view of children as moral agents. This should be a strong argument for the granting of information rights to all adoptees, irrespective of their country of origin or residence.

Conclusion

The purpose of this chapter has been to investigate child-centrism in current adoption from care practice, and to compare adopted children's rights with their non-adopted peers'. While adoption clearly has its place within child welfare measures by providing substitute families to many children who cannot be cared for by their birth families, more needs to be done to ensure that the child remains firmly at the centre of adoption throughout the process, and beyond.

The examples of adoption language and birth records may seem academic issues but they reveal who currently controls the discourse. Child-centrism urges us to put the adopted child first, and to listen to adoptee voices in progressing adoptions from care. An urgent starting point would be to put adopted children's rights on an equal footing with those of non-adopted children. As moral individuals, children should not be marketed, and they should not have to show cause when it comes to information about their family history. Current access practices reveal a disconnect between many adopted children's holistic social and emotional family, and the family created through the legal act of adoption. How much this matters can be seen from recent events in New York State, where a new law came into force in January 2020 that enabled adoptees to obtain copies of their original birth certificates, with thousands of requests being filed within days (Engel, 2020). Signing the legislation, Governor Cuomo (2020) said:

> Every person has the right to know where they come from, and this new law grants all New Yorkers the same unrestricted rights to their original birth records. ... After years of being denied this basic human right, adoptees will finally be able to obtain critical information about their origins, family histories and medical backgrounds.

While names, certificates and website descriptions may not matter to all adopted children equally, and possibly not at all to some, the key issue is that all children must have their rights respected, and adopted children should have their perspectives taken into consideration. Since preferences cannot be determined a priori, flexibility is required to accommodate the individuality of adopted children (Krutzinna, forthcoming). This might require the state to use its powers to create records that allow for multiple sets of parents and combinations of birth and adoptive names, to ease access to information held on file, and to facilitate contact between separated family members if they so wish.

Adoption as a moral decision requires us to consider how it affects the child, and the adult that child eventually becomes. This chapter has highlighted only some aspects of adoptions from care that could be improved to become more child-centric; many others exist. Thus, our collective goal must be to work towards ensuring that adoptions from care always treat children as the moral agents they are.

Acknowledgements
This project has received funding from the Research Council of Norway under the Independent Projects – Humanities and Social Science program (grant no. 262773) and European Research Council under the European Union's Horizon 2020 research and innovation programme (grant agreement No 724460). Disclaimer: This chapter

reflects only the authors' views and the funding agencies are not responsible for any use that may be made of the information contained therein.

Notes

[1] System differences and lack of comprehensive data render inter-country comparisons of adoption breakdown rates challenging (see Palacios et al, 2018).
[2] Exceptions include older children wishing to be adopted by adults they have a close relationship with, including step-parents they are already living with.
[3] The search was conducted using 'adoption + COUNTRY' as the search term and identifying the top-listed government website. Where this yielded no description, capital city was used instead (England, Spain). For England, the second-largest metropolitan area, Greater Manchester, was chosen for simplicity as London has multiple adoption authorities.
[4] Except where paternity (and sometimes maternity) is unknown.

References

Adoption Counts (2019) 'Adoption explained'. Available at: https://adoptioncounts.org.uk/adoption-explained (accessed 31 March 2020).

AdoptUSKids (no date) 'Meet the children'. Available at: www.adoptuskids.org/meet-the-children/search-for-children/search (accessed 31 March 2020).

Andersson, G. (2009), 'Foster children: a longitudinal study of placements and family relationships', *International Journal of Social Welfare*, 18: 13–26.

Archard, D. (2010) *The Family: A Liberal Defense*, Basingstoke: Palgrave Macmillan.

Baden, A. (2016) ' "Do you know your real parents?" and other adoption microaggressions', *Adoption Quarterly*, 19(1): 1–25.

Blake, L. (2017) 'Parents and children who are estranged in adulthood: a review and discussion of the literature', *Journal of Family Theory and Review*, 9(4): 521–36.

BMFSJ (Bundesministeriums für Familie, Senioren, Frauen und Jugend) (2019) 'Adoption'. Available at: www.bmfsfj.de/bmfsfj/themen/familie/schwangerschaft-und-kinderwunsch/adoptionen-und-adoptionsvermittlung/73952 (accessed 31 March 2020).

Breen, C., Krutzinna, J., Luhamaa, K. and Skivenes, M. (2020) 'Family life for children in state care. An analysis of the European Court of Human Rights' reasoning on adoption without consent', *International Journal of Children's Rights*, 28: 715–47.

Bufdir (2019) 'Adoptere fra utlandet gjennom en organisasjon' ['Adopting from abroad via an organisation']. Available at: www.bufdir.no/Adopsjon/Jeg_onsker_a_adoptere/Adoptere_fra_utlandet/ (accessed 31 March 2020).

Bundeskanzleramt (2020) 'Allgemeines zur Adoption' ['General information concerning adoption']. Available at: www.oesterreich. gv.at/themen/familie_und_partnerschaft/adoption/Seite.720001. html (accessed 31 March 2020).

Burns, K., Križ, K., Krutzinna, J., Luhamaa, K., Meysen, T., Pösö, T., Segado, S., Skivenes, M. and Thoburn, J. (2019) 'The hidden proceedings – an analysis of accountability of child protection adoption proceedings in eight European jurisdictions', *European Journal of Comparative Law and Governance*, 6(4): 339–71.

Comunidad de Madrid (2019) 'Adopción'. Available at: www. comunidad.madrid/servicios/asuntos-sociales/adopcion (accessed 31 March 2020).

Cuomo, A.M. (2020) 'Governor Cuomo announces new law allowing adoptees to obtain a certified birth certificate at age 18 goes into effect January 15'. Available at: www.governor.ny.gov/news/governor-cuomo-announces-new-law-allowing-adoptees-obtain-certified-birth-certificate-age-18 (accessed 31 March 2020).

De Wispelaere, J. and Weinstock, D. (2018) 'Ethical challenges for adoption regimes', in A. Gheaus, G. Calder and J. De Wispelaere (eds) *The Routledge Handbook of the Philosophy of Childhood and Children*, Abingdon: Routledge, pp 213–24.

Engel, C. (2020) 'Signed and unsealed, New York delivers on its promise for open birth records', *NY City Lens*. Available at: http://nycitylens.com/2020/03/adoption-law-history/ (accessed 31 March 2020).

European Union Agency for Fundamental Rights (2018) 'Accessing adoption files and information on the biological family'. Available at: https://fra.europa.eu/en/publication/2017/mapping-minimum-age-requirements/accessing-adoption-files (accessed 31 March 2020).

Featherstone, B., Gupta, A., Morris, K. and White, S. (2018) *Protecting Children*, Bristol: Bristol University Press.

Fenton-Glynn, C. (2013) 'The child's voice in adoption proceedings: a European perspective', *The International Journal of Children's Rights*, 21(4): 590–615.

Ferguson, L. and Brake, E. (2018) 'Introduction: the importance of theory to children's and family law', in E. Brake and L. Ferguson (eds) *Philosophical Foundations of Children's and Family Law*, Oxford: Oxford University Press, pp 1–37.

Garber, K.J. and Grotevant, H.D. (2015) '"YOU were adopted?!": microaggressions toward adolescent adopted individuals in same-race families', *The Counseling Psychologist*, 43(3): 435–62.

Glover, V. and Capron, L. (2017) 'Prenatal parenting', *Current Opinion in Psychology*, 15: 66–70.

Hoad, T.F. (2003) 'Adopt', *The Concise Oxford Dictionary of English Etymology*. Available at: www.oxfordreference.com/view/10.1093/acref/9780192830982.001.0001/acref-9780192830982-e-188 (accessed 31 March 2020).

Krutzinna, J. (forthcoming) 'Who is "the child"? Best interests and individuality of children in discretionary decision-making'.

Leighton, K. (2005) 'Being adopted and being a philosopher: exploring identity and the "desire to know" differently', in S. Haslanger and C. Witt (eds) *Adoption Matters: Philosophical and Feminist Essays*, New York: Cornell University Press, pp 146–70.

Lindemann, H. (2019) 'Why families matter', in M. Verkerk, H. Lindemann and J. McLaughlin (eds) *What About the Family? Practices of Responsibility in Care*, Oxford: Oxford University Press, pp 16–46.

Malm, K. and Welti, K. (2010) 'Exploring motivations to adopt', *Adoption Quarterly*, 13(3/4): 185–208.

National Supervisory Authority for Welfare and Health (2020) 'Adoption'. Available at: www.valvira.fi/web/en/social_welfare/adoption (accessed 31 March 2020).

One Adoption (no date) 'Child profiles'. Available at: www.oneadoption.co.uk/north-humber/child-profiles (accessed 31 March 2020).

OriginsCanada (2009) 'The language of adoption'. Available at: www.originscanada.org/adoption-practices/adoption-language/language-of-adoption/ (accessed 31 March 2020).

Orwell, G. (2013) *Politics and the English Language (First Published in 1945)*, London: Penguin Classics.

Palacios, J., Rolock, N., Selwyn, J. and Barbosa-Ducharne, M. (2018) 'Adoption breakdown: concept, research, and implications', *Research on Social Work Practice*, 29(2): 130–42.

Palacios, J., Adroher, S., Brodzynski, D., Grotevant, H., Johnson, D., Juffer, F., Martínez-Mora, L., Muhamedrahimov, R., Selwyn, J., Simmonds, J. and Tarren-Sweeney, M. (2019) 'Adoption in the service of child protection: an international interdisciplinary perspective', *Psychology, Public Policy, and Law*, 25(2): 57–72.

Republic of Estonia Social Insurance Board (2020) 'Adoption'. Available at: www.sotsiaalkindlustusamet.ee/en/family-and-child-protection/adoption (accessed 31 March 2020).

Sandel, M. (2012) *What Money Can't Buy: The Moral Limits of Markets*, London: Penguin Books.

Satz, D. (2017) 'Feminist perspectives on reproduction and the family', in E.N. Zalta (ed) *The Stanford Encyclopedia of Philosophy*. Available at: https://plato.stanford.edu/archives/sum2017/entries/feminism-family/ (accessed 31 March 2020).

The Adoption Authority of Ireland (2019) 'Domestic adoption'. Available at: https://aai.gov.ie/en/who-we-are/domestic-adoption.html (accessed 31 March 2020).

Tutu, D. (1999) 'Bill Moyers' conversation with Archbishop Tutu'. Available at: www.pbs.org/moyers/journal/12282007/transcript2.html (accessed 31 March 2020).

UNCRC (United Nations Committee on the Rights of the Child) (2013) 'General comment no. 14 (2013) on the right of the child to have his or her best interests taken as a primary consideration (Art. 3, para. 1)'.

US Government Services (2020) 'Adoption, foster care, and other child related issues'. Available at: www.usa.gov/child-care (accessed 31 March 2020).

Van Ijzendoorn, M., Juffer, F. and Klein Poelhuis, C. (2005) 'Adoption and cognitive development: a meta-analytic comparison of adopted and nonadopted children's IQ and school performance', *Psychological Bulletin*, 131(2): 301–16.

Verrier, N. (2009) *The Primal Wound: Understanding the Adopted Child* (UK edn), London: Coram-BAAF Adoption and Fostering Academy.

Vinnerljung, B. and Hjern, A. (2011) 'Cognitive, educational and self-support outcomes of long-term foster care versus adoption. A Swedish national cohort study', *Children and Youth Services Review*, 33(10): 1902–10.

Wijedasa, D. and Selwyn, J. (2017) 'Examining rates and risk factors for post-order adoption disruption in England and Wales through survival analyses', *Children and Youth Services Review*, 83: 179–89.

Winnicott, D. (2012) *The Family and Individual Development*, London and New York: Routledge.

Witt, C. (2005) 'Family resemblances: adoption, personal identity, and genetic essentialism', in S. Haslanger and C. Witt (eds) *Adoption Matters: Philosophical and Feminist Essays*, New York: Cornell University Press, pp 135–45.

13

Understanding attachment in decisions on adoption from care in Norway

Hege Stein Helland and Sveinung Hellesen Nygård

Introduction

The attachments between a child and their caregivers are of vital importance for the well-being of a child and for their development as a person. In Norwegian child welfare legislation and policy, there are few definitions or substantive descriptions of what is meant by attachment or of how it is supposed to be assessed in decisions concerning adoptions from care without parental consent. This is despite the fact of 'attachment' being one of two alternative basic conditions for consenting to adoption pursuant to Article 4–20 (para 3a) of the Norwegian Child Welfare Act 1992 (CWA), which states that adoption can be consented to if the child 'has become so attached to persons and the environment where he or she is living that, on the basis of an overall assessment, removing the child may lead to serious problems for him or her'. Decision-makers are provided with significant room for discretion to interpret what attachment entails. Even though adoption is considered to be the strongest measure available in the CWA, we know little about how decision-makers' discretion is applied and of how attachment is understood and used as a parameter in actual decisions. By studying decisions from the decision-making body for involuntary measures by the CWA, the County Social Welfare Board (the Board), the aim of this chapter is to explore how the concept of attachment is interpreted in decisions on adoption and how decision-makers apply it to inform their decisions.

In the first part of this chapter, adoption is linked with the concept of attachment via a short introduction on attachment theory from the psychological perspective. This is followed by an overview of the formal decision-making structure for decisions on adoptions from care in Norway. Next, we connect the challenges of knowledge application by professionals in the decision-making process with questions of legitimate decisions and use of discretion, while utilising perspectives inspired by institutional theory and system-theoretical thinking. Further, we present the methods and limitations of the study before presenting and discussing the findings. Finally, some concluding remarks are made.

Background

From the early 2000s and onwards, the development of policies in the field of adoptions from care in Norway has been increasingly influenced by expert knowledge. In recent years, knowledge from the field of psychology has dominated this expert discourse (Tefre, 2020). Tefre (2020) finds that developmental psychology has become a prominent supplier of terms in justifying state interventions on behalf of children in the Norwegian political discourse and, furthermore, that the psychological concept of attachment has attained an increasingly significant position in the political discourse on adoption. Illustrative of this is the authorities' discussion some years back of introducing the principle of 'developmentally supportive attachment' into the child welfare system (NOU, 2012:5). The recommendation entailed that the quality of attachment between children and their caregivers should be given decisive weight in the decision-making process and, if necessary, should be given precedence over the biological principle. This development is not without challenges, and we do not know to what degree decision-makers in Norwegian child welfare matters rely on a psychological understanding of attachment in their practice. The use of expert knowledge and concepts across professional fields requires that the meaning and inherent qualities of the knowledge and concepts are sustained throughout the process, and that it is applied according to its intended purpose. As decision-makers are provided with considerable room for discretion in their interpretation and application of attachment in assessments of adoption, challenges can arise with regards to the legitimacy of both the institutions responsible for the decisions and the decisions being made.

To our knowledge, no previous studies have analysed how attachment is interpreted and applied in public administration or the court system in Norway. There are, nonetheless, studies that have investigated which considerations different decision-making groups and bodies emphasise in their decisions on adoptions from care (Bendiksen, 2008; Skivenes, 2010; Skivenes and Tefre, 2012; Helland, forthcoming). From these studies, it is apparent that attachment is a significant factor in adoption assessments and in the considerations of a child's best interests. In research covering other areas of child welfare practice, it is claimed that the employment of attachment theory in professional recommendations for placement practice for smaller children is not nuanced enough (Smeplass, 2009). Internationally, more research exists and the general message is that while attachment theory and knowledge deserve a place in the family court's deliberations, its application remains flawed due to the lack of consistency and common understanding of the concept (McIntosh, 2011[1]; for a discussion, see also Cashmore and Parkinson, 2014). Based on previous research, there is reason to anticipate that we will find variation in the interpretation and application of the concept across, and possibly also within, decisions on adoption.

A concept that can be understood in different ways can mislead reasoning (Copi et al, 2014) and expand the discretionary space in which decisions are made. With few guidelines from the legislators to guide child welfare decision-makers, it becomes pertinent to examine if and how attachment is applied in decision-making by the Board. Is attachment utilised in congruence with psychological theory or more along the lines of common speech? If the latter is the case, what implications could this have for the quality of the decisions that are made?

Formal structures for decisions on adoption from care

The four legal conditions (Art 4–20 para 3 CWA) for an adoption to be consented to are that: (1) the placement is permanent, either due to the parents' inability to provide the child with proper care or the child's attachment to persons and the environment around them (condition a); (2) adoption is in the best interest of the child (condition b); (3) the adoption seekers are the child's foster parents and have proven fit to raise the child as their own (condition c); and (4) the conditions to consent to adoption pursuant to the Adoption Act are fulfilled (condition d). The decision is made by the Board, which is headed by a lawyer qualified as a judge and further composed of an expert (in most cases, a psychologist) and a layman[2] (for a detailed outline of the conditions for decision-making on adoption in Norway, see Helland and Skivenes, this volume).

Few discussions or directives about how to understand attachment are found in the preparatory work for the CWA, in relevant policy or circulars, or in the guidelines for internal quality proceedings in the Board. Yet, some brief descriptions of attachment do exist. In a Bill from the Ministry of Children and Families (Prop. 106, p 82) from 2013, it was suggested that attachment and relational quality, understood as 'interaction, relational quality and form of attachment seen in relation to the child's age', should be one of several principles on which to base a child's best interest decision.

Adoption and attachment

The concept of attachment appears frequently in discussions regarding children and their development, and stands as a principal element when professionals in the field of child welfare comment on a child's current and future situation of care and well-being (Azar et al, 1998; Kuehnle et al, 2000; Hennum, 2016). Attachment has a specific position in decisions on adoption as it is included as one of two alternative basic conditions for adoption. According to Ofstad and Skar (2015), the child's age, the duration of the placement and the extent of access between the child and her parents are important elements for consideration in an assessment of attachment pursuant to Article 4–20 of the CWA. Based on case law (see, for example, Rt. 2007 s. 561), circulars, international conventions and obligations (CRC, 2013; The Norwegian Directorate for Children, Youth and Family Affairs, 2017), and research on assessments of the child's best interest in decisions on adoption (Skivenes, 2010; Skivenes and Tefre, 2012; Helland, 2020), we expect attachment to be a part of the Board's assessments.

The concept of attachment and attachment theory

Attachment, in the sense of being attached to something, is a term that frequently occurs in everyday speech. We feel connected to persons, things and places, and are able to establish emotional bonds to things and persons that we relate to, as well as with places that feel important to us. This 'common sense' understanding of attachment is reflected in our daily use of the term and is related to the concept of 'belonging' but not directly connected to the psychological understanding of attachment derived from attachment theory. When we say that we feel attached to something or someone, it is implicit in the statement that the subject of our attachment has an emotional value to us. The essential criteria for such an attachment to arise is exposure over time. Quantitative measures, such as duration and intensity of the relation, are important when describing this form of attachment.

Attachment is also understood as a relational concept in psychology. Yet, in attachment theory, it signifies a relationship that develops between young children and caregivers in a specific time period of a child's development (Ainsworth, 1982). This is a comprehensive and complex theory, and there is not room to go into detail about the theory here. The main sentiment of the theory is that it links attachment patterns (children's behaviour) with conditions of care. Attachment theory, developed by John Bowlby in the 1950s and further elaborated by Mary Ainsworth and others, is a framework that seeks to explain how children develop in relation to their closest caregivers, how a child's relational experiences shape the child's later expectations and the consequences this may have for the development of psychopathology (Wallin, 2007). What constitutes a comprehensive theory of child development today, for Bowlby, started out with a desire to highlight the consequences for children of experiencing separation and loss of a caregiver (primarily maternal) (Rutter, 1981). Assessing children's attachment within the framework of psychological attachment theory is conducted by applying the 'strange situation' procedure, a test developed by Ainsworth and Bell (1970) to identify patterns in children's responses when exposed to a stressful situation and, subsequently, their response when being reunited with the caregiver. Using this procedure, four 'attachment patterns' can be identified: 'secure', 'insecure-ambivalent', 'insecure-avoidant' and 'insecure-disorganised' (Main and Solomon, 1986). For the purpose of analysis, we understand the psychological use of the attachment concept as emphasising aspects related to the *quality* of the relationship over *quantitative* parameters, such as the length of the relationship, and employ the four categories for classifying attachment within the psychological understanding of attachment.

Based on these two understandings of attachment, we make the distinction between a *psychological* and *non-psychological* understanding of attachment in our analysis, where the latter refers to the 'common sense' utilisation of attachment found in everyday speech. This entails descriptions of attachment as, for example, 'strong' or 'weak', or where it is described as 'lacking' or merely as existing or not. These are ideal types and are, accordingly, simplified representations of reality. Nonetheless, they do provide us with a constructive set of concepts for the purpose of our analysis.

Discretion and legitimate decisions

In interaction with rules, discretion is an indispensable component in decisions made by the courts (Dworkin, 1963) and court-like bodies like the Board. That decision-makers have discretion means that they are provided with a certain freedom that is bound by a set of standards to decide how to interpret and give meaning and form to the law in each specific case (Hawkins, 1986). Under a democratic rule of law, one is entitled to have an expectation of how the legal text is interpreted and on what basis. Discretion challenges fundamental principles of predictability and that equal cases should be treated equally and different cases differently.

From an institutional perspective, it is problematic if essential concepts are interpreted and applied differently as cultural-cognitive consistency is one of several premises for the legitimacy of an institution (Scott, 2001). In this sense, an institution and its practice can only be legitimate as long as the actors within that institution define a situation similarly and within the same frame of reference. The legitimacy of an institution is also dependent on the quality of the decisions that are made and that the decisions are made according to the existing laws and regulations (Scott, 2001). One could also claim that decision-makers should have a consistent use of expressions in order for an argumentation to be logical and rational (see Feteris, 2017: 81).

Professional discourses and the use of psychological expert knowledge in the decision-making process

Our analysis is informed by the system-theoretical tradition of Niklas Luhmann (King and Piper, 1995; Luhmann, 1995; see also King and Thornhill, 2003), which sees the law as an autopoietic system. That is to say, the judicial system is self-referential and substantiates statements about the world by referring back to the system's own internal means and procedures. Even though the Board is not a court, it operates by judicial procedure and is thus situated within the judicial system. The challenge in child welfare cases is that the judicial system has to take into consideration perspectives that follow different logics than the legal. Through the judicial discourse, legal decision-makers operate with two sets of rationalities or ideologies when deciding on child welfare matters: that of *justice* and that of *welfare* (King and Piper, 1995; Ottosen, 2006). Where the binary justice perspective characterises the logic within the judicial system – that something is legal or illegal, right or wrong – child welfare matters demand that one also takes the welfare perspective – of what is good or bad for the child.

Following this line of thought (King and Thornhill, 2003), the judicial system is considered closed in the sense that information tends to be considered valid only when it can be reproduced by the system's own procedures and criteria. At the same time, the judicial system is by its own means unable to produce the necessary knowledge relevant for a child welfare case. The judicial system is therefore dependent on externally produced knowledge, and here is where the psychological perspective enters the equation. From the psychological discourse, the decisions are informed on matters concerning the child's social and psychological well-being – of what is harmful or beneficial for children. The influence from this discourse can be found both on an individual level, reflected in decision-making and methods for retrieving information, and on a more general or abstract level, such as in laws and policies relating to child welfare matters (Ottosen, 2006), as seen in the earlier discussion about the increasing influence from the psychological field of expert knowledge on Norwegian child welfare policy.

Methods and data

The data for the study underpinning this chapter consist of all the decisions made on adoption by the Board in the year of 2016 – 58 decisions in total, with 56 of them resulting in an adoption order. The Board is obligated to give written reasons for its decision, and these documents are structured as follows: a presentation of the facts of the case; the parties' argumentation, both the public party (the municipality) and the private party (the parent[s] and/or the child); and the Board's assessment and decision. On average, the Board's assessment constitutes six pages. The expert on the Board was a psychologist in 67 per cent of the cases,[3] a psychiatrist in 14 per cent, a (clinical) social worker in 9 per cent, a child welfare officer in 7 per cent and a special education teacher in 3 per cent.

The 58 written documents were analysed in five steps[4]: (1) we started by reading all the decision documents to identify how attachment was described; (2) we thereafter identified all references to attachment and attachment-related terms[5] in the decisions by searching and registering references; (3) we identified to whom and how (non-psychological or psychological character) attachment was described; (4) we registered which terms were used to describe the attachment; and, lastly, (5) we explored the meaning of attachment as a concept by identifying how the Board makes use of and operationalises attachment in their argumentation. We used the analytical tool Nvivo 12 for steps three to five, and only the Board's assessment is analysed. All data were reviewed and registered manually, and, with the exception of step four, the occurrence of references is counted per case and the number of occurrences within each case is not considered. The coding in step five was reviewed in three steps, where the researchers systematically reviewed their own coding, each other's coding and conducted a joint review. As a reliability measure, strict conditions were set for which parts of the text were eligible for coding. The text had to either: (1) contain direct references to the term; or (2) be an identifiable part of the discussion related to the second alternative of the basic condition (a) given in Article 4–20 (para 3) of the CWA. Direct references to the law and when the term 'attachment' was not used to describe a relation were excluded from analysis.

Limitations

Our analysis is based on written material – authored in retrospect and for a certain purpose – and does not provide a complete representation of the cases. These documents do not contain all the information available to the Board during the negotiation. Still, the Board is required to account for the formal decision, and the content of the decision will thus reflect the justifications that the Board wishes to account for in the official decision (see Magnussen and Skivenes, 2015). Another limitation is that we cannot say anything about the quality of the investigations made by experts and other professionals in the cases.

Findings

Where and how often?

The results reveal that attachment is a significant element in decisions on adoption (see Table 13.1). Given the wording of the law, this was expected. It is furthermore evident that, in most cases, attachment is addressed as part of the public party's argumentation for adoption. In the private parties' argumentation, there are references to attachment in about half the cases.

Table 13.1: Cases with references to one or more attachment-related terms in the decision documents

Part of decision document	Number of cases with references to attachment
I. Public party (the municipality)	55 (95%)
II. Private party (parent[s])	30 (52%)
III. Private party (the child)	2 (3%)[a]
IV. The Board's assessment	57 (98%)

Note: Distributed by the section in the document where the references were identified. Number of cases and percentage of total number of cases (n = 58).[a] For a child to be party to the case, they have to be 15 years or older; thus, the child is rarely party to the case.

Table 13.2: Conditions of Article 4–20 where attachment is assessed/described in the Board's assessment

	Conditions (letter) for adoption (Art 4–20)				
	(a) Permanence	(b) Best interest	(c) Foster parents' fitness	(d) Legality	Other/ unknown
N (%)	55 (95%)	50 (86%)	4 (7%)	1 (2%)	3 (5%)

Note: Number of cases and percentage of total number of cases (n = 58)

Table 13.3: Attachment described with relation to persons or environment, differentiated by type of attachment understanding (non-psychological or psychological)

	Non-psychological			Psychological	
	Foster parents (family)	Biological parents (family)	Environment (extended family)	Foster parents (family)	Biological parents (family)
N (%)	54 (93%)	41 (71%)	18 (31%)	22 (38%)	9 (16%)

Note: Number of cases and percentage of total number of cases (n = 58)

In relation to the four legal criteria for adoption (see Table 13.2), we find that attachment is mentioned and described in relation to the permanency condition (a) in the law in all cases except three.[6] Attachment is also a highly relevant factor in best interest assessments: 86 per cent of the cases include a description of the child's attachment to persons or environment, related to condition (b). Attachment is rarely mentioned in assessments of the foster parents' fitness (condition c) or of the legality (condition d) of the decision in relation to the adoption law.

To whom is attachment assessed by the Board?

When reviewing to whom the child's attachment is described and if the described attachment is of a 'non-psychological' or 'psychological' character (see earlier definitions and Table 13.3), we find that the non-psychological understanding of attachment is dominant compared to the psychological. Descriptions of attachment between the child and their foster parents occur more often than between the child and their biological parents. Furthermore, our analysis revealed that attachment is assessed in terms of existing or not existing – it either is or is not. Where the Board finds that there *is* an attachment – in positive terms – between the child and their foster parents, no such attachment is found between the child and their biological parents. In about one third of the

Table 13.4: Psychological-oriented terms used to describe attachment

Psychological references	Distribution of the 36 references	The child's attachment to
Secure	29 references	The foster parents (family)
Insecure	6 references	Biological parents
Disorganised	1 reference	Biological parents

Note: Terms used and between whom attachment is described. Number of references by term (n = 25 cases)

cases, the child's attachment to their environment or extended family is also described, usually depicting an attachment with extended family (grandparents, aunts, uncles and so on) or the 'environment around the family'. Considering that the law only requires an assessment of foster parents, it is interesting to find that attachment to biological family is assessed in relation to both condition (a) and (b) – in about one third of the cases for the former and just above half for the latter.

How is attachment described by the Board?

When studying the adjectives applied to describe attachment (see Table 13.4), we find that it is less common that notions of attachment occur in the psychological form as described with terms from attachment theory, as previously noted. A further exploration, revealed 225 occurrences of 'attachment' being accompanied by a descriptive adjective (distributed among 40 of the 58 cases). Among these, 36 adjectives (distributed among 25 of the 58 cases) had a distinct reference to a psychological use of the term (secure, insecure and disorganised). The 29 times that 'secure attachment' was mentioned (distributed among 22 cases), it was always as a description of the relation between the child and their foster parents. When 'insecure attachment' (six instances) or 'disorganised attachment' (one instance) were mentioned, they concerned the child's attachment to biological parents.

In contrast, we identified 82 instances (distributed among 34 cases) of attachment being accompanied by an adjective adhering to the non-psychological understanding of the term and that expressed a quantitative evaluation of the attachment, such as 'strong', 'weak', 'lacking', 'complete', 'absence of' or 'none'. Multiple adjectives are sometimes used to describe attachment in the same sentence; non-psychological and psychological descriptions of attachment were combined 32 times (for example, 'safe and secure'). Moreover, the Board frequently describes attachment as 'fundamental', 'basic',

Table 13.5: Assessments and descriptions of all forms of attachment

	Thematic dimension		
	Time	Identity, integration and belonging	Care and contact
N (%)	52 (90%)	44 (76%)	35 (60%)

Note: Number of cases and percentage of total number of cases (total n = 58). N = 30 cases also containing a variety of other themes

'rooted', 'real', 'primary' or 'psychological'. When such designations are used, they refer to the assessed intensity of the attachment, and allude to a qualitative property of the attachment.

How does the Board understand attachment?

We explored how the Board understands and operationalises attachment in its argumentation (see Table 13.5), and found that time is the most common parameter for assessing attachment (in 90 per cent of the cases). The age of the child when they were first placed out of home or in the care of the adoption seekers, the length of the placement, and the age of the child at the time of the decision in the Board are factors that are mentioned. Thus, the permanency of the placement appears key. Furthermore, we find that attachment was assessed on conditions related to 'care and contact' in 60 per cent of the cases. Most often, we find this expressed as the lack of attachment to biological parents, where the (low) frequency and quality of contact between parents and the child apply as relevant conditions. Within this category, we also find that parents' previous neglect or failure to provide the child with adequate care is found to inform the assessment as a disadvantaging factor of the attachment between the child and their biological parent(s). In contrast, the foster parents' care is seen to have provided fertile ground for attachment bonds to grow. The child's identity, integration and belonging are referred to in 76 per cent of the cases. Considerations within this category are tightly intertwined, and are interpreted as expressions related to identity and the child's feeling of self and safety (see, for example, Triseliotis, 1983). Mentions include descriptions: of whom the child sees and experiences as their de facto parents (family), and of not knowing any other family; of being a natural part of the family and that it is 'as if the child was the foster parents' biological child'; of being integrated into the family and the environment around it; of calling the foster parents 'mom' and 'dad'; and of wanting to or using the family name of the foster family.

Such considerations are, with two exceptions, only used to describe attachment bonds to the foster family.

Discussion

We find that attachment figures as an important concept in the written statements from the Board when it makes decisions concerning adoption from care. However, a wide range of meanings is prescribed to the attachment concept and there is no obvious common denominator or understanding of what attachment is or how it should be described, as illustrated by the fact that, among other things, attachment was accompanied by a multitude of different adjectives. Although we identified some common practices for where and how attachment is assessed, and were able to describe the parameters that were widely used to inform an assessment – time; identity, integration and belonging; and care and contact – the decisions do not display any apparent convergence on the conceptual understanding of attachment, neither between nor within cases. Even though we cannot claim that there is a single pathway or factor that determines attachment security (see George et al, 2011), or that the variety we have observed would have substantial implications for the outcome of the decision and, in turn, for the parties involved, the unpredictability could pose a considerable challenge for the quality of the decisions. Considering that similar assessments to those analysed here are highly relevant for both decisions on reunification and care orders, the issues identified could potentially have implications for a wider range of decision-making processes.

What primarily characterises how attachment is described in the decisions is the marked binary distinction between the presence and absence of attachment. This could be a consequence of the procedural process. The law requires that the person(s) seeking to adopt have fostered the child and that they have been proven fit to care for the child as their own, and the cases that are tried for adoption are, in all the essentials, cases where reunification is not considered a viable option. This probably explains why attachment is more commonly discussed in relation to the child's foster parents compared to biological parents. It also sheds some light on the fact that the child's identity and belonging were, in all essentials, discussed related to the foster home, though the lack of attention to the child's 'birth identity' and to considerations related to the child's biological origin could be problematised (see, for example, recommendations in 'General comment no. 14' of the CRC Committee [2013]). At the same time, our analysis revealed that in relation to the legal permanence condition (a), the Board assesses attachment not only in relation to foster parents, which is what the law requires, but also in relation to biological parents. This could be interpreted as an argumentative strategy, where the Board contrasts the child's attachment to their foster parents with the lack of such attachment to their biological parents with the purpose of reinforcing the argument that the attachment between the foster parents and the child is of such a nature that removing the child may lead to serious problems for them. In this perspective, the discretionary reasoning is exercised by applying contrast as an argumentative tool.

The findings hint at an outline of a binary juridical discourse. It is the task of the Board to assess where and whether attachment exists or not in order for the decision to be right or justifiable. In line with a judicial logic, attachment may become a question of presence or absence. Although it is easily imaginable that attachment can be present in one situation and not in another, this binary logic might become problematic if it forces attachment into being or not being present, among other things, because research has shown that children may have several attachment relations (Killén, 2007). It can also pose a problem for the quality of the decision if complex constructs such as attachment are simplified and understood in binary terms. According to Groze and Rosenthal (1993), such dichotomies can appear when it is difficult to gather around a uniform understanding of a concept. This usage of the term can be misleading and it is a question whether attachment, rather than being understood as being or not being, should be seen as a continuum or as having multiple levels.

We also find traces of a tension between welfare and justice. The psychological understanding of attachment has a less explicit position in the assessments. At the same time, it is obvious that the Board combines non-psychological and psychological understandings of the concept; the judicial discourse alludes to the psychological discourse on several occasions. This makes the interpretation of the Board's utilisation of the construct challenging. One explanation for this practice is that the influence from psychological expert knowledge, as seen at the policy level, has manifested itself at the concrete level in the actual decision-making. In addition, it may be a result of the Board's composition given the high prevalence of psychologists acting as members of the Board.

We found that attachment was dominantly discussed in relation to the permanency condition (a). As the basic condition of Article 4–20 provides two alternatives for determining the permanency of a placement, this implies that attachment could be the preferred alternative to be addressed. In practice, because of how the law is outlined, it becomes somewhat redundant to address the often more complex and difficult question of the likelihood that the parents will be permanently unable to provide the child with proper care if a relocation of the child is already considered to cause serious problems for the child based on an assessment of attachment (Lindboe, 2011). It could also be the (most) relevant alternative to assess, or it could be that attachment is assessed irrespective of which alternative is decisive for the permanence decision. Given that quality of care is understood as an indicator for an attachment bond, it might also be intercorrelated with an assessment of the birth parents' ability to provide care. It is interesting that we also find that attachment is a frequently mentioned factor in best interest assessments. Taking into consideration that the child's identity, integration and belonging, conditions of care, and de facto family situation are provided as parameters for an attachment, it is not surprising that it would also become a part of a best interest assessment. Yet, the question of whether attachment is seen as an umbrella concept that covers most concerns relevant for an adoption assessment, or whether it is merely considered as pivotal in the balancing of adoption or continued foster care, remains unclear.

Conclusion

Our analysis shows that attachment has a prominent position in decisions on adoption, both in terms of determining the permanency of the placement and for assessing if adoption is in the best interest of the child. The quality of the assessments is thus vital for the overall quality of the decisions. At the same time, our analysis shows that there is variation in the conceptualisation of attachment. This was expected given the comprehensive room for discretion that decision-makers are given. Furthermore, while it is beyond the scope of this chapter to consider whether attachment is better understood as a psychological or a non-psychological construct in these decisions, it is clear that problems may arise when predictability is at stake and if the same concept entails different meanings. This begs the question of whether the legislators should provide stronger and more substantial guidance for decision-makers as to how to assess and give meaning to attachment in adoption cases. That could be a useful measure to minimise ambiguity and ensure greater consistency in the understanding and application of attachment by the courts and the Board.

Acknowledgements

This project has received funding from the Research Council of Norway under the Independent Projects – Humanities and Social Science program (grant no. 262773) and European Research Council under the European Union's Horizon 2020 research and innovation programme (grant agreement No 724460). Disclaimer: This chapter reflects only the authors' views and the funding agencies are not responsible for any use that may be made of the information contained therein.

Notes

1   Results based on a survey of 298 respondents from the US, Canada, Norway, Australia, New Zealand, South Africa and Israel.
2   The Board could be composed of five members, should the case in question require it.
3   In seven cases, there were two experts on the Board, and in another in seven cases, the case was decided by the Board leader alone. In the cases where an expert was actually assigned to the Board, they were a psychologist in 75 per cent of the cases.
4   A full description of the analytical approach and code descriptions are available at: www.discretion.uib.no/projects/supplementary-documentation/
5   In Norwegian, 'knyttet til', 'tilknytning', 'tilknytningen', 'tilknyttet' and 'tilknytningspsykologisk'.
6   In one case, such an assessment was not relevant, while in the two other, the permanence condition (a) is only assessed in relation to the birth parents' inability to provide care.

References

Ainsworth, M.D. (1982) 'Attachment: retrospect and prospect', in C.M. Parkes and J. Stevenson-Hinde (eds) *The Place of Attachment in Human Behavior*, New York: Basic Books, pp 3–30.

Ainsworth, M.D. and Bell, S.M. (1970) 'Attachment, exploration, and separation: illustrated by the behavior of one-year-olds in a strange situation', *Child Development*, 41: 49–67.

Azar, S.T., Lauretti, A.F. and Loding, B.V. (1998) 'The evaluation of parental fitness in termination of parental rights cases: a functional-contextual perspective', *Clinical Child and Family Psychology Review*, 1(2): 77–100.

Bendiksen, L.R.L. (2008) *Barn i langvarige fosterhjemsplasseringer—Foreldreansvar og adopsjon* [*Children in Long-Term Placements – Parental Responsibility and Adoption*], Bergen: Fagbokforlaget.

Cashmore, J. and Parkinson, P. (2014) 'The use and abuse of social science research evidence in children's cases', *Psychology, Public Policy, and Law*, 20(3): 239–50.

Copi, I., Cohen, C. and McMahon, K. (2014) *Introduction to Logic* (14th edn), New York: Pearson.

CRC (Committee on the Rights of the Child) (2013) 'General comment no. 14 (2013) on the right of the child to have his or her best interests taken as a primary consideration (Art. 3, para. 1)', CRC/C/GC/14.

Dworkin, R. (1963) 'Judicial discretion', *The Journal of Philosophy*, 60(21): 624–38.

Feteris, E.T. (2017) *Fundamentals of Legal Argumentation: A Survey of Theories on the Justification of Judicial Decisions*, Dordrecht: Kluwer Academic Publishers.

George, C., Isaacs, M. and Marvin, R. (2011) 'Incorporating attachment assessment into custody evaluations: the case of a two-year old and her parents', *Family Court Review*, 49(3): 483–500.

Groze, V. and Rosenthal, J. (1993) 'Attachment theory and the adoption of children with special needs', *Social Work Research and Abstracts*, 29(2): 5–13.

Hawkins, K. (1986) 'Discretion in making legal decisions. On legal decision-making', *Washington and Lee Law Review*, 43: 1161–242.

Helland, H.S. (2020) 'Tipping the scales: The power of parental commitment in decisions on adoption from care' *Children and Youth Services Review*, 119: 105693.

Helland, H.S. (forthcoming) 'In the best interest of the child? Justifying decisions on adoption without parental consent in the Norwegian Supreme Court'.

Hennum, N. (2016) 'Kunnskapens makt i beslutninger' ['The power of knowledge in decisions'], in Ø. Christiansen and B.H. Kojan (eds) *Barnevernets beslutninger* [*Child Welfare Decisions*], Oslo: Universitetsforlaget, pp 48–61.

Killén, K. (2007) *Barndommen varer i generasjoner. Forebygging er alles ansvar* [*Childhood Lasts for Generations. Prevention Is Everyone's Responsibility*] (2nd edn), Oslo: Kommuneforlaget.

King, M. and Piper, C. (1995) *How the Law Thinks about Children* (2nd edn), Aldershot: Ashgate.

King, M. and Thornhill, C. (2003) *Niklas Luhmann's Theory of Politics and Law*, Basingstoke: Palgrave Macmillan.

Kuehnle, K., Coulter, M. and Firestone, G. (2000) 'Child protection evaluations: the forensic stepchild', *Family and Conciliation Courts Review*, 38: 368–91.

Lindboe, K. (2011) *Barnevernloven* [*The Child Welfare Act*] (7th edn), Oslo: Gyldendal Akademiske.

Luhmann, N. (1995) *Social Systems*, Stanford, CA: Stanford University Press.

Magnussen, A.-M. and Skivenes, M. (2015) 'The child's opinion and position in care order proceedings', *The International Journal of Children's Rights*, 23(4): 705–23.

Main, M. and Solomon, J. (1986) 'Discovery of a new, insecure-disorganized/disoriented attachment pattern', in M. Yogman and T.B. Brazelton (eds) *Affective Development in Infancy*, Norwood, NJ: Ablex, pp 95–124.

McIntosh, J.E. (2011) 'Guest editor's introduction to special issue on attachment theory, separation, and divorce: forging coherent understandings for family law', *Family Court Review*, 49(3): 418–25.

NOU 2012:5 (Noregs offentlege utgreiingar) (2012) *Bedre beskyttelse av barns utvikling – ekspertutvalgets utredning om det biologiske prinsipp i barnevernet* [*Better Protection of Children's Development – The Expert Panel Inquiry on the Biological Principle in the Child Welfare System*], Oslo: Barne-, Likestillings- og Inkluderingsdepartementet.

Ofstad, K. and Skar, R. (2015) *Barnevernloven med kommentarer* [*The Child Welfare Act with Comments*] (6th edn), Oslo: Gyldendal juridisk.

Ottosen, M.H. (2006) 'In the name of the father, the child and the holy genes: constructions of "the child's best interest" in legal disputes over contact', *Acta Sociologica*, 49(1): 29–46.

Rutter, M. (1981) *Maternal Deprivation Reassessed* (2nd edn), Harmondsworth: Penguin.

Scott, W.R. (2001) *Institutions and Organizations* (2nd edn), Thousand Oaks, CA: Sage.

Skivenes, M. (2010) 'Judging the child's best interests: rational reasoning or subjective presumptions?', *Acta Sociologica*, 53(4): 339–53.

Skivenes, M. and Tefre, Ø.S. (2012) 'Adoption in the child welfare system – a cross-country analysis of child welfare workers' recommendations for or against adoption', *Children and Youth Services Review*, 34(11): 2220–8.

Smeplass, S.F. (2009) 'Tilknytningsteori i møtet med praksisfeltet ved plassering av små barn i fosterhjem' [Attachment theory meets the practice field in the placing of small children in foster care], *Tidsskriftet Norges Barnevern*, 86(3): 158–71.

Tefre, Ø.S. (2020) 'The child's best interests and the politics of adoptions from care in Norway', *International Journal of Children's Rights*, 28(2): 288–321.

The Norwegian Directorate for Children, Youth and Family Affairs (2017) 'Saksbehandlingsrundskrivet' ['Circular for case processing'] Available at: https://bufdir.no/en/Barnevern/Fagstotte/saksbehandlingsrundskrivet/ (accessed 9 December 2020).

Triseliotis, J. (1983) 'Identity and security in adoption and long-term fostering', *Adoption and Fostering*, 7: 22–31.

Wallin, D. (2007) *Attachment in Psychotherapy*, New York: Guilford.

14

The adoptive kinship network: issues around birth family contact in adoption

June Thoburn

Introduction

The legislation, protocols and practice relevant to relationships between birth family members, adopters and adoptees (as children and adults) has changed over time and varies across countries in light of their particular models of adoption in general and adoption from care specifically. This is apparent in the past and present language used. In England, the more rights-based term 'access' changed in legal and practice terminology to 'contact', and the term preferred by some members of adoptive and birth families is now 'family time'. Some authors of the chapters in this book refer to 'visitation' for meetings and use the broader term 'open adoption' for a wider range of arrangements. These changes in terminology recognise movements in legislation and practice that have occurred in recent years. Acknowledgement has grown that post-adoption links will vary over the lifetime of the adopted child/adult and with differing lifetime events of the birth and adoptive family members. For their research on contact in adoptive families, Neil et al (2015) use the term 'communicative openness' (first used and summarised by Brodzinsky [2006] and more recently by Grotevant et al [2013]) when referring to the approach of adopters who have succeeded in making a range of contact arrangements work well for children with differing needs.

Although the impact on the day-to-day social and inner worlds of the adults and children involved in post-adoption contact have much in common across national boundaries, the way in which it is experienced by adults and children will also depend on the legal provisions or professional approaches to adoptions from care. For countries such as Norway and Ireland, where most adoptions from care have been by existing foster parents with whom the child has lived for years rather than months, arrangements for family links for children in long-term foster family care are very relevant to post-adoption arrangements. The Norway chapter reports movement towards encouraging 'open adoption', and in New South Wales, being willing to facilitate continuing birth family links is a requirement for prospective adopters in a specialist 'permanence' programme (Tregeagle et al, 2014). For England, where, in recent years, most placements for adoption from care are of young children with families not previously known to them, the emphasis moves very quickly to a consideration of pre- and post-placement links between birth families and adopters, and the relational transfer of the child from the foster family to the new family. For countries that have a more 'mixed' system (including 'high' users of adoption from care, as with the US, and 'low' users, as with Finland), the relevant protocols, practice and research have to take account of contact with foster families as well as with adopters. For the US, where adoption by kin is fairly frequent, post-adoption contact will bring in different issues. Where post-adoption secrecy is still the prevalent model of adoption, continuing contact is unusual but can happen if persistent social workers, birth relatives, adopters and older children take steps to facilitate it.

This chapter focuses on birth family contact for children placed for adoption from care in jurisdictions in which the practice is fairly extensive and has existed for long enough for the development of a knowledge base for practice, as well as for some corresponding adaptations to legislation. As is clear from the other chapters in this volume, this is mainly the US and the UK nations, though the main focus for this chapter is England.[1] It starts with an overview of the context and growing understanding in the literature on what is now generally referred to as 'contact' for children in care needing placements with substitute families (sometimes referred to, especially by professionals and the children and adopters themselves, as 'families for life' or 'forever families'). The term 'contact' is used as shorthand for a range of practices for setting up and maintaining meaningful links between members of the birth family and the child as they grow to maturity in the adoptive family.

The context and developing practice of contact within UK child placement services

There are overarching principles and understandings from child development and the social sciences (see, especially, Kirk, 1964; Brodzinski, 1987; Fahlberg, 1994) that have informed adoption practice in general and adoptions from care in particular, and that underpin practice when deciding on and facilitating appropriate continuing links. Thoburn (1994) has summarised the broadly agreed conclusion that success when placing children in care, to which the appropriate contact arrangements for each child and family will contribute, is for the child to have a strong sense of identity and self-esteem that enables them to feel confident in making new relationships. This involves careful assessment and reassessment in order to best meet each child's needs at each stage of the journey through care, adoption and beyond.

To summarise a great deal of relevant child development and child placement research, children entering care whose long-term needs cannot be met by returning to birth parents or relatives need security, love, stability and to be 'part of a family' – what has come to be known as a 'sense of permanence' and belonging. However, they also need knowledge of their birth family and their personal and cultural history, and to be helped to come to an understanding of 'why' they needed to first leave their birth family and then become a member of another family. This involves being helped by their adopters, social workers and sometimes specialist therapists to work through and manage the distress of separation, loss and other traumas they have suffered, and (other than in exceptional circumstances) to maintain appropriate and meaningful links with adult and sibling members of their birth families. For those whose new family is of a different ethnic or cultural background, and especially if they are visibly different from their adopters, there is the additional task of integrating their birth heritage with the culture they grow up in, and for some, preserving family links will be an important part of that (Thoburn et al, 2000).

Those adopted from care when past infancy (whether by current foster carers or by adoptive families not previously known to them) may retain an attachment with one or more adult birth family members, as well as (in most, though not all, cases) becoming attached to their adoptive parents. In some cases, when sibling groups are adopted into the same family, there may be a difference in this respect between those joining the new family at different ages.

Moving on from overarching principles when thinking about birth family links, there are commonly held but 'unevidenced myths' that have been identified by researchers who have interviewed social workers and other practitioners (see, for example, Thoburn et al, 2000; Adams, 2012; Neil et al, 2015). These include:

- Birth family (and former foster family) contact will impede the growth of attachments when a child moves to an adoptive family.

- Contact will make it more likely that the child will wish to return to the birth family at some point.
- Contact between adopted children and siblings still living with or in contact with birth parents is likely to be unhelpful or even harmful as it is less easy for adopters to maintain their confidentiality and to control the information their child has about the birth family.
- Children past infancy who have 'strong' attachments to birth families will not be able to/should not be expected to form new attachments.
- Children who have a secure attachment in a planned short-term foster family will be able to 'transfer the attachment' with little difficulty. Although it is sometimes unavoidable, separation from and loss of a loved foster carer will always be stressful and the new parents need to be prepared for this, including, where appropriate, facilitating continuing contact with the foster carers.

An overview of the research on birth family links for children placed for adoption

The following sections summarise the lessons for policy and practice from this body of research (much of it coming directly from adoptees, birth relatives and adopters), as well as from the practice literature (see, for example, Fahlberg, 1994; Argent, 2002; Adams, 2012; for a research-based practice handbook, see also Macaskill, 2002). There is a body of research (mainly from the US) on (mainly consensual) adoption that reports on continuing birth family contact when children are placed as infants, most notably, the longitudinal study by Grotevant and colleagues (2013), which used case record data, in-depth interviews and standardised tests for different aspects of well-being to report on changing patterns of contact. The lack of post-adoption birth family contact in most 'consensual' adoption placements made before the 1970s is the main focus of the 'adoption search and reunion' studies of Howe and Feast (2000) and Triseliotis et al (2005). Much of the earlier UK research on birth family contact for children in care focuses on children in foster family care, and this is relevant to those adopted by their current foster carers (see, for example, Neil and Howe, 2004).

Among the government-commissioned research tracking child placement arrangements before and after the Children Act 1989 and the Adoption Act 2002 were studies that include information on contact for children in long-term care and adopted (Thomas, 2013). There are, however, very few longitudinal studies that specifically focus on contact arrangements at the different stages of a child's journey through care into an adoptive family and as they grow up and into adult life. Boyle

(2017) scopes the more recent research (all published after 2004). She provides a content analysis of 11 publications that meet the standards for inclusion, identifying 'attachment', 'separation and loss' and 'identity' as key themes. Numbers of children in these studies range from two to 87 and they refer to seven separate research studies, four of which include long-term foster placements as well as adoption.

The larger number of UK studies of adoption from care usually combine case record data with anonymised case examples and direct quotes from birth relatives, children and adopters. Some include whether or not there is family contact as a variable that may be associated with positive or less positive outcomes. Fratter et al (1991) have 'contact' as a variable when reporting on 1,165 children placed from care with adoptive or permanent foster families, and Thoburn et al (2000) used quantitative and qualitative data to follow up 297 of those of minority ethnic heritage when they were between the ages of 17 and 25.

Fratter (1996) and Smith and Logan (2004) report on the views of adopters and birth parents who made arrangements for direct post-adoption contact, and, most recently, Neil et al (2015) report on a 16-year follow-up study of varying contact arrangements for children placed for adoption, most of whom were aged under two at the time of placement. The longitudinal study of Selwyn et al (2014) includes some children entering care and placed with adopters when past infancy. The longer pre-placement experience of traumatic events of some, often together with a mixture of positive and negative memories of birth relatives, in part, explains some differences in these two studies with respect to the benefits and stresses of contact. Older-placed children, for example, are reported to show more distress before and after face-to-face meetings than tends to be the case with younger-placed children who have not formed an attachment with the birth relative they are meeting.

Contact arrangements at the different stages of adoption from care

As noted in Chapter 2 in this volume, in England, there was a shift in age at placement for adoption between the 1980s, when 'hard-to-place' specialist agencies placed children across the age groups from residential and foster care with adoptive and 'permanent' foster families, and the present time, when the majority join their adoptive families when under the age of three (Fratter et al, 1991; Selwyn et al, 2014; Neil et al, 2015, 2018). Over this period, in line with legislation and statutory guidance, requirements for a 'permanence plan' for all children in care have strengthened and have to include a section on birth family links in the short and longer term. Depending on the year of placement, from the mid-1990s onwards, between 80 per cent and 90 per cent of children adopted from care in England had a plan for some form of contact (mostly indirect) with at least one adult birth family member.

There is very little research specifically exploring contact during the early period of care and the move to an adoptive family. An area that has been touched on concerns very young children during care proceedings, where researchers have explored a tension regarding contact: on the one hand, not pre-empting the court decision and therefore having contact arrangements that allow infants to maintain and (for those removed at birth) make attachments so that return can be facilitated if it becomes the preferred plan; and, on the other hand, the likely negative impact on the infant of the disruption of routines necessitated by frequent meetings with birth relatives. Researchers reporting on a 'concurrent planning' service report the views of a small number of prospective adopters and birth parents on what makes birth family contact during this period more or less stressful (Monck et al, 2003; Kenrick, 2009). Schofield and Simmonds (2011) draw on this research to identify questions about the impact of contact on the infant's development that need to be considered and the importance of allowing for change in contact arrangements and frequency during court proceedings.

The majority of the studies referred to earlier provide data and insights from the 'adoptive kinship network'[2] after the decision for adoption has been made. Some specifically report on the views of birth relatives and adoption workers, while most include information on the views of adopters and adoptees as children and young adults.

Neil and colleagues (2015) report on a 16-year follow-up study of different contact arrangements for children placed mainly under the age of two. The start of the study coincided with a period when some adoption agencies specifically sought adopters who were interested in facilitating direct contact with a parent or adult relative, so the sample of adoptive families allowed for a consideration of both direct meetings (mostly once a year but sometimes more frequent) and 'indirect' contact. In some cases, the adopted child shares in an age-appropriate way in these indirect exchanges (which are usually moderated by a specialist adoption worker), but in others, anything received from the birth family is 'saved' for the child to see 'when old enough'. Some adopters in the 'indirect contact' group met a birth parent before or shortly after placement and, over time, arrangements changed, some direct contact becoming indirect and stopping, and some indirect arrangements moving to direct contact between adopters, birth relatives and the child, or just between the older child and birth relatives. Contrary to the research evidence that well-managed, agreed, direct contact is usually less problematic for all concerned than 'letter-box' contact, in recent years, face-to-face contact has become less frequent and 'letter-box contact' has become the norm, even for older-placed children.

These researchers also report that, over the past ten years or so, some adoptive children have begun to have contact with birth family members via social media. These reconnections are often driven by unmet needs of adoptees and birth parents to know about each other; however, this often sudden, and covert and unsupported contact can sometimes lead to difficulties for young people. Virtual or online contact may also be used by adults and young people just to gather information, or it may be a welcomed 'add-on' to existing face-to-face contact plans – allowing less formal and more frequent contact to take place, and making contact over large geographical distances more possible. Comments in the professional journals and social media indicate that online methods for retaining or re-establishing links are prompting professionals and adoptive parents to consider that a closed adoption cannot be guaranteed, and that the best way to avoid 'out of the blue' contact is to maintain open communication that meets adopted young people's needs. Research into the recent widespread use of digital technology to keep children in care in touch with birth family during the 'lockdown' necessitated by the COVID-19 pandemic suggests that digitally mediated contact could be a useful option for some adopted children to stay connected with members of their birth families (Neil et al, 2020).

A growing source of information comes from 'experts by experience' in the form of reports both from post-adoption or parent advocacy groups and on social media. One recent example is the 'Two Good Mums' series of podcasts, in which a birth parent and an adoptive parent talk of the moves they made from the trauma of loss through compulsory removal into care and the sadness of involuntary childlessness, to the rewards of their present regular emails and annual family meetings.[3] Another adoptive parent blogger and post-adoption counsellor (Mummy Tiger Blogs, 2018), along with her adopted daughter, advocates for more flexible contact arrangements and away from formulaic practices based on age of the child and reason for care rather than individual circumstances: 'Last weekend I left my children with the woman courts decided couldn't care for them and social workers had said was too volatile for me to meet' (Twitter@ mummytiger1, 18 November 2018). For others, the experience was more stressful, as with the following adoptive mother interviewed by Neil et al (2015: 97) who kept up with the infrequent family meetings she had committed herself to at the start of the process:

> you're spending time with people that you don't really know all that well. You have this odd link with them that's not based on friendship or family or background or anything. ... And then there's also, it's just another reminder that she's not 100% yours. So, I have to cope with that.

What do we know about how contact arrangements impact on outcomes in the longer term?

Researchers use a wide range of outcome measures, which makes it difficult to compare what different studies have to say about the impact of contact arrangements on satisfaction with adoption and child well-being outcomes. Outcome measures that are used differently according to research method are:

- the placement lasts/disrupts (though duration of follow-up varies) (Expressed more positively: did the adoptive family become the child's 'family for life'?);
- Physical and psychological well-being (treatment aims achieved), including resilience, self-efficacy and self-esteem;
- educational/employment aims achieved;
- making satisfactory relationships as an adult;
- awareness of and comfort with personal, ethnic and cultural identity as an adopted person; and
- satisfaction of child/young person, birth parents and adopters with their adoptive family experience and with placement practice.

The last two of these specifically require a consideration of any ongoing birth family links.

The research, especially on placements that have disrupted or come under severe stress, points to the conclusion that the wrong match (with respect to legal arrangements but especially to the matching of adopters' needs, wishes and motivations with the child's needs) cannot be 'mended' by even high-quality practice and services; it can only be 'patched up'. Adopters and adopted young people have argued that the child's need for the maintenance of meaningful links should be more central to the matching process and detailed placement plans than it usually is (see, for example, the 'blogs' referred to earlier; see also Featherstone et al, 2018).

As noted elsewhere in this volume, numbers adopted from care in England have increased but the proportion placed beyond infancy has decreased and there has been a decline in the numbers who have ongoing post-placement direct contact. Recent longitudinal research has found no statistically significant link between the type of contact arrangements and placement stability or other well-being outcomes. However, along with US researchers, Neil et al (2015) report that the characteristic of 'communicative openness' was more likely to be found among the adopters of children in the 'more successful outcome' group, and that this characteristic was more likely when there was some direct contact with at least one adult birth family member. These researchers and others who have directly sought the views of children in adoptive families (Thomas et al, 1999; Thoburn et al, 2000; Smith and Logan, 2004; McSherry and Fargas Malet, 2018) report that those who do have contact with a birth relative are generally broadly content with their contact arrangements. Of those who were not content, rather more wanted more frequent than less frequent contact, and with more rather than fewer family members.

From their detailed conversations with young adoptees as they grew up, Neil et al (2015) concluded that:

- satisfaction with contact varied within all types of openness, being associated with contact quality and stability more than type or frequency;
- dissatisfaction was often associated with gaps in or unexplained cessation of contact, and this was most likely with 'letter-box' than with 'direct' contact; and
- most saw some benefits in having contact and argued that the option should be there ('Even if the contact is only brief ... I think social workers should ensure that the option of staying in contact is always left open' [Neil et al, 2015: 255]).

For whom and why is contact important and what are the risks of inappropriate or badly managed contact?

The evidence about possible harms is sparse, and conclusions are mainly about direct contact and mainly drawn from case analyses of very small numbers (see, for example, Howe and Steele, 2004). This tends to be mainly about pre-placement contact since direct post-adoption contact for very young children is unusual, and tends to mainly concern slightly older children who have had more extensive experience of abuse or rejection. Authors writing from a psychological or child psychiatry perspective argue that even young children may be re-traumatised on seeing the parent they associate with harm, or that a child's sense of safety and trust in the new family may be impaired. Some researchers, including Selwyn et al (2014), report cases when parental contact has contributed to destabilising a placement (especially in adolescence and when social media is used by a birth relative or teenager to renew or increase contact without the knowledge of the adoptive parents).

The research and practice texts have more to say about the potential benefits of appropriate and well-managed contact, and note that benefits may be gained when links are maintained with some family members (often grandparents and siblings) and not others. From the range of studies and research syntheses from across continents that are drawn upon here, the potential benefits of seeking to maintain appropriate meaningful links with the birth family, if ways of doing so can be safely arranged, for the child and young adult are as follows:

- it helps the child and young adult to have a clearer sense of genetic and cultural identity (contact with family members can be especially important to a sense of ethnic and cultural identity if the adopters are of a different ethnicity);
- it helps the developing child and young adult to have an understanding of and be comfortable with their identity as an adopted person;
- it can contribute to higher self-esteem in the young person and adult;
- for some who have knowledge of a parent and of the parent's difficulties, it helps stop them worrying that the parents are coming to harm, and also any siblings they are aware of who are still with the parent;
- when carefully managed, it can reduce the risk of the placement breaking down (before or after the adoption order) and the child returning to care;
- for children placed past infancy (including young children for whom birth family ties improved during the period of temporary foster care), it can offer continuity of relationships and can help overcome the grief associated with separation and loss;
- it may provide a contingency plan if a placement does not work out (there are examples, especially for children with disabilities, when a birth family member has stepped in to provide 'short break' care for the adoptive family); and

- by retaining links that can possibly come into their own as the child goes through adult life, there is an increased chance that the adopted person will have at least one 'family for life' (this applies especially to maintaining sibling links).

The potential benefits for adopters (see Thoburn et al, 2000; Jones and Hackett, 2007; Neil, 2010; Neil et al, 2015, Featherstone et al, 2018) are as follows:

- it gives them a more rounded picture and fuller understanding of the birth family;
- it helps them to communicate with their child and to adapt how they do so as the child's understanding changes;
- it helps them both early on and as their love for the child deepens to manage anxieties ('For me, a mother popping up out of the blue would feel very threatening. ... I don't have that threat because we already have that relationship with her' [Neil et al, 2015: 84]); and
- it can bring them closer to their child ('I think it actually makes them feel more part of our family. ... Every contact we come away feeling more secure really ... more certain that they need us as parents and that they are our children' [Neil et al, 2010: 162]).

The potential benefits for birth family members

The members of the 'adoptive kinship network' who speak most appreciatively to researchers about their experience of appropriate continuing links are birth parents and relatives (Neil et al, 2010). In England, placement practice and judicial decision-making over the past ten years or so follows the 'formula' that has grown from custom and practice. Contact is discussed (as required in the legislation) and the decision is taken that there will be no direct contact, but there will be agency-monitored 'letter-box' contact. This practice results in very few birth relatives being asked if they would like to retain direct contact, even when they have been important parts of the child's life before and during care. Some birth parents are too distressed or emotionally low to respond to the (infrequent) invitation of a social worker to discuss possible contact arrangements. Often, the assumption is made by social workers and matching panels, even for older children with fairly positive existing links, that an initial reaction of birth parents to the decision that their child will not return to them is a once-and-forever response, and no attempt is made to help them through their anger or distress and reach an arrangement that can benefit their child and themselves. The predominant response made to researchers by birth parents and relatives having any form of sustained contact, though especially planned and facilitated meetings, is gratitude that this allows them to 'still be a mum [dad or grandparent]' even though not able to be a full-time parent. Researchers cite birth relatives who find actual meetings or even sensitively written letters to be sources of comfort that their child is loved and cared for (Featherstone et al, 2018). The other response is that having regular updates frees them from 'thinking the worst' – they want to know, though do not need details, if not all is well. For some, the opportunity to 'still be a mum' has meant that they decided against having other children.

The importance of pre- and post-placement services that support contact arrangements

The qualitative research studies are rich with ideas from children, young adults, birth relatives, adopters, social workers and foster carers about how to make, maintain or change arrangements for maintaining appropriate links. Researchers emphasise that the benefits of contact are less likely to be achieved if the support of trusted professionals (and often for birth parents and kinship carers, practical services and help with transport) is not there at the start and at times of change. Neil et al (2015) found that many contact arrangements petered out without explanation to the other party to the arrangements: a third of the young people in their study had lost the (mostly indirect) contact they started off with by the time they were in their mid-teens. This was most often because of adopters not seeing the benefits for their family as a whole but also because some birth parents dropped out of sight, as well as the unreliability, cumbersome nature and lack of sensitivity of the agency's letter-box service. Contact with parents was less likely to be maintained than contact with grandparents and siblings (sometimes unavoidably because a parent had died). However, there was some increase in contact for some in adolescence (often unknown to their adoptive parents) via social media.

The characteristics of services that achieve successful contact are discussed by Neil and Howe (2004), who advocate a 'transactional model' for thinking about contact. Researchers and practitioners conclude that successful contact arrangements are most likely to be achieved and endure when adopters and birth relatives can establish a positive, or at least neutral, relationship. However, birth relatives can be helped by sensitive social work to become more accepting of the adoption, and continuing monitoring can pick up on the fact that early hostility has turned into acceptance, making appropriate contact possible (Neil et al, 2010).

Contact arrangements should start to be discussed among placement team members and with parents as soon as adoption becomes a serious possibility. Local authorities that routinely set up family meetings have an advantage in this respect as this is a forum for seeking the views of birth parents and close relatives whose children may be placed for adoption. The way in which this discussion is approached can make a big difference. Too often, it is put as 'our policy on contact is ...' or, slightly better, 'What contact would you be seeking?', though more appropriate would be 'What role might you be able to play in your child's life as they settle into a new family?' and 'What sort of arrangements for staying in touch will work best for you/will you be able to manage to keep up with?'. A meeting between the likely foster or adoptive family and the parent(s), relatives or carers of siblings placed elsewhere who will be part of contact arrangements can be particularly helpful around the time of the 'matching' decision (Cossar and Neil, 2013). The timing of such a meeting will vary and it should not be combined with a contact meeting with the child or between siblings. Also, a plea from birth relatives, especially as some form of contact is maintained or happens later with most children placed from adoption, is that there should be an end to the inappropriate and hurtful language and practice of 'goodbye visits'. Many agencies, for example, use the language of 'a family meeting to wish you well as you move to your new family'.

Conclusion

The most important determinant of good outcomes is the quality of the child's experience in the adoptive family and the match between the needs and wishes of the child and the skills, hopes and expectations of the adopters. *However*, skilled and informed care planning and the quality of social work practice with children, foster carers, adopters and birth relatives will make a difference in maximising the potential of any placement to give children and young people the start in life they need. Arrangements for maintaining appropriate links with birth family members are just one component, though likely to be an important one. There is no formula that works in all cases and no slide rule on frequency at different ages, but it is important to know that most children who have been asked for their views want more contact with a larger number of family members than is actually arranged for them. Care is needed to identify the small minority of children, especially among those who have been severely maltreated or cruelly rejected, who are likely to be harmed by some forms of contact with some (and occasionally all) members of the birth family. However, overall, the research supports a presumption of some form of contact that results in meaningful links with some (though not necessarily all) members of the birth family. For England, there is clear evidence to support a move from standardised decisions about continuing links based on a child's age and the preferences of potential adopters, to one based on the needs and particular circumstances and relationships of each child.

Notes

[1] Adoption practice in the four UK nations has many similarities but also differences (Featherstone et al, 2018).

[2] This term is used by the Grotevant et al team in the US (Grotevant et al, 2013).

[3] See: www.twogoodmums.co.uk

References

Adams, P. (2012) *Planning for Contact in Permanent Placements*, London: BAAF.

Argent, H. (ed) (2002) *Staying Connected: Managing Contact in Adoption*, London: BAAF.

Boyle, C. (2017) 'What is the impact of birth family contact on children in adoption and long-term foster care?', *Child and Family Social Work*, 22: 22–33.

Brodzinsky, D. (1987) 'Adjustment to adoption: a psychosocial perspective', *Clinical Psychological Review*, 7: 25–47.

Brodzinsky, D. (2006) 'Family structural openness and communication openness as predictors in the adjustment of adopted children', *Adoption Quarterly*, 9: 1–18.

Cossar, J. and Neil, E. (2013) 'Making sense of siblings: connections and severances in post-adoption contact', *Child and Family Social Work*, 18: 67–76.

Fahlberg, V. (1994) *A Child's Journey through Placement*, London: BAAF.

Featherstone, B., Gupta, A. and Mills, S. (2018) *The Role of the Social Worker in Adoption – Ethics and Human Rights*, Birmingham: BASW.

Fratter, J. (1996) *Adoption with Contact: Implications for Policy and Practice*, London: BAAF.

Fratter, J., Rowe, J., Sapsford, D. and Thoburn, J. (1991) *Permanent Family Placement: A Decade of Experience*, London: BAAF.

Grotevant, H.D., McRoy, R.G., Wrobel, G. and Ayres-Lopes, S. (2013) 'Contact between adoptive and birth families: perspectives from the Minnesota/Texas Adoption Research Project' *Child Development Perspectives*, 7(3): 193–8.

Howe, D. and Feast, J. (2000) *Adoption, Search and Reunion: The Long-Term Experience of Adopted Adults*, London: BAAF.

Howe, D. and Steele, M. (2004) 'Contact in cases in which children have been traumatically abused or neglected by their birth parents', in E. Neil and D. Howe (eds) *Contact in Adoption and Permanent Foster Care*, London: BAAF.

Jones, C. and Hackett, S. (2007) 'Communicative openness within adoptive families: adoptive parents' narrative accounts of the challenges of adoption talk and the approaches used to manage these challenges', *Adoption Quarterly*, 10(2/3): 157–78.

Kenrick, J. (2009) 'Concurrent planning: a retrospective study of the continuities and discontinuities of care and their impact on the development of infant and young children placed for adoption by the Coram Concurrent Planning Project', *Adoption and Fostering*, 33(4): 5–18.

Kirk, D. (1964) *Shared Fate*, London: Collier Macmillan.

Macaskill, C. (2002) *Safe Contact? Children in Permanent Placement and Contact with Their Birth Relatives*, Lyme Regis: Russell House.

McSherry, D. and Fargas Malet, M. (2018) 'The extent of stability and relational permanence achieved for young children in care in Northern Ireland', *Children Australia*, 43(2): 124–34.

Monck, E., Reynolds, J. and Wigfall, V. (2003) *The Role of Concurrent Planning*, London: BAAF.

Mummy Tiger Blogs (2018) 'Contact'. Available at: http://mummytigerblogs.com/contact/ (accessed 7 June 2020).

Neil, E. (2010) 'The benefits and challenges of direct post-adoption contact: perspectives from adoptive parents and birth relatives', *Aloma: Revista de Psicologia, Ciències de l'Educació i de l'Esport*, 27. Available at: http://revistaaloma.net/index.php/aloma/article/view/23/12

Neil, E. and Howe, D. (eds) (2004) *Contact in Adoption and Permanent Foster Care: Research, Theory and Practice*, London: BAAF.

Neil, E., Cossar, J., Lorgelly, P. and Young, J. (2010) *Helping Birth Families: Services, Cost and Outcomes*, London: BAAF.

Neil, E., Beek, M. and Ward, E. (2015) *Contact after Adoption: A Longitudinal Study of Post Adoption Contact Arrangements*, London: Coram-BAAF.

Neil, E., Young, J. and Hartley, L. (2018) *The Joys and Challenges of Adoptive Family Life: A Survey of Adoptive Parents in the Yorkshire and Humberside Region*, Norwich: UEA Centre for Research on Children and Families. Available at: www.researchgate.net/publication/337171004_THE_JOYS_AND_CHALLENGES_OF_ADOPTIVE_FAMILY_LIFE_A_SURVEY_OF_ADOPTIVE_PARENTS_IN_THE_YORKSHIRE_AND_HUMBERSIDE_REGION (accessed 11 December 2020).

Neil, E., Copson, R. and Sorensen, P. (2020) *Contact During Lockdown: How Are Children and Their Birth Families Keeping in Touch?*, London: Nuffield Family Justice Observatory.

Schofield, G. and Simmonds, J. (2011) 'Contact for infants during care proceedings', *Family Law*, 41: 617–22.

Selwyn, J., Wijedasa, D.N. and Meakings, S.J. (2014) *Beyond the Adoption Order: Challenges, Interventions and Disruptions*, London: DfE.

Smith, C. and Logan, J. (2004) *After Adoption: Direct Contact and Relationships*, London: Routledge.

Thoburn, J. (1994) *Child Placement: Principles and Practice*, Aldershot: Avebury.

Thoburn, J., Norford, L. and Rashid, S.P. (2000) *Permanent Family Placement for Children of Minority Ethnic Origin*, London: Jessica Kingsley.

Thomas, C. (2013) *Adoption for Looked after Children: Messages from Research*, London: BAAF.

Thomas, C., Beckford, V., Lowe, N. and Murch, M. (1999) *Adopted Children Speaking*, London: BAAF.

Tregeagle, S., Moggash, L., Cox, E. and Voigt, L. (2014) 'A pathway from long-term care to adoption: findings from an Australian permanency programme', *Adoption and Fostering*, 38(2): 115–30.

Triseliotis, J., Feast, J. and Kyle, J. (2005) *The Adoption Triangle Revisited*, London: BAAF.

Making sense of adoption from care in very different contexts

Tarja Pösö, Marit Skivenes and June Thoburn

Introduction

This book has its focus on a very special group of children, namely, children in public care for whom adoption may be appropriate. It is about children who, for various reasons, are the responsibility of the child protection system and the government in a country. The traditional division of responsibilities between the family and the state has been altered for these children; for them, it is the state that has the formal responsibility to raise them and evoked the *parens patriae*. Of course, in practice, children are raised by foster parents, kin and extended family, and residential care workers; however, it is nevertheless the state that has the formal authority to make decisions about the child, and to ensure that the child's needs are appropriately met, as would any good parent.

The recent WHO–UNICEF–Lancet Commission article 'A future for the world's children?' (Clarke et al, 2020) measures the foundational conditions for today's children, across the world, to survive and thrive. The nine countries in this book are, with two exceptions, among the top 20 in terms of children's living conditions. The exceptions are Estonia (ranked 27) and the US (ranked 39) (Clarke et al, 2020). As we remarked upon in the introductory chapter, the countries approach their responsibilities towards children in different ways, with those approaches varying from risk-oriented child protection systems[1] to family service systems with a focus on the family and on children's rights (Gilbert et al, 2011). Although different forms of child protection removals and alternative care have been highlighted before in conjunction with the states' responsibilities towards children and the different child protection systems, this book's focus on adoptions from care is unique in its ambition to provide in-depth analyses of country policies, practices and key themes regarding adoption from care. It complements the analysis by Palacios et al (2019), in which an interdisciplinary group of researchers, based on their broad knowledge of research in this area, conclude that adoption provides a legitimate model for the alternative care of children if undertaken within a rights and ethics framework that emphasises children's best interests, as set out in international conventions and national laws. In this concluding chapter, we will summarise the key messages from the previous chapters, look at the strengths and weaknesses of the use of adoption as a child protection measure, and suggest ways ahead for research, policy and practice.[2]

The types of adoption from care

We presented the definition for the term 'adoption from care' in the introductory chapter in the following way:

> adoptions from care ... are to be understood as those adoptions where a child who is currently in public care or is under guardianship of the state, after full or partial removal of custody from the parents, is placed with prospective adopters and/or legally adopted by their foster carers with or without the consent of the parents.

We have included only domestic adoptions from care in this book. Family reunification is an aim in all child protection systems (Berrick et al, forthcoming a); however, unfortunately, the statistical information on reunification seems to be scarcely available and even information about the length of time spent in public care is not available for cross-country comparisons. Nevertheless, several country authors report that children rarely leave long-term care. Although the term 'adoption from care' is not an established and comprehensively used term, children who are in public care are adopted in every jurisdiction included in this book. We found two main types of adoptions from care. They take place: first, in those situations in which children are already in long-term public care and are then adopted by the foster parents (or a relative) with whom they already live; or, second, when the child moves to live with specially recruited adopters, sometimes fairly quickly but sometimes after a period of months or years in public care. In the first path, the foster parents who become adoptive parents are already familiar to the child, whereas the adoptive parents will usually be strangers in the second path. Some of the countries in this book use mainly one approach, while others use both.

For almost all countries, adoption is an integral part of the child protection system (the exceptions are Austria and Finland). For most, it is the same decision-making body that makes the decision about a care order that also makes the decision about an adoption from care (the exceptions are Finland and Spain). Although all systems can decide on adoption without the agreement of the parent(s), in four countries, cooperation and consent from the parent(s) are the norm: Austria, Finland, Germany and Ireland (in Ireland, there are two pathways depending on the consent). Children's consent is equally required (we will return to the age limits later in this chapter). A comprehensive overview of the proceedings and decision-making bodies in eight of the nine jurisdictions (minus the US) included in this volume is laid out in Burns et al (2019: esp 365, Table 4).

Two important, and recently recognised, themes in discussions about adoptions from care (see Helland and Skivenes, 2019; Breen et al, 2020; see also ECtHR Strand Lobben v Norway 2017) are: first, that decisions in these cases are about continued public care *versus* an adoption, and rarely about an adoption or a reunification with the birth parents; and, second, an adoption decision shifts the public care responsibility for the child to the private care of a family. An adopted child is no longer directly under the *parens patriae* responsibility of the state, but included in the private sphere of the family (Tefre, 2015). This resonates with a view that children not only have formal rights, but are also recognised as individuals within the family unit that both the state and courts must relate to directly. From a family perspective, and regarding the child's right to family life, this is an under-reported dimension in our view and something we believe is immensely important. In an article by Breen and colleagues (2020), the status of and respect for the child's de facto family life is discussed, and based on an analysis of 20 judgments regarding adoption from care made by the European Court of Human Rights (ECtHR), the authors argue that the discourses are changing. The interesting and paradoxical theme in cases of adoption from care is that, in case law and principles, the birth family is regarded as the superior family, even for children who will never be reunified with their birth parents, but will grow up in care (Breen et al, 2020). What Breen et al find is that the ECtHR's view on and understanding of family for children increasingly entails a recognition and stronger protection of children's non-biological and de facto family life.

The adoptive family of a child previously in public care is as any family in all countries included in this book, with some exceptions regarding financial and other post-adoption support (the US and England). The same applies to adopted children: as they are adopted, they rely on their adoptive family's support and, if needed, on the support given to any other child with a similar need. We will look at the issues related to pre- and post-adoption services raised by the country authors after we first look at the numbers of children adopted from care.

Adoption from care in numbers

The nine jurisdictions included in this book cover a range of welfare state models and child protection systems. Examining the statistics, it is of importance to examine how many of the children placed in public care by the child protection system are subsequently adopted. We asked every country author to provide the numbers of children adopted from care, as well as the numbers of children in care by a care order. Underscoring that the bases for the calculations are not always similar and that comparing statistics across countries is notoriously difficult (for example, in terms of stock or flow numbers, or defining what a care order means in different jurisdictions), the overview gives a very clear picture of the countries that make most frequent use of adoption from care. In the US, 14.44 per cent of children in care on a given day were adopted during the year, and in England, it was 6.2 per cent. In Spain, 1.7 per cent of children in care were adopted, and in the remaining countries, less than 1 per cent of children in care were adopted. An interesting observation is that we see some correlation between adoption policies in a country and the child protection system in place. England and the US are high users of adoptions (see Table 15.1). However, Ireland also has a risk-oriented system but has few adoptions from care.

An important reason for the use of adoption in England and the US, as both Thoburn (in Chapter 2) and Berrick (in Chapter 5) point out, is that research demonstrated that too many children were not reunited with their families and experienced too many placement changes. In the US, a child rights orientation among congressional leaders focusing on children's right to permanency resulted in new legislation (the Adoption and Safe Families Act 1997) that set adoption as the preferred alternative if reunification was not possible (see Chapter 5). Tefre (2015) argues that an important driver for the new legislation in the US was research that revealed the importance of permanency and the improved outcomes for children that were adopted compared to children in foster care. Similar reasons are evident in Norway (see Chapter 9; see also Tefre, 2020) and Ireland (see Chapter 4). In England, the emphasis on children's rights to stability and family membership

Table 15.1: Overview of children in public care and adoption from care for nine countries

1	2	3	4	5	6
Country and child population (0–17) (year)	Children in public care by care order decision, total at year end (year)	Rate of children in public care by care order decision per 100,000	Number of children adopted from care	Rate per 100,000 child population adopted from care	Adopted from care as a percentage of children in care
Austria 1,535,958 (2018)	13,325[a]	868	110 (2018)	7.1	0.83%
England 11,776,562 (2018)	61,710	524	3,820 (2017/18)	32	6.2%
Estonia 252,117 (2018)	2,451	972	22 (2018)	8	0.9%
Finland 1,058,091 (2018)	9,295	878	10 (2015)	0.9 (2015)	0.1% (2015)
Germany 13,470,300 (2016)	147,258 (2016)	1,082	269	2	0.18%
Ireland 1,190,478 (2017)	5,974 (2018)	501	25 (2018)	2	0.42%
Norway 1,122,508 (2018)	8,868 (2018)	790	55 (2018)	4.8	0.62%
Spain 8,119,000 (2015)	34,644 (2017)	426	588 (2016)	7.2	1.7%
USA 73,600,000 (2016)	437,283 (2018)	595	63,123 (2018)	85.9	14.44%

Note: [a] For Austria, the statistics include all types of out-of-home placements during a year.

resulted in both an increase in adoptions and also improvements in long-term foster care so that it could be regarded as a permanence option for some children, though young entrants to long-term care are mainly placed quickly for adoption (see Chapter 2).

When we look at the trends of adoptions from care over the last 15 years or so (depending on the data available in different chapters), the US and England stand out again. The use of adoptions from care has expanded in both contexts. However, England has experienced a decline in the most recent years. We can see trends in Austria, Norway, Estonia and Germany as well, and the trends show either some decrease (Estonia) or very slight increase (Austria and Norway). The ways in which adoptions from care have been included in the statistics have, however, changed in many countries over the years. Those trends follow the overall pattern of decreasing domestic adoptions across the globe (Palacios et al, 2019).

Indeed, adoptions from care are not common forms of placement for children needing long-term care in the family service-oriented child protection systems. The research about the public's view and opinion on child protection interventions is scarce but the few studies that do exist display that a majority have a positive view of adoptions from care and would choose adoption over foster care in certain circumstances (Skivenes and Thoburn, 2017; Helland et al, 2020; Berrick et al, forthcoming b). This is somewhat surprising, and for some countries, such as Norway and Finland, research indicates that public opinion may be on a collision course with ongoing practice.

Children as the standpoint

In the course of its long history, adoption has very much been seen from the perspective of those who wish to adopt, and only quite recently – since the 1960s and 1970s – has a more child-centred view on adoption emerged (Triseliotis et al, 1997). That view has brought the child more into focus, and issues such as children's capacities to recover from early childhood adversity and to adjust to adoptive life have been studied and findings used to improve planning and practice (Palacios and Brodzinsky, 2010). Currently, that view has been expanded to a more rights-based view, with an emphasis on human rights and children's rights in particular (see Chapter 11). This emphasis suggests that if we examine adoptions from care from the perspective of the child, it is also a story of a child given the opportunity to belong within a family for life, recreating the bonds of belonging so vital for an individual's self-esteem and perception of self-worth. It is discouraging that, more often than not, it is adoption from the perspective of the birth and prospective adoptive parents that is promoted (Breen et al, 2020), as pointed out in Chapters 9 and 12. Research focusing on children's experiences of inter-country adoptions is not fully transferable to the issues of adoptions from care, though some notions of identity and belonging are most likely relevant to both types of adoption. For example, from the point of view of making decisions, Helland and Skivenes (see Chapter 9; see also McEwan-Strand and Skivenes, 2020) conclude that, in Norway, 'To a large degree, available research has left unanswered questions about: if and how Norwegian children are involved; whether children give their consent; whether children have views on foster care versus adoption as a placement alternative; and whether children have a view on their contact with the birth family.' Most countries represented in this book require that children above a certain age give their consent to adoption. The exceptions are England and Ireland, though in England, the wishes of children of all ages must be independently ascertained and reported to the court. In Estonia, the age is ten years; in Norway, Spain and Finland the 'qualifying' age is 12 years; and in Germany and Austria, the age is 14 years (see Burns et al, 2019). For most of these countries, younger children may give consent if considered legally competent.

It is indeed a gap in the knowledge base not to know more about children's views on their own placement histories and involvement in decision-making regarding adoption. In their 1999 study reporting on interviews with 41 children adopted from care in England, Thomas and colleagues reported that half of the children were concerned about the court proceedings, not only in terms of the actual court hearing, meeting a judge and being in the courtroom, but also about the outcome of the proceedings and whether the judge would, for example, say 'no' to an adoption, and what would happen then: 'I was worried whether I would be allowed to get adopted or not. And if I was not, what would I do and where would I go' (Thomas et al, 1999: 69). The long waiting period before the court hearing was also mentioned as difficult for about half of the children. For their ten-year follow-up study, Neil et al (2015) interviewed 32 adoptees aged between 16 and 20. As part of their follow-up study of 265 children of minority ethnic heritage permanently placed from care (mostly with adopters), Thoburn et al (2000) spoke with 24 young people aged between 16 and 21. Both these studies record that the young people themselves had a wide range of experiences and opinions about the positive but also negative aspects of adoption, and especially the regrets some had at having to lose all links with adult birth relatives and siblings (see

Chapter 14). Based on a small qualitative study in Norway on families experiencing involuntary adoption from care, including interviews with six children that were adopted from care, Berg (2010) reports that children who were 17 or older at the time of the interviews said that they were fully aware that they were adopted, of the family they came from and why they had been adopted. All the children said that they were happy they had been adopted and that they believed they had had more opportunities and a better life in their new families than they would have had in their families of origin.

However, children's standpoint should not be narrowed down to only asking for their views. It is much wider as it should guide the fundamental way of thinking of adoption as an alternative to long-term care for some children. This standpoint challenges us to think carefully about the two premises evident in all countries employing adoptions from care: the principle of the child's best interest; and the ambition to create families by adoption. These two premises can complement each other but children can also be objectified and treated as means to create a family by adults wishing to have a family through adoption. In this respect, Breen et al (2020) provide a promising view as a result of their analysis of all ECtHR judgments on adoptions from care, concluding:

> The Court's understands 'family unit', in the context of adoptions from care, to mean biological relationships between children and parents, but more recently, also between children and foster parents, and to a more limited extent in terms of recognition, between siblings themselves. To this extent, our findings with regard to the Court's understanding of family composition are in line with the theoretical literature, wherein the concept of family reflects the bonds created by personal, caring relationships and activities.

The bonds created by personal, caring relationships and activities are important for any child. It is equally important for children who may be adopted that their existing relationships and the likely relationships with the prospective adoptive parents are assessed correctly. Chapter 13, examining the ways in which the Norwegian court views attachment as part of its decisions on adoption, demonstrates how important the high quality of assessments of such key psychological terms is and what challenges the courts may have when working in this juncture of legal and welfare reasoning.

Birth parents and adoption from care

Domestic adoptions were more common in the first part of the 20th century than later in many Western countries as single motherhood was not supported. Social stigma attached to single mothers, as well as lack of economic support and childcare, was reflected in higher numbers of children abandoned and/or given up for adoption. Since the 1960–1970s, the increasing welfare state services addressed to single mothers, the expansion of contraception and the decreasing stigma attached to 'illegitimate' children and mothers have resulted in decreasing numbers of children released for domestic adoption. Nevertheless, the country chapters still report on abandoned children. The baby hatches in Germany and newborn babies given up for adoption in Austria, Estonia, Finland and Spain may point to gaps in services supporting mothers to look after their babies (see Luhamaa et al, 2021), and that there are social and cultural norms that make this kind of abandonment possible. It is noteworthy that when talking about babies 'left' for adoption, the focus is still on mothers, excluding the role of fathers. Although the background of and motives for 'baby adoptions' are only lightly discussed in this book, and they may be different from abandonment (see Chapter 7), the very existence of babies adopted in this way is relevant from the point of view of the existing legal and ethical guidelines for adoptions.

There are differences between countries in the routes taken from birth family to adopters, which impact on the legislative provisions for and understandings of the impact of adoptions from care on birth family members and the services provided. However, whatever route to adoption is taken, once the 'supply' of infants for consensual adoption (who came from across social backgrounds) diminished, those whose children were considered for adoption from care have tended to come from materially deprived or otherwise disadvantaged backgrounds. In countries with a longer history of the provision of family support services, inadequate resources are rarely – or should not be – the sole reason for adoption from care (Luhamaa et al, 2021), and poverty and deprivation as sources of parental difficulty are compounded by physical and mental health problems, addictions, and inter-parental violence.

Of particular note in those countries (especially England and the US in this volume), where a large proportion of those adopted from care enter care as infants, is that some of the birth parents are themselves under the age of 18 and have special rights as children themselves, and especially so if they are also still 'in care'. The research on birth parents of children adopted from care does, however, demonstrate that mothers and, even more so, fathers cross the age range, and this is especially so for those who lose more than one child (either as a sibling group or infants born sequentially) to non-consensual adoption. Some of the studies of adoptions from care referenced in the country chapters show detailed information at the time of entry to care and adoption placement, though fewer provide information on birth families over the longer term (see Chapter 14; see also Howe and Feast, 2000; Triseliotis et al, 2005; Neil et al, 2015; Broadhurst et al, 2018).

Becoming an adoptive parent for a child adopted from care

In every type of adoption, prospective adoptive parents need to be declared not only eligible (legal criteria), but also suitable (health and psychosocial criteria), according to the international treaties and ethical standards in this area (see Chapter 11). Prospective adoptive parents should also receive skilled preparation and services before, during and after the child's placement. When children are adopted from care in the countries represented in this book, it is often foster parents who adopt the child. In some countries (for example, Norway), it is *only* foster parents who can, in fact, adopt a child in public care, and in some countries (for example, Estonia and Finland), it is especially foster parents who initiate the adoption process of a child in care. Obviously, children and foster parents have learnt to know each other before the adoption proceedings, and the new form of an adoptive family is based on existing relationships. At the same time, this means that the recruitment of foster carers is important for adoption and that what is done at that stage regarding matching children and foster carers has an impact on the future interest and likelihood of adoption. When people are recruited by fostering services, they are assessed and trained to be foster carers, which is a different task and commitment from that of being adoptive parents.

It is not, however, only assessment of the suitability of foster parents to become adoptive parents that matters, but also their understanding of what it means to become adoptive parents. 'Adoptive parenthood' is an aspect of psychosocial counselling in some countries, required as a part of adoption proceedings (Triseliotis et al, 1997). The process of preparing for the adoption is considered to be an important part of a successful adoption (see Chapter 8). Counselling aims to support prospective adoptive parents to also prepare themselves on the emotional and psychological level for what it means to shift from being foster carers to being adoptive parents. That kind of support is also given to other members of the prospective adoptive family as the adoption of a former foster child has an impact on the whole family structure and relations. Some country contributors, for example, Bovenschen and Meysen, express concerns that the period of foster care may have an impact on the assessment and counselling, that is, as the family is already known to the public authorities, the assessment may be lighter.

When those other than foster parents apply to adopt a child who is already in public care, matching children and prospective adoptive parents is part of the adoption process. There needs to be a way for prospective adoptive parents to learn about the children available for adoption, which is sometimes done through adoption parties, mentioned in Chapter 2 on England. In order to recruit prospective adopters, campaigns to encourage interest in adoptive parenthood, especially for older children and teenagers, also take place (McRoy et al, 2009). The role of counselling prospective adoptive parents may not, however, be well developed – the chapters describing practice in the US and England in this book focus on matching in particular and give less attention to psychosocial guidance for prospective adoptive parents. The definitions of suitable adoptive parents, however, have a prominent, yet contested, role in some countries, addressing the issues of ethnicity, race, marital status or sexual orientation (see Chapter 5).

The suitability and commitment of prospective adoptive parents, whether foster carers or strangers, is crucial for children adopted from care. The history of adoptions includes too many tragic stories of children being badly cared for or even exploited (Briggs and Marre, 2009). Traditional ways of undertaking pre-adoption assessments have resulted in some prospective adopters being deemed non-suitable, resulting in their exclusion from public and formal adoption proceedings. For example, the issue of the age of prospective adopters excludes some from adoption. Currently, much attention has been given to whether the prospective adopters can be single or in same-sex relations, and whether heterosexual or same-sex couples are legally registered or not, resulting in some variation across the countries (European Parliamentary Research Services, 2016). Indeed, if adoption is to succeed in its aim of providing legal, residential and relational permanence to children in care, the adoptive parents (and families) play a centrally important role. Prospective adopters known to the child through fostering have several advantages for providing permanence of this type but they still need information, support and understanding of what the shift from fostering to adoption means for them legally, socially and psychologically. Those prospective adoptive parents who are strangers to the child to be adopted have even more learning to do at this preparation stage, not only about becoming an adoptive parent, but also about the special needs and characteristics of the child who will be joining their family.

Pre- and post-adoptive services when children from care are adopted

The country chapters demonstrate that pre-adoption services exist to a varying degree. The main type of pre-adoption service is counselling for birth parents, children to be adopted and prospective adopters. In general, counselling aims to provide information to different parties and to support them psychosocially and emotionally to come to terms with the changes brought about by adoption. Counselling may include assessment of the eligibility and suitability of prospective adopters, as well as checking on the commitment and consent of the birth parents, and it may be regarded as an essential precondition for the proceedings towards adoption, as required in Finland, for example. Counselling may be replaced and/or accompanied by training, with some countries, Austria as an example, providing 'preparatory courses' for prospective adopters, consisting of lectures and exercises. Counselling is provided by social workers specialised in adoption in most countries. Only the Estonian chapter describes practices to prepare and support the wider network of the child, including 'biological relatives, siblings and everyone who is connected to the child' (see Chapter 3). The country chapters do not, however, report on any particular adaptations of adoption counselling to serve the situations in which children in care are adopted. In a similar way, although adoption counselling is also provided for children to be adopted, the particularities of adoptions from care are not described in the country chapters. For a child, this shift from foster care into adoption will often mean a change in the family name (or even the 'given' first name in some countries); these markers of the changes, some more mundane than others, are not meaningless and should not take place without preparing the child for the change. It is, after all, well known that children in care struggle with a variety of issues of social belonging. Therefore, the shift from foster care into adoption should pay enough attention to the counselling needs of children, in addition to their wishes and views on the decision itself.

After the child has been adopted, adoptive families and adoptees are, in general, the same as any other family with children regarding the services they may receive. In most countries, former foster families lose the support and payments given previously. In this collection of countries, it is only the US and England chapters which state that some or most adoptive parents continue to receive state funding as adoptive parents. In the US, 'adoptive parents typically receive an initial tax credit; thereafter they usually receive a monthly subsidy, similar to the foster care subsidy, until the child turns 18' (see Chapter 5). Furthermore, it is not only the former foster parents that may lose the support, but also the children. The Finnish chapter, for example, demonstrates how children who grow up in care receive aftercare services to support their independent young adulthood; however, children who have been adopted from care will not have that same public support, but will be dependent on the support given by their adoptive families. In most countries, post-adoption services to adoptive families are more likely to respond, though only when asked to do so, to requests for assistance by adoptive parents, as well as the child, with respect to issues around identity. This is most likely to be as the adoptee reaches adolescence and moves towards adulthood, when they may wish to seek information or reconnect with birth family members. The post-adoption service to birth parents is also most likely to concern providing assistance with post-adoption contact, though mental health services may also provide counselling with respect to the grief reactions experienced by many birth parents, especially of children placed for adoption shortly after birth.

Conclusion

The motivation for this book has been to explore adoption from care and to thereby learn how children's rights are practised and weighed against parents' and adopters' rights in present-day societies, as well as how governments and legal and welfare professionals balance those rights and discharge their duties of care to those children who cannot grow up in their parents' care. This edited volume has demonstrated that children in care for protective reasons are more likely to be adopted in the US and England, and that these two countries have well-developed guidelines and practice frames. In the other seven countries, including countries with a risk, family service and children's rights orientation to child protection, children are rarely, if ever, adopted from care and interest in adoption within child welfare policy is not, in general, strong. There is also surprisingly little country-specific research providing information about the different stakeholders in adoption from care. The characteristics, views and coping mechanisms of children, birth parents and adopters at the time of the adoption decision and afterwards, are only rarely studied outside the countries making more frequent use of adoption from care. Thus, child protection systems have to make policy and practice decisions based on the limited information they do have. As the rationales of child protection systems, welfare states and the history and cultural meanings of adoption vary, the messages from research elsewhere have to be adapted to specific country contexts and their understandings of private and public responsibilities, rights to family life, and children's rights. Children needing long-term care from the state should be given the best possible option to grow up in every jurisdiction, and the provision of options should be based on research-based knowledge of their strengths and weaknesses.

Acknowledgements
This project has received funding from the Research Council of Norway under the Independent Projects – Humanities and Social Science program (grant no. 262773) and European Research Council under the European Union's Horizon 2020 research and innovation programme (grant agreement No 724460). Disclaimer: This chapter reflects only the authors' views and the funding agencies are not responsible for any use that may be made of the information contained therein.

Notes
1   England is positioned between these two approaches, with family service-oriented legal provisions but operating in practice within a risk-oriented framework.
2   When we comment on practices in different countries, we are aware that, with limited word length, authors have had to be selective about what they include and miss out. Therefore, if something is not mentioned, it cannot be assumed to mean that it does not happen.

References
Berg, T. (2010) 'Adopsjon som barneverntiltak – hvordan gikk det med barna? Rapport fra praksis' ['Adoption as a child welfare measure – how did it work out for the children? A report from praxis'], *Tidsskriftet Norges Barnevern*, 87(1): 48–59.

Berrick, J.D., Gilbert, N. and Skivenes, M. (eds) (forthcoming a) *International Handbook of Child Protection Systems*, New York: Oxford University Press.

Berrick, J.D., Skivenes, M. and Roscoe, J. (forthcoming b) 'Right orientation and citizens views of adoption from care in U.S. and Norway'.

Breen, C., Krutzinna, J., Luhamaa, K. and Skivenes, M. (2020) 'Family life for children in state care. An analysis of the European Court of Human Rights' reasoning on adoption without consent', *International Journal of Children's Rights*, 28(2020): 715-747. Available at: https://brill.com/view/journals/chil/aop/article-10.1163-15718182-28040001/article-10.1163-15718182-28040001.xml?language=en

Briggs, L. and Mare, D. (2009) 'Introduction. The circulation of children', in D. Mare and L. Briggs (eds) *International Adoption. Global Inequalities and the Circulation of Children*, New York: New York University Press, pp 1–28.

Broadhurst, K., Alrouh, B., Mason, C., Ward, H., Holmes, L., Ryan, M. and Bowyer, S. ,(2018) *Born into Care Proceedings in England*, London: Nuffield Foundation.

Burns, K., Kriz, K., Krutzinna, J., Luhamaa, K., Meysen, T., Pösö, T., Sagrario, S., Skivenes, M. and Thoburn, J. (2019) 'The hidden proceedings – an analysis of accountability of child protection adoption proceedings in eight European jurisdictions', *European Journal of Comparative Law and Governance*, 6(4): 339–71.

Clark, H., Coll-Seck, A.M., Banerjee, A., Peterson, S., Dalglish, S.L., Ameratunga, S., Balabanova, D., Bhan, M.K., Bhutta, Z.A., Borrazzo, J., Claeson, M., Doherty, T., El-Jardali, F., George, A.S., Gichaga, A., Gram, L., Hipgrave, D.B., Kwamie, A., Meng, Q., Mercer, R., Narain, S., Nsungwa-Sabiiti, J., Olumide, A.O., Osrin, D., Powell-Jackson, T., Rasanathan, K., Rasul, I., Reid, P., Requejo, J., Rohde, S.S., Rollins, N., Romedenne, M., Singh Sachdev, H., Saleh, R., Shawar, Y.R., Shiffman, J., Simon, J., Sly, P.D., Stenberg, K., Tomlinson, M., Ved, R.R. and Costello, A. (2020) 'A future for the world's children? A WHO–UNICEF–Lancet Commission', *The Lancet*, 395(10224): 605–58.

European Parliamentary Research Service (2016) 'Briefing. Adoption of children in the European Union'. Available at: www.europarl.europa.eu/RegData/etudes/BRIE/2016/583860/EPRS_BRI(2016)583860_EN.pdf (accessed 24 June 2020).

Gilbert, N., Parton, N. and Skivenes, M. (eds) (2011) *Child Protection Systems. International Trends and Emerging Orientations*, New York: Oxford University Press.

Helland, H. and Skivenes, M. (2019) *Adopsjon som barneverntiltak [Adoption from Care as a Child Welfare Measure]*, Bergen: University of Bergen.

Helland, H., Pedersen, S. and Skivenes, M. (2020) 'Befolkningens syn på adopsjon' ['Population's view on adoption from care'], *Tidsskrift for Samfunnsforskning*, 61(2): 124–39.

Howe, D. and Feast, J. (2000) *Adoption, Search and Reunion: The Long Term Experience of Adopted Adults*, London: BAAF.

Luhamaa, K., McEwan-Strand, A., Ruiken, B., Skivenes, M. and Wingens, F. (2021) 'Services and support to mothers and newborn babies in vulnerable situations: A study of eight countries', *Children and Youth Service Review*, 120: 105762.

McEwan-Strand, A. and Skivenes, M. (2020) 'Children's capacities and role in matters of great significance for them. An analysis of the Norwegian county boards' decision-making in cases about adoption from care', *International Journal of Children's Rights*, 28(3): 632–65.

McRoy, R., Lynch, C., Chanmugam, A., Madden, E. and Ayers-Lopez, S. (2009) 'Children from care CAN be adopted', in G. Wrobel and E. Neil (eds) *International Advances in Adoption Research and Practice*, Chichester: Wiley-Blackwell, pp 97–118.

Neil, E., Beek, M. and Ward, E. (2015) *Contact after Adoption: A Longitudinal Study of Post Adoption Contact Arrangements*, London: Coram-BAAF.

Palacios, J. and Brodzinsky, D. (2010) 'Adoption research: trends, topics, outcomes', *International Journal of Behavioral Development*, 34(3): 270–84.

Palacios, J., Brodzinsky, D., Grotevant, H., Johnson, D., Juffer, F., Marninez-Mora, L., Muhamedrahimov, R., Selwyn, J., Simmons, J. and Tarren-Sweeney, M. (2019) 'Adoption in the service of child protection. An international interdisciplinary perspective', *Psychology, Public Policy, and Law*, 25(2): 57–72.

Skivenes, M. and Thoburn, J. (2017) 'Citizens' views in four jurisdictions on placement policies for maltreated children', *Child and Family Social Work*, 22(4): 1472–9.

Tefre, Ø. (2015) 'The justifications for terminating parental rights and adoption in the United States', *Children and Youth Service Review*, 48: 87–97.

Tefre, Ø. (2020) 'The child's best interest and the politics of adoptions from care in Norway', *The International Journal of Children's Rights*, 28(2): 288–321.

Thoburn, J., Norford, L. and Rashid, S.P. (2000) *Permanent Family Placement for Children of Minority Ethnic Origin*, London: Jessica Kingsley.

Thomas, C., Lowe, N.V., Lowe, N., Beckford, V. and Murch, M. (1999) *Adopted Children Speaking: A Whole New World*, London: British Association for Adoption and Fostering.

Triseliotis, J., Shireman, J. and Hundelby, M. (1997) *Adoption. Theory, Policy and Practice*, London: Cassell.

Triseliotis, J., Feast, J. and Kyle, J. (2005) *The Adoption Triangle Revisited*, London: BAAF.

Index

Page numbers in *italic* type refer to figures and tables. References to endnotes show both the page number and the note number (231n3).